DRYAD

VOLUME ONE

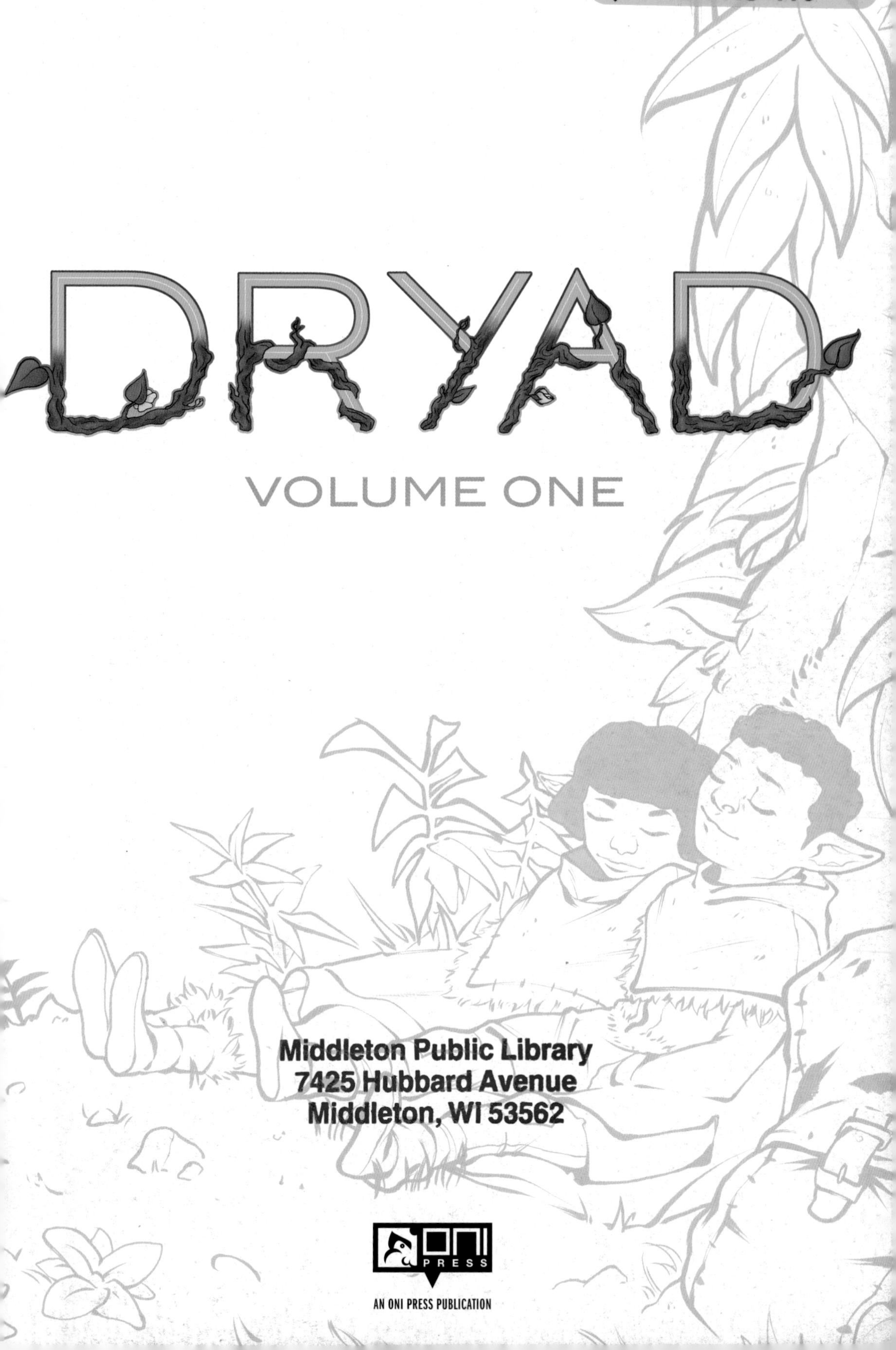

AN ONI PRESS PUBLICATION

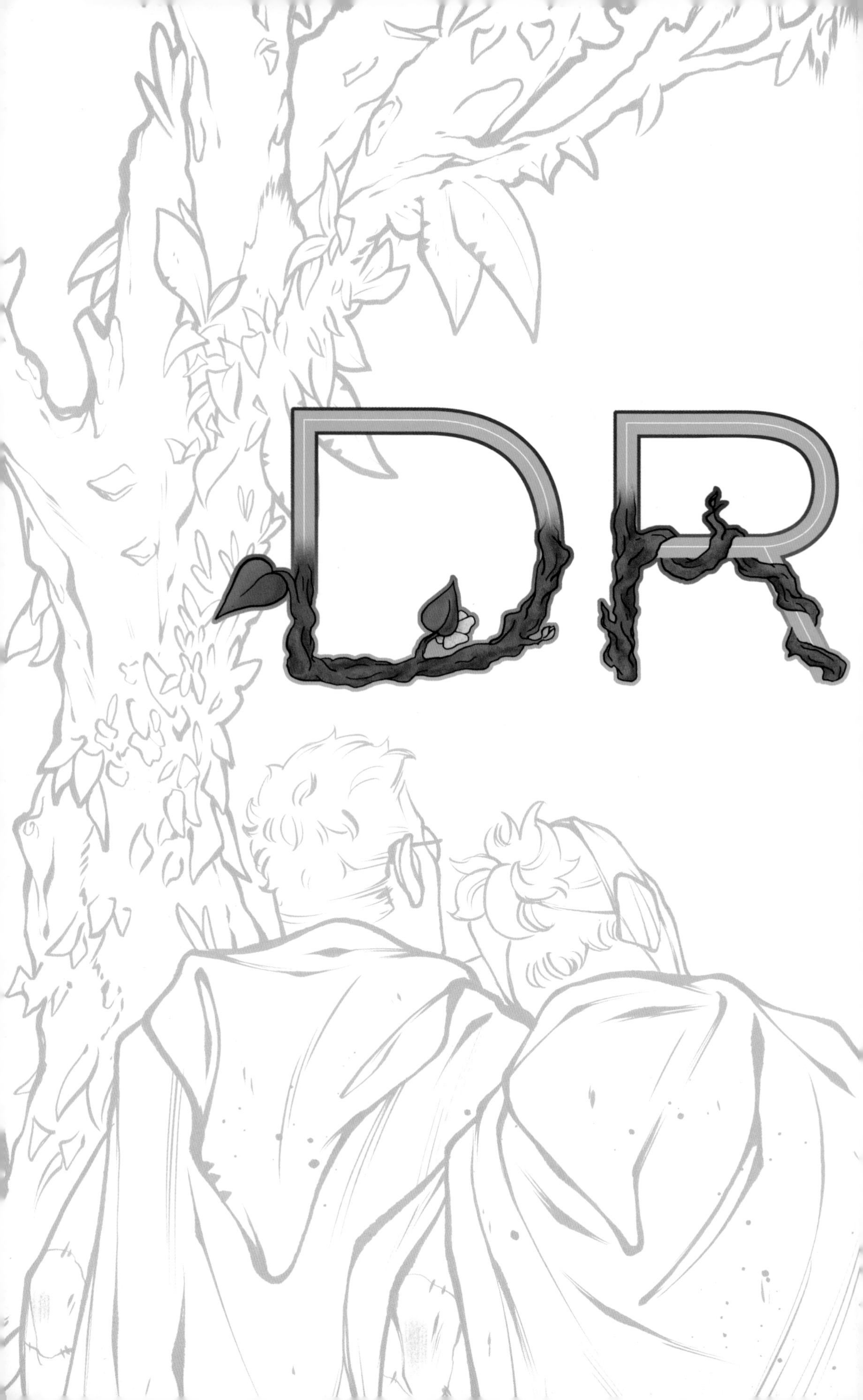
DR

VOLUME ONE

CREATED BY KURTIS WIEBE AND JUSTIN BARCELO

Written by **Kurtis Wiebe**
Illustrated by **Justin Barcelo**

Colored by **Justin Barcelo** [Chapters 1 and 2]
Meg Casey [Chapter 3]
and **Francesco Segala** [Chapters 4 and 5]

Lettered by **Jim Campbell**

Cover by **Tomas Oleksak**

Edited by **Jasmine Amiri**
Designed by **Kate Z. Stone**

PUBLISHED BY ONI PRESS, INC.

James Lucas Jones, president & publisher **Sarah Gaydos**, editor in chief **Charlie Chu**, e.v.p. of creative & business development **Brad Rooks**, director of operations **Amber O'Neill**, special projects manager **Harris Fish**, events manager **Margot Wood**, director of marketing & sales Jeremy Atkins, director of brand communications **Devin Funches**, sales & marketing manager **Katie Sainz**, marketing manager **Tara Lehmann**, publicist **Troy Look**, director of design & production **Kate Z. Stone**, senior graphic designer **Sonja Synak**, graphic designer **Hilary Thompson**, graphic designer **Sarah Rockwell**, junior graphic designer **Angie Knowles**, digital prepress lead **Vincent Kukua**, digital prepress technician **Shawna Gore**, senior editor **Amanda Meadows**, senior editor **Robert Meyers**, senior editor, licensing **Jasmine Amiri**, editor **Grace Bornhoft**, editor **Zack Soto**, editor **Chris Cerasi**, editorial coordinator **Steve Ellis**, vice president of games **Ben Eisner**, game developer **Michelle Nguyen**, executive assistant **Jung Lee**, logistics coordinator **Joe Nozemack**, publisher emeritus

onipress.com
facebook.com/onipress
twitter.com/onipress
instagram.com/onipress

lionforge.com
facebook.com/lionforge
twitter.com/lionforge
instagram.com/lionforge

@KurtisWiebe
@ohnoJustinO
@spookymeaghan
@FrancescoSegala
@CampbellLetters

First Edition: January 2021
ISBN 978-1-62010-790-4
eISBN 978-1-62010-811-6

Printed in China.

Library of Congress Control Number: 2020937769

1 3 5 7 9 10 8 6 4 2

CHAPTER ONE

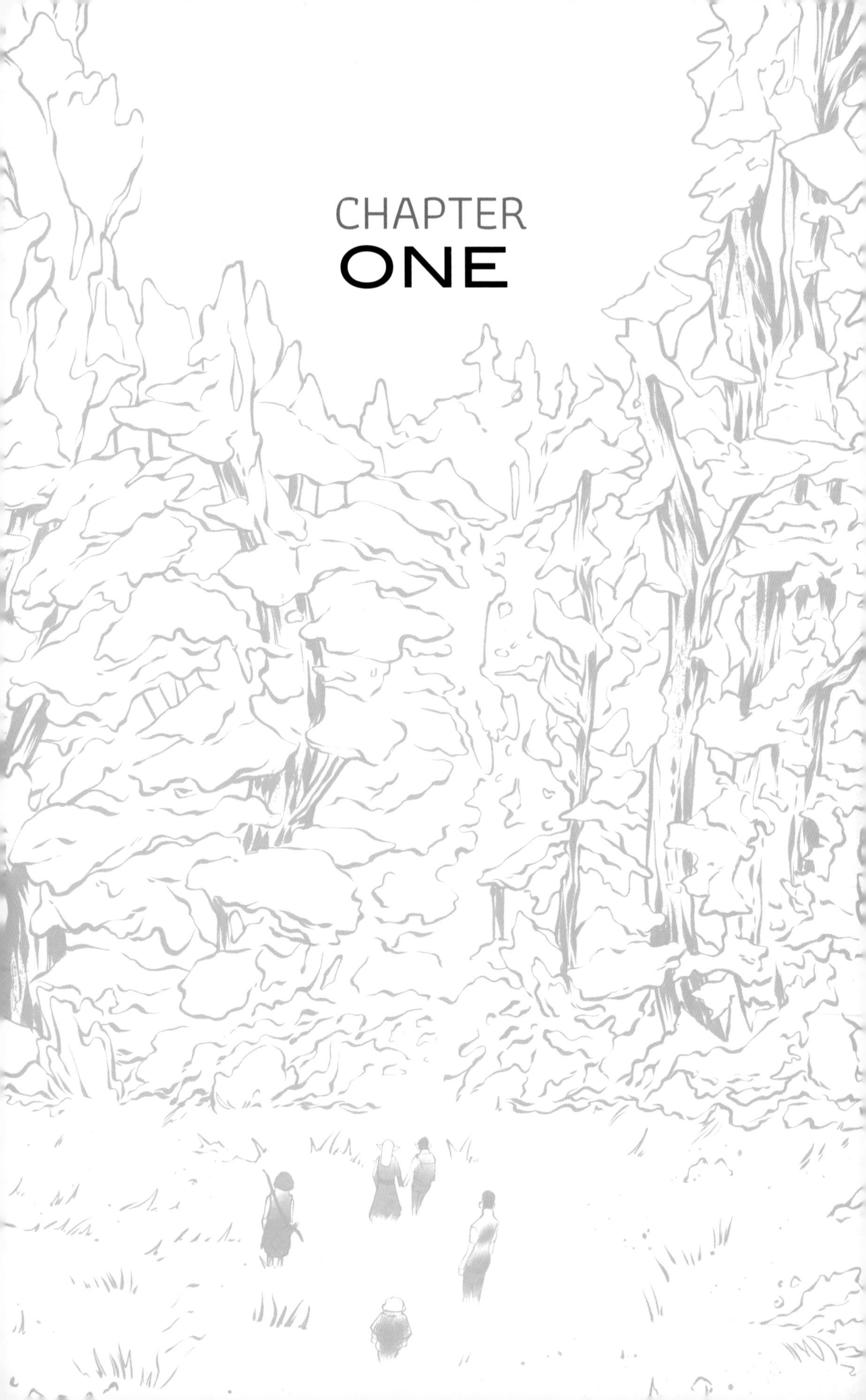

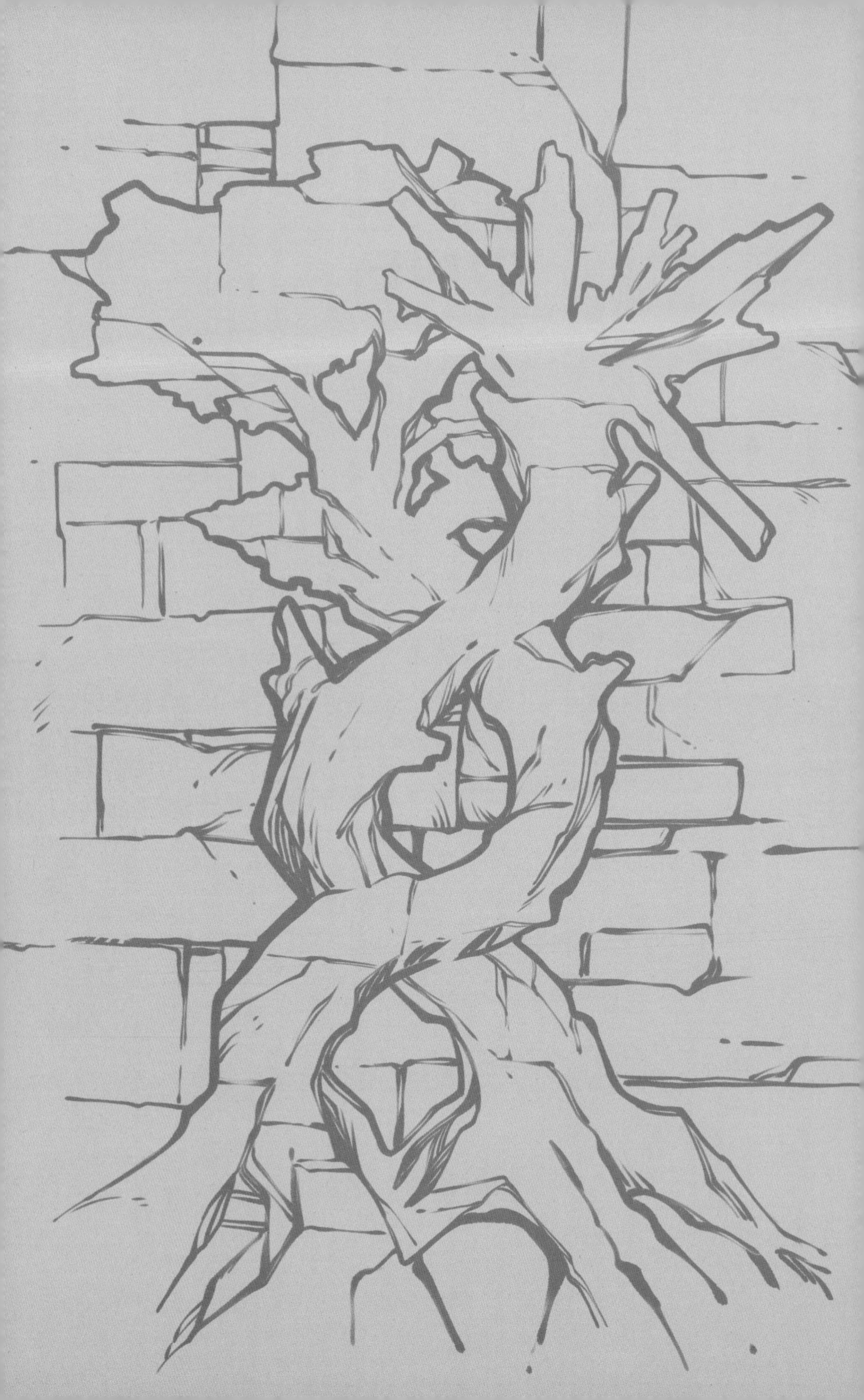

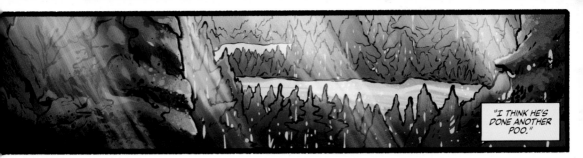

"I THINK HE'S DONE ANOTHER POO."

AND SOMEHOW YOU STILL HAVEN'T FIGURED OUT THAT THEY GO MORE THAN ONCE IN THEIR LIVES.

IT'S BEEN AN HOUR!

RIGHT...

...

HE'S TWO, MORGAN! TWO! HOW'S THIS AMOUNT EVEN *POSSIBLE?*

AND WHAT THE HELL IS THAT? STRING?

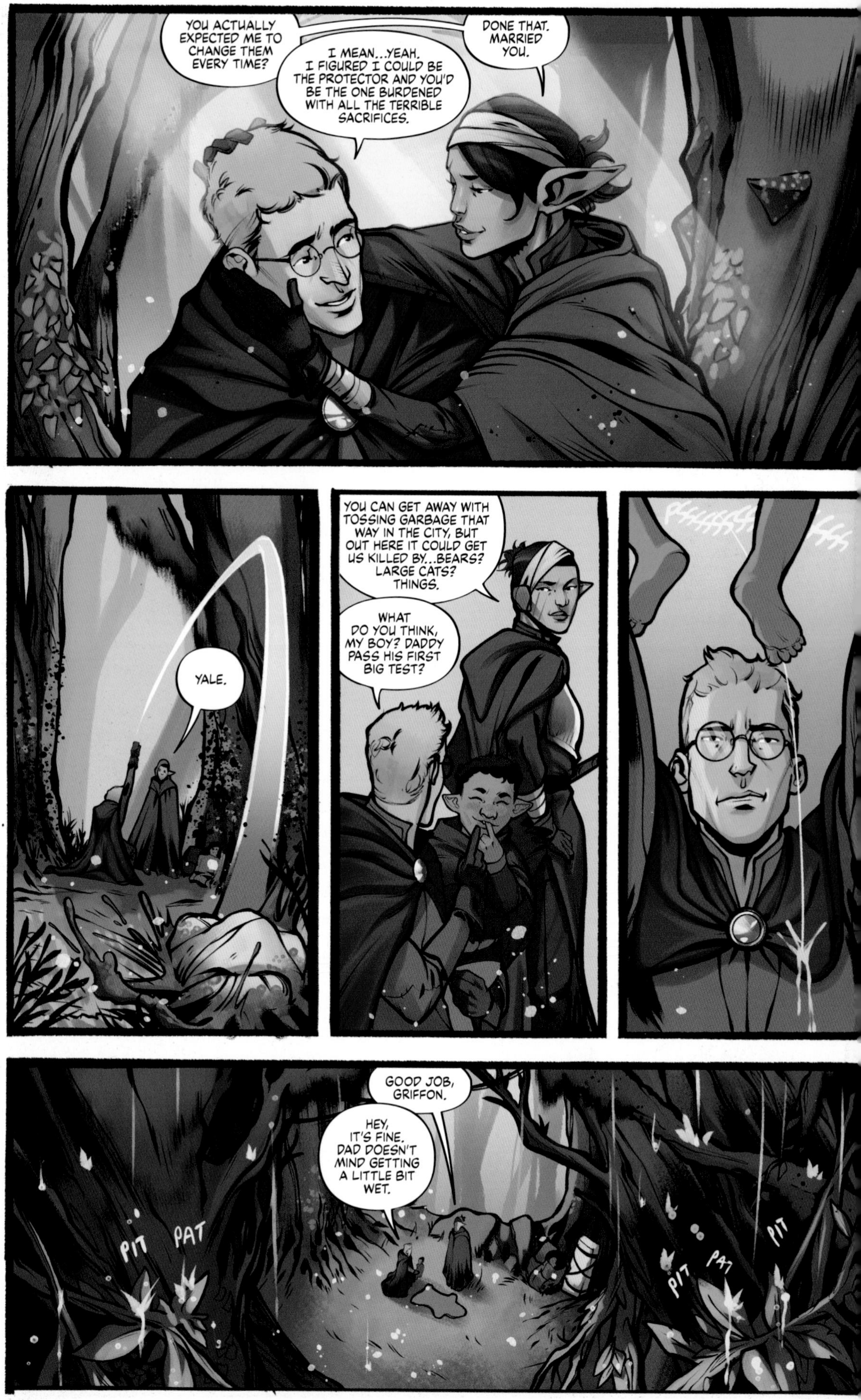
YOU ACTUALLY EXPECTED ME TO CHANGE THEM EVERY TIME?
I MEAN...YEAH. I FIGURED I COULD BE THE PROTECTOR AND YOU'D BE THE ONE BURDENED WITH ALL THE TERRIBLE SACRIFICES.
DONE THAT. MARRIED YOU.
YALE.
YOU CAN GET AWAY WITH TOSSING GARBAGE THAT WAY IN THE CITY, BUT OUT HERE IT COULD GET US KILLED BY...BEARS? LARGE CATS? THINGS.
WHAT DO YOU THINK, MY BOY? DADDY PASS HIS FIRST BIG TEST?
PSSSSSSSSSSSSS
GOOD JOB, GRIFFON.
HEY, IT'S FINE. DAD DOESN'T MIND GETTING A LITTLE BIT WET.
PIT PAT
PIT PAT PIT

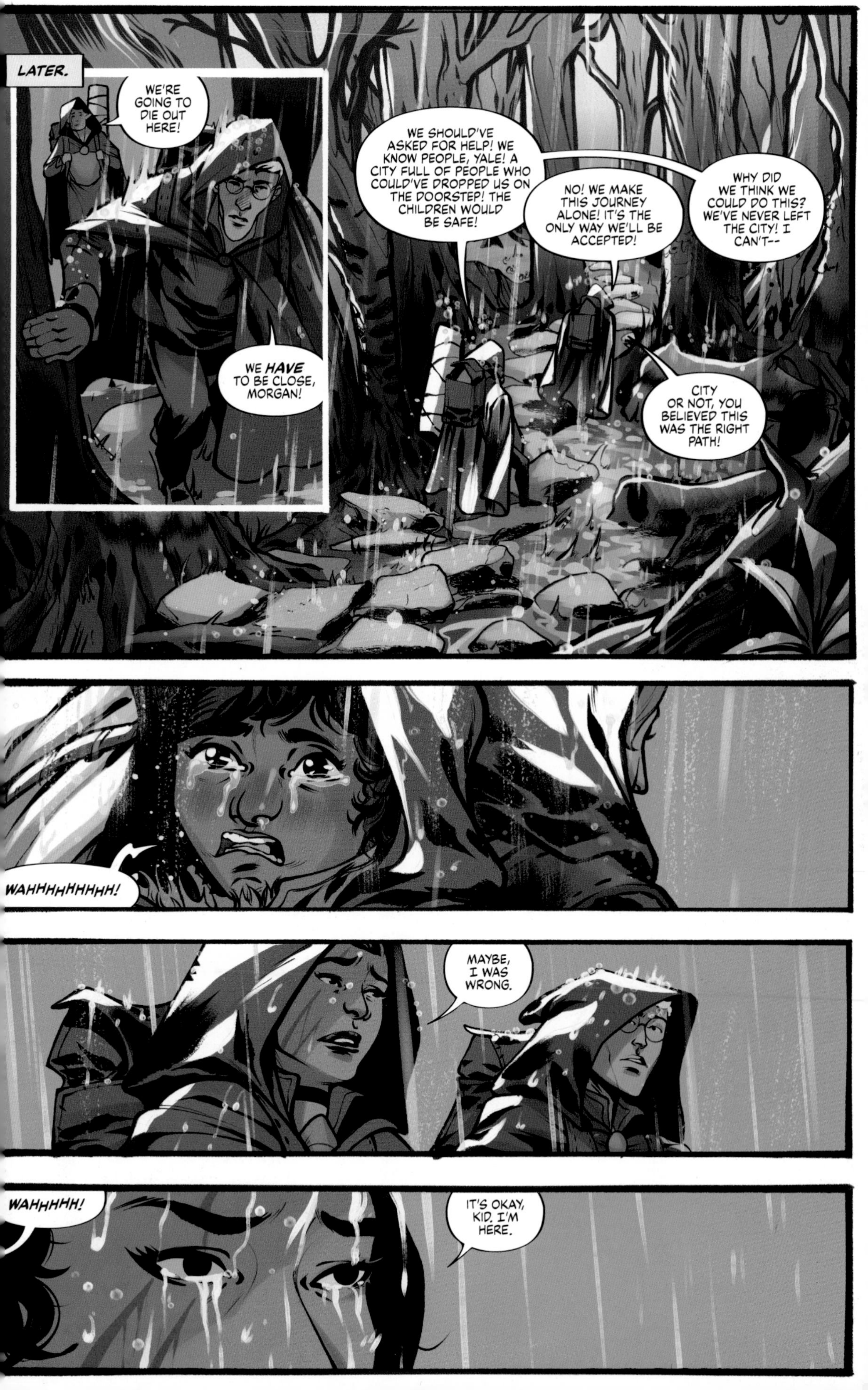
LATER.
WE'RE GOING TO DIE OUT HERE!
WE *HAVE* TO BE CLOSE, MORGAN!
WE SHOULD'VE ASKED FOR HELP! WE KNOW PEOPLE, YALE! A CITY FULL OF PEOPLE WHO COULD'VE DROPPED US ON THE DOORSTEP! THE CHILDREN WOULD BE SAFE!
NO! WE MAKE THIS JOURNEY ALONE! IT'S THE ONLY WAY WE'LL BE ACCEPTED!
WHY DID WE THINK WE COULD DO THIS? WE'VE NEVER LEFT THE CITY! I CAN'T--
CITY OR NOT, YOU BELIEVED THIS WAS THE RIGHT PATH!
WAHHHHHHHHH!
MAYBE, I WAS WRONG.
WAHHHHH!
IT'S OKAY, KID. I'M HERE.

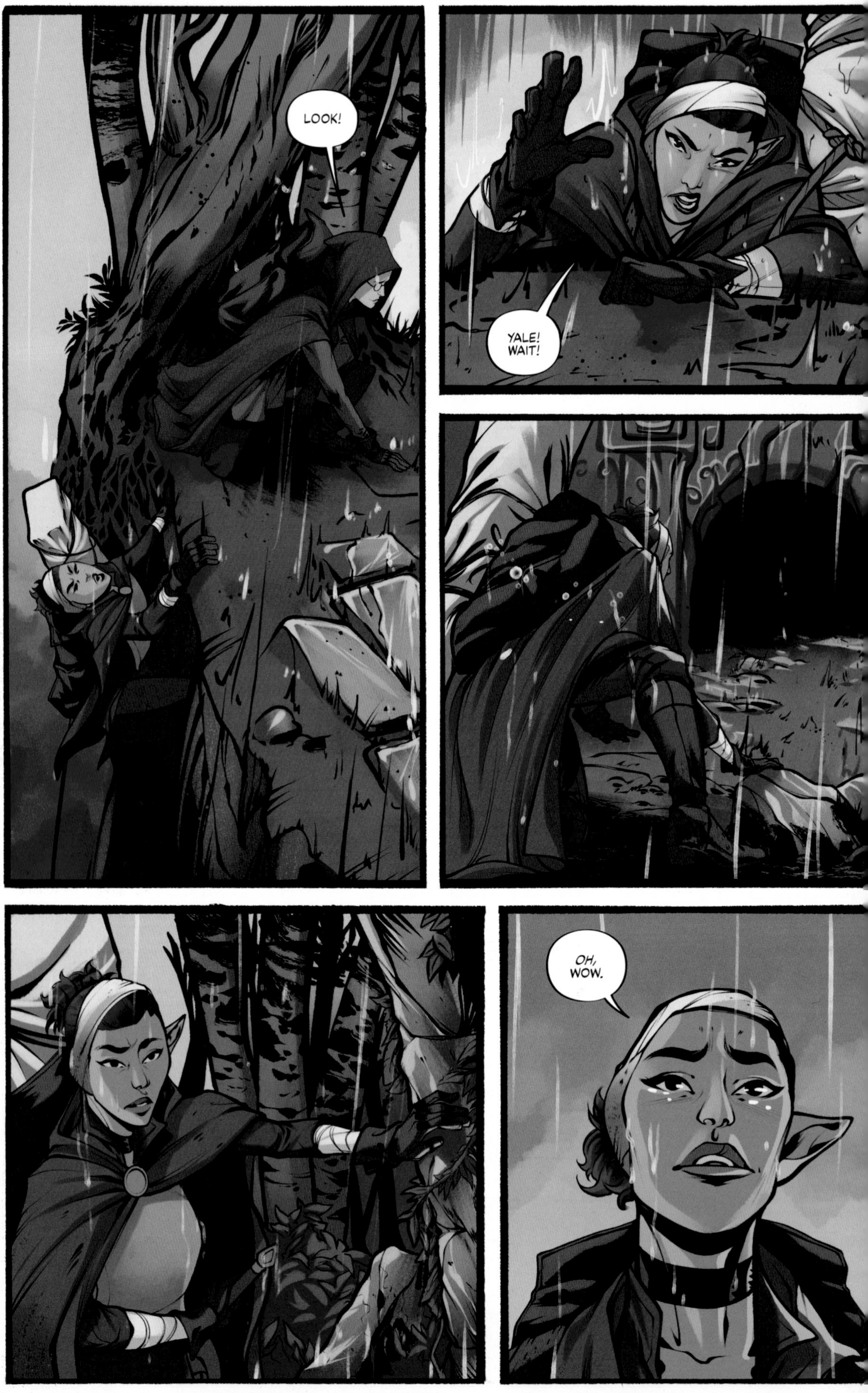
LOOK!
YALE! WAIT!
OH, WOW.

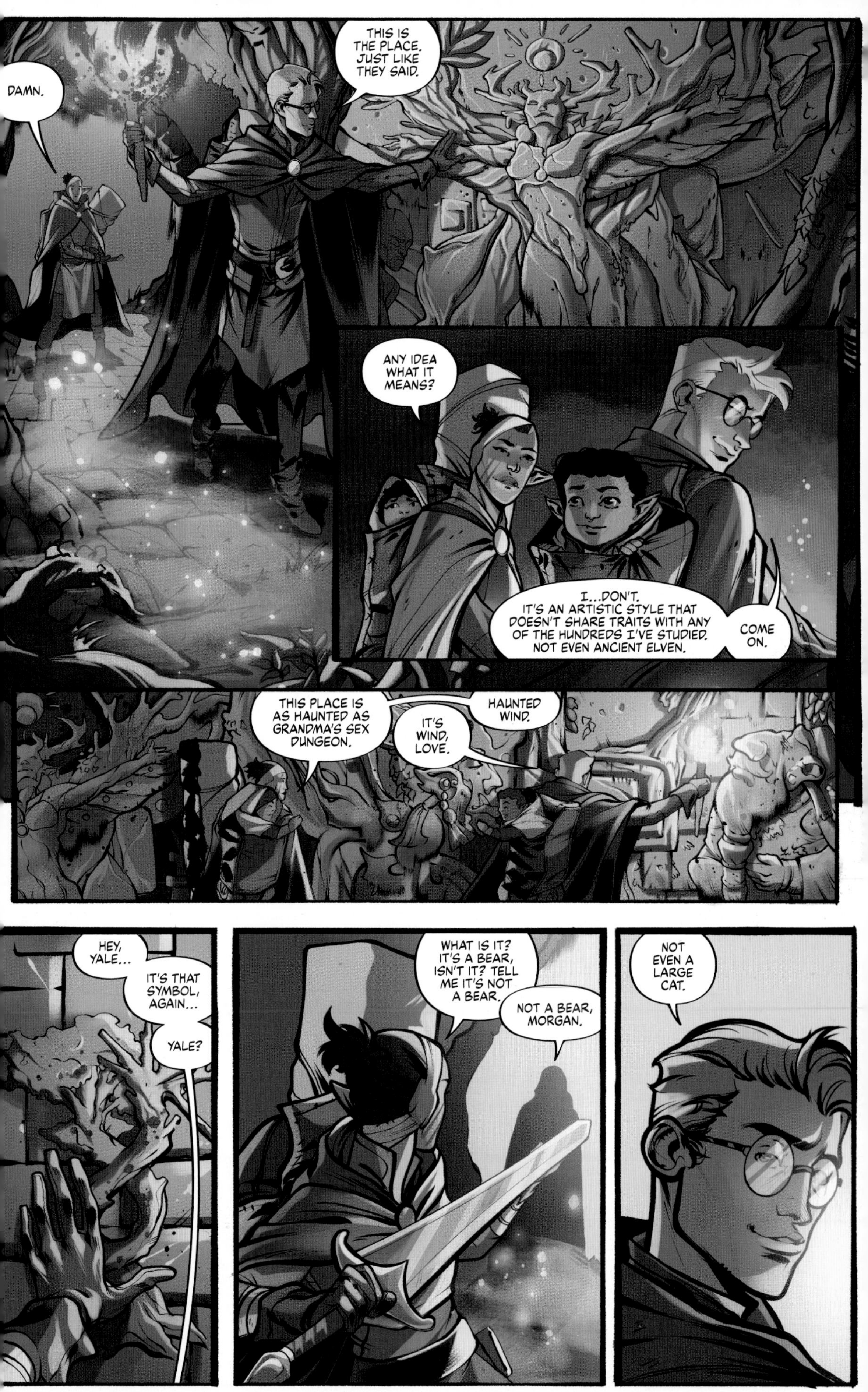
DAMN.
THIS IS THE PLACE. JUST LIKE THEY SAID.
ANY IDEA WHAT IT MEANS?
I...DON'T. IT'S AN ARTISTIC STYLE THAT DOESN'T SHARE TRAITS WITH ANY OF THE HUNDREDS I'VE STUDIED. NOT EVEN ANCIENT ELVEN.
COME ON.
THIS PLACE IS AS HAUNTED AS GRANDMA'S SEX DUNGEON.
HAUNTED WIND.
IT'S WIND, LOVE.
HEY, YALE...
IT'S THAT SYMBOL, AGAIN...
YALE?
WHAT IS IT? IT'S A BEAR, ISN'T IT? TELL ME IT'S NOT A BEAR.
NOT A BEAR, MORGAN.
NOT EVEN A LARGE CAT.

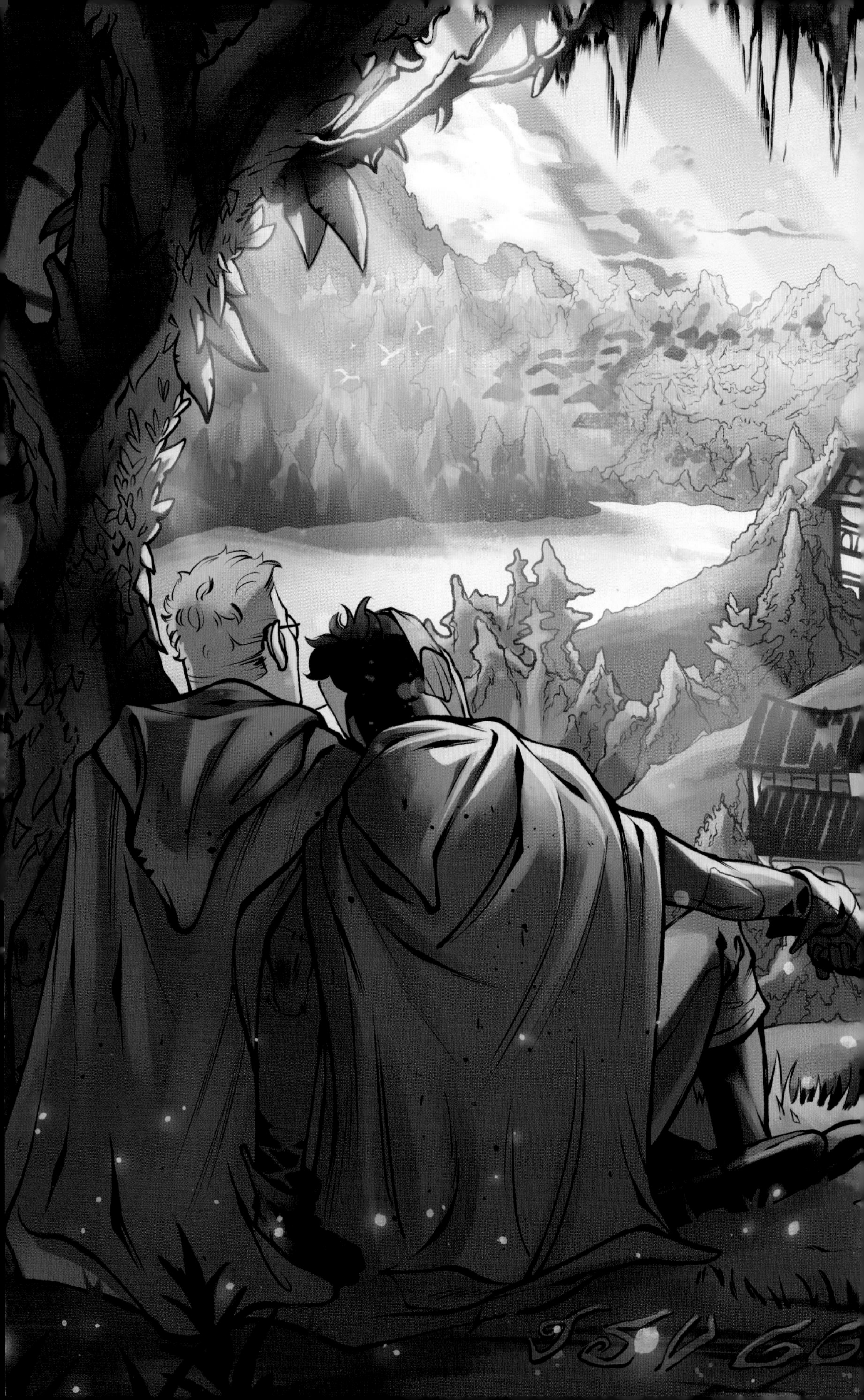

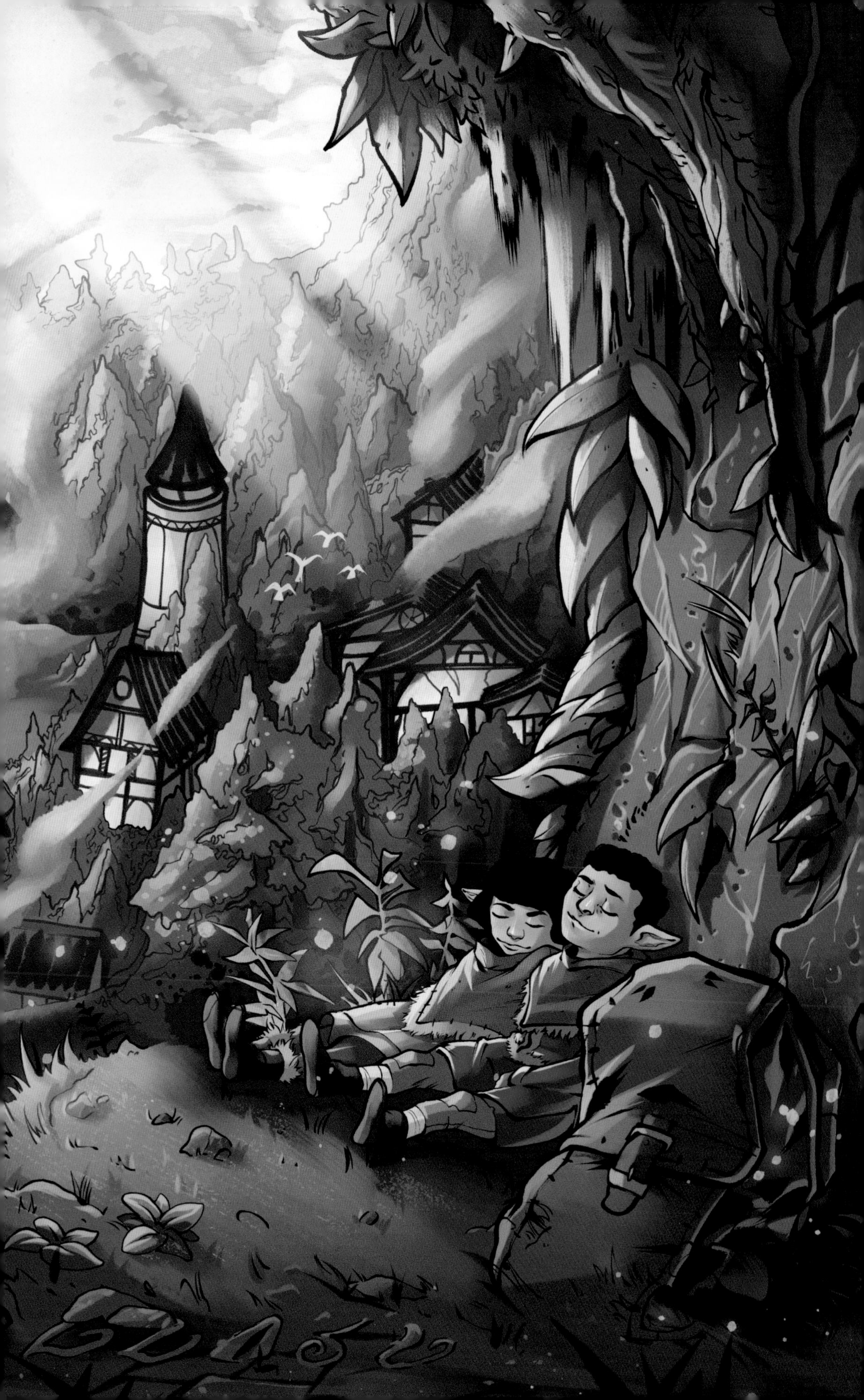

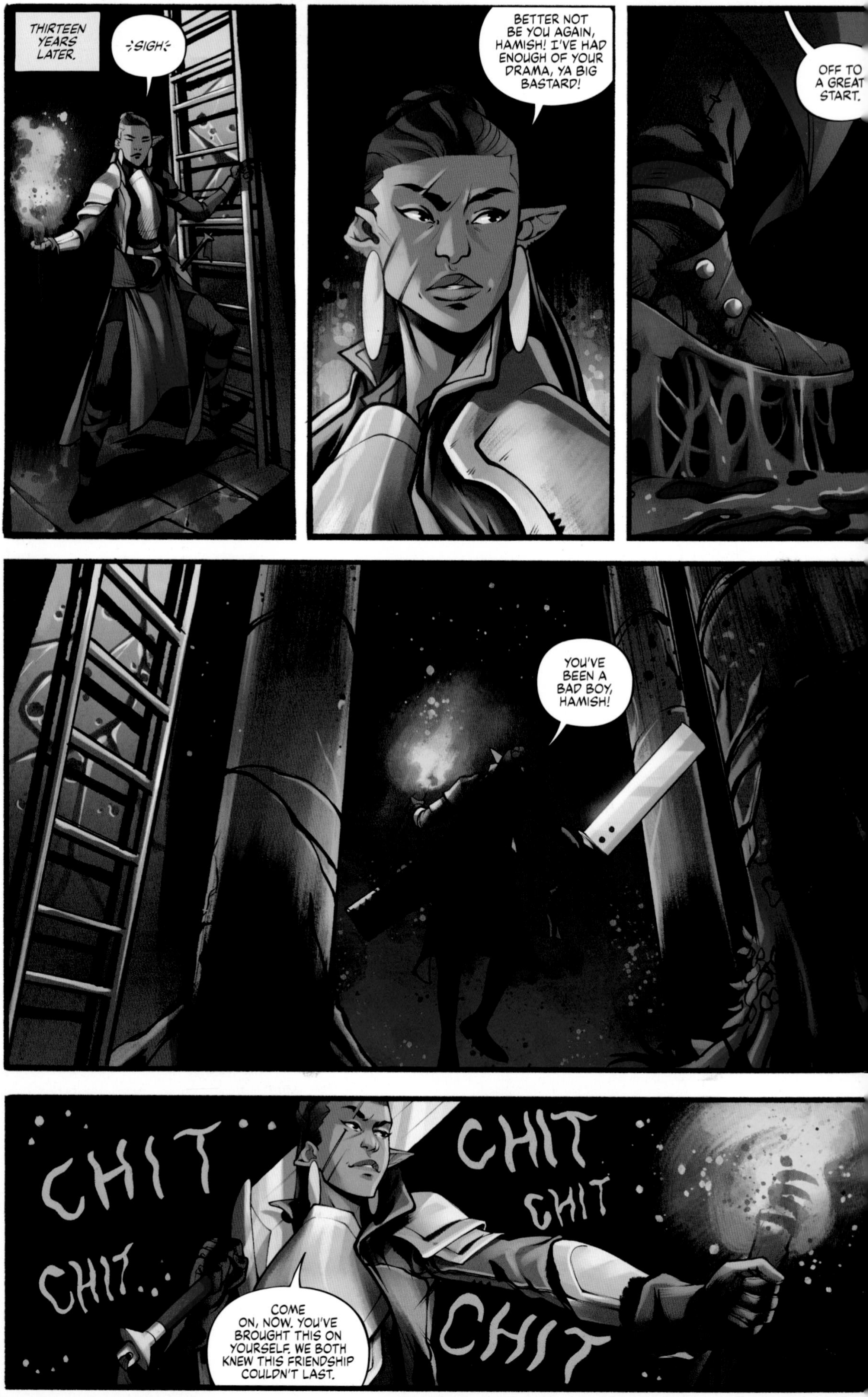
THIRTEEN YEARS LATER.
SIGH
BETTER NOT BE YOU AGAIN, HAMISH! I'VE HAD ENOUGH OF YOUR DRAMA, YA BIG BASTARD!
OFF TO A GREAT START.
YOU'VE BEEN A BAD BOY, HAMISH!
CHIT
CHIT CHIT
CHIT...
CHIT
COME ON, NOW. YOU'VE BROUGHT THIS ON YOURSELF. WE BOTH KNEW THIS FRIENDSHIP COULDN'T LAST.

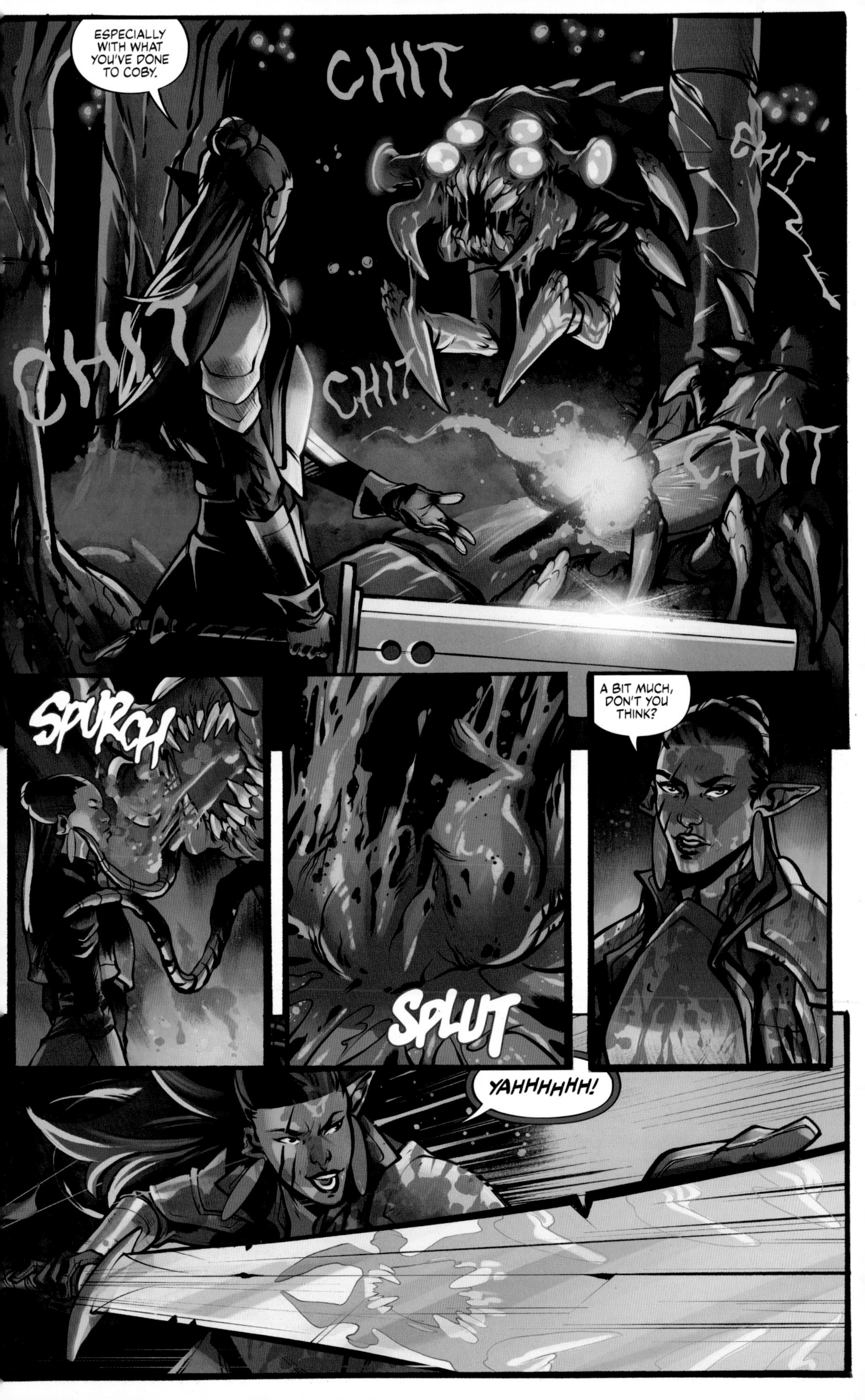
ESPECIALLY WITH WHAT YOU'VE DONE TO COBY.
CHIT
CHIT
CHIT
CHIT
CHIT
SPURCH
SPLUT
A BIT MUCH, DON'T YOU THINK?
YAHHHHHH!

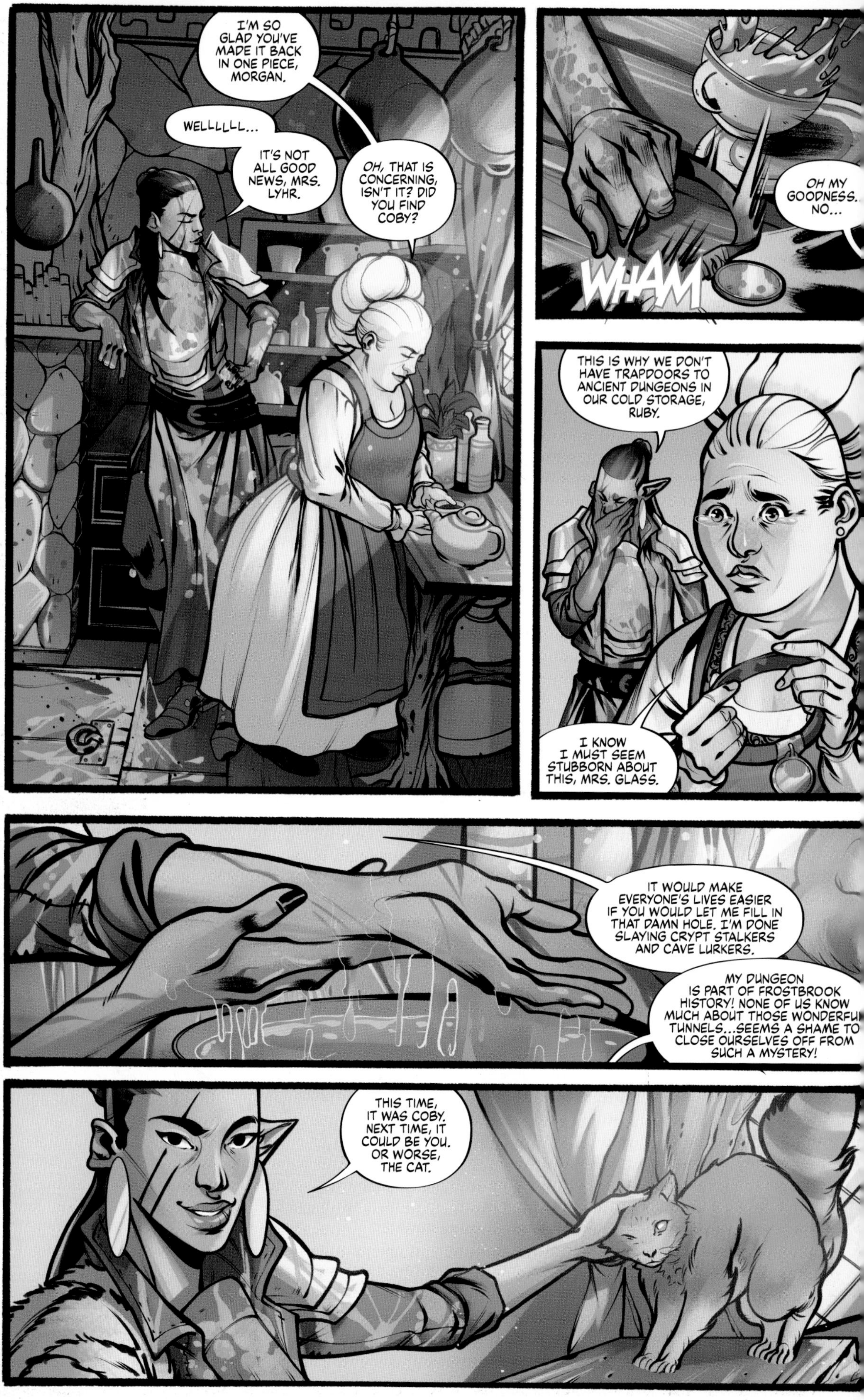
I'M SO GLAD YOU'VE MADE IT BACK IN ONE PIECE, MORGAN.
WELLLLLL...
IT'S NOT ALL GOOD NEWS, MRS. LYHR.
OH, THAT IS CONCERNING, ISN'T IT? DID YOU FIND COBY?
WHAM
OH MY GOODNESS. NO...
THIS IS WHY WE DON'T HAVE TRAPDOORS TO ANCIENT DUNGEONS IN OUR COLD STORAGE, RUBY.
I KNOW I MUST SEEM STUBBORN ABOUT THIS, MRS. GLASS.
IT WOULD MAKE EVERYONE'S LIVES EASIER IF YOU WOULD LET ME FILL IN THAT DAMN HOLE. I'M DONE SLAYING CRYPT STALKERS AND CAVE LURKERS.
MY DUNGEON IS PART OF FROSTBROOK HISTORY! NONE OF US KNOW MUCH ABOUT THOSE WONDERFU TUNNELS...SEEMS A SHAME TO CLOSE OURSELVES OFF FROM SUCH A MYSTERY!
THIS TIME, IT WAS COBY. NEXT TIME, IT COULD BE YOU. OR WORSE, THE CAT.

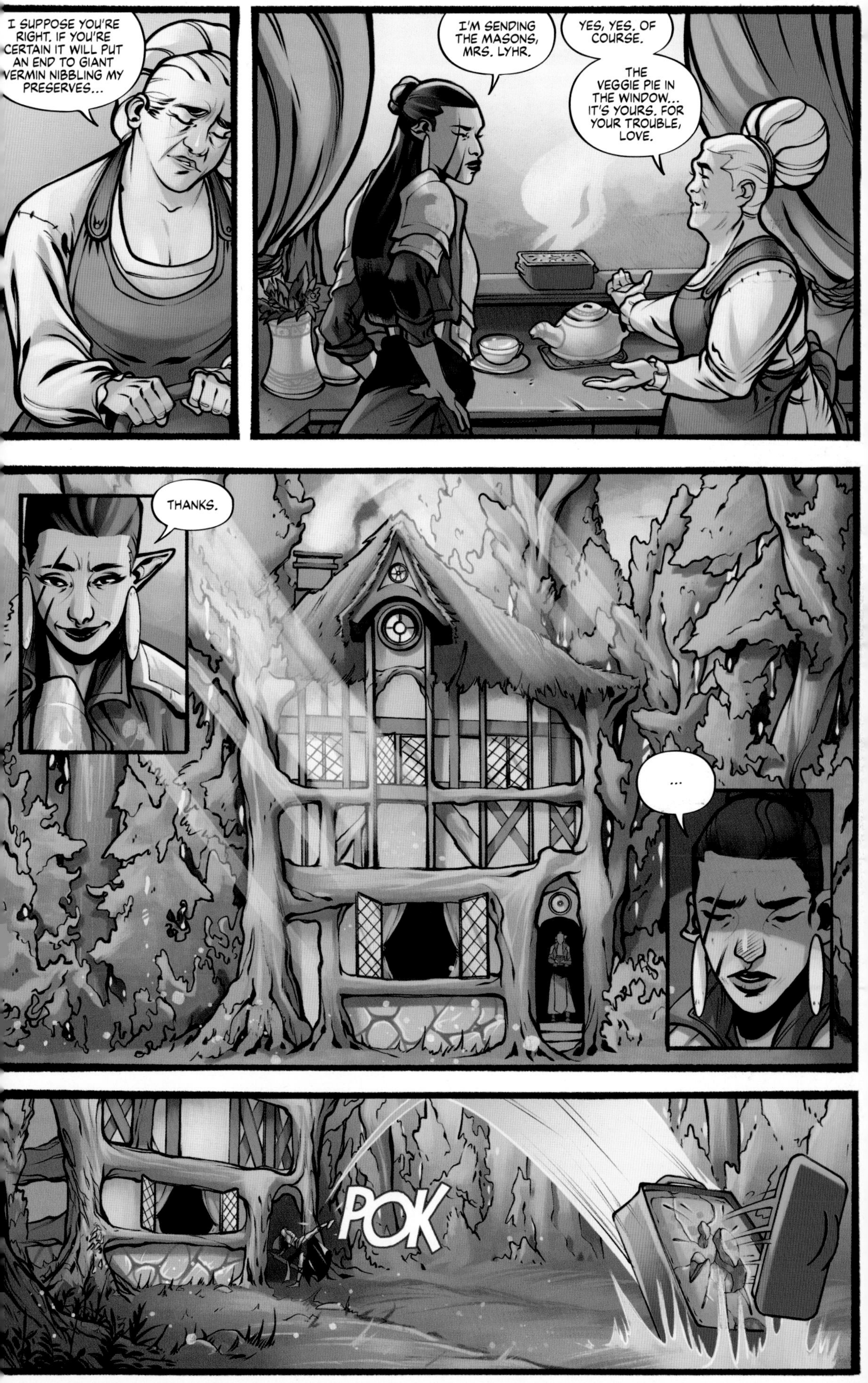

I SUPPOSE YOU'RE RIGHT. IF YOU'RE CERTAIN IT WILL PUT AN END TO GIANT VERMIN NIBBLING MY PRESERVES...
I'M SENDING THE MASONS, MRS. LYHR.
YES, YES. OF COURSE.
THE VEGGIE PIE IN THE WINDOW... IT'S YOURS. FOR YOUR TROUBLE, LOVE.
THANKS.
...
POK

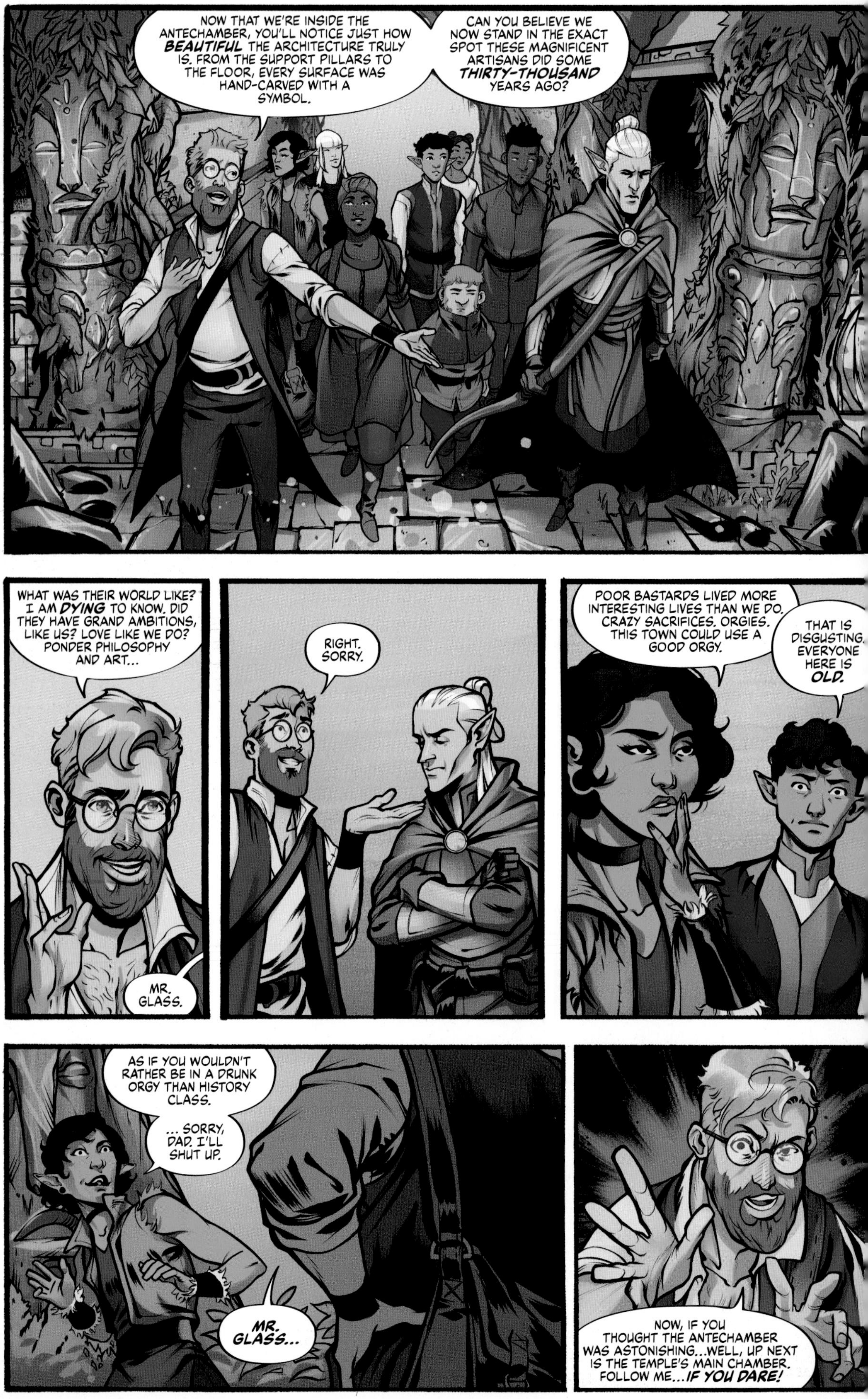
NOW THAT WE'RE INSIDE THE ANTECHAMBER, YOU'LL NOTICE JUST HOW BEAUTIFUL THE ARCHITECTURE TRULY IS. FROM THE SUPPORT PILLARS TO THE FLOOR, EVERY SURFACE WAS HAND-CARVED WITH A SYMBOL.
CAN YOU BELIEVE WE NOW STAND IN THE EXACT SPOT THESE MAGNIFICENT ARTISANS DID SOME THIRTY-THOUSAND YEARS AGO?
WHAT WAS THEIR WORLD LIKE? I AM DYING TO KNOW. DID THEY HAVE GRAND AMBITIONS, LIKE US? LOVE LIKE WE DO? PONDER PHILOSOPHY AND ART...
MR. GLASS.
RIGHT. SORRY.
POOR BASTARDS LIVED MORE INTERESTING LIVES THAN WE DO. CRAZY SACRIFICES. ORGIES. THIS TOWN COULD USE A GOOD ORGY.
THAT IS DISGUSTING. EVERYONE HERE IS OLD.
AS IF YOU WOULDN'T RATHER BE IN A DRUNK ORGY THAN HISTORY CLASS.
... SORRY, DAD. I'LL SHUT UP.
MR. GLASS...
NOW, IF YOU THOUGHT THE ANTECHAMBER WAS ASTONISHING...WELL, UP NEXT IS THE TEMPLE'S MAIN CHAMBER. FOLLOW ME...IF YOU DARE!

WELCOME TO THE BEATING HEART OF HISTORY, CLASS. WE'RE UNCERTAIN IF THERE WAS A GARDEN IN THE TEMPLE BEFORE IT WAS ABANDONED. WE *DO* KNOW THAT THE ACOLYTES OF THIS DEAD RELIGION WERE WELL-VERSED IN HERBALISM.

HOW?

THAT IS AN EXCELLENT QUESTION. WHILE THERE'S VERY LITTLE EVIDENCE ABOUT THIS PARTICULAR CULTURE, WE CAN LEARN A GREAT DEAL BY THEIR ART.

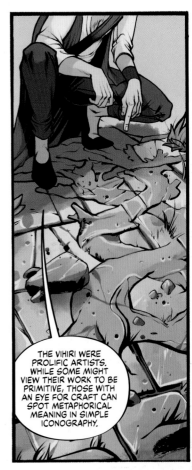

THE VIHIRI WERE PROLIFIC ARTISTS. WHILE SOME MIGHT VIEW THEIR WORK TO BE PRIMITIVE, THOSE WITH AN EYE FOR CRAFT CAN SPOT METAPHORICAL MEANING IN SIMPLE ICONOGRAPHY.

THE VIHIRI ART WITHIN THE TEMPLE WAS MADE BY TWO, OR THREE INDIVIDUALS WITH A PREDOMINANT THEME OF NATURE. PLANTS, ANIMALS.

A BALANCE OF LIFE BETWEEN THOSE THAT WORSHIPPED IT AND THAT WHICH NATURE, ITSELF WAS MADE UP OF.

THESE PEOPLE COMMITTED THEIR LIVES TO THIS PLACE. I DON'T UNDERSTAND WHY GOD WOULD ABANDON THEM.

IT *IS* A MYSTERY. NO ONE KNOWS WHY GOD ABANDONED THIS WORLD.

PERHAPS HE FELT IT WAS TIME FOR US TO MAKE A GO OF LIFE ON OUR OWN.

DID HE TAKE MAGIC WITH HIM, TOO, MR. GLASS?

SOME BELIEVE.

WHAT DO *YOU* BELIEVE?

I'D SAY IT'S NEVER REALLY GONE AWAY--IT LIVES IN ALL OF US.

AHHHHH!

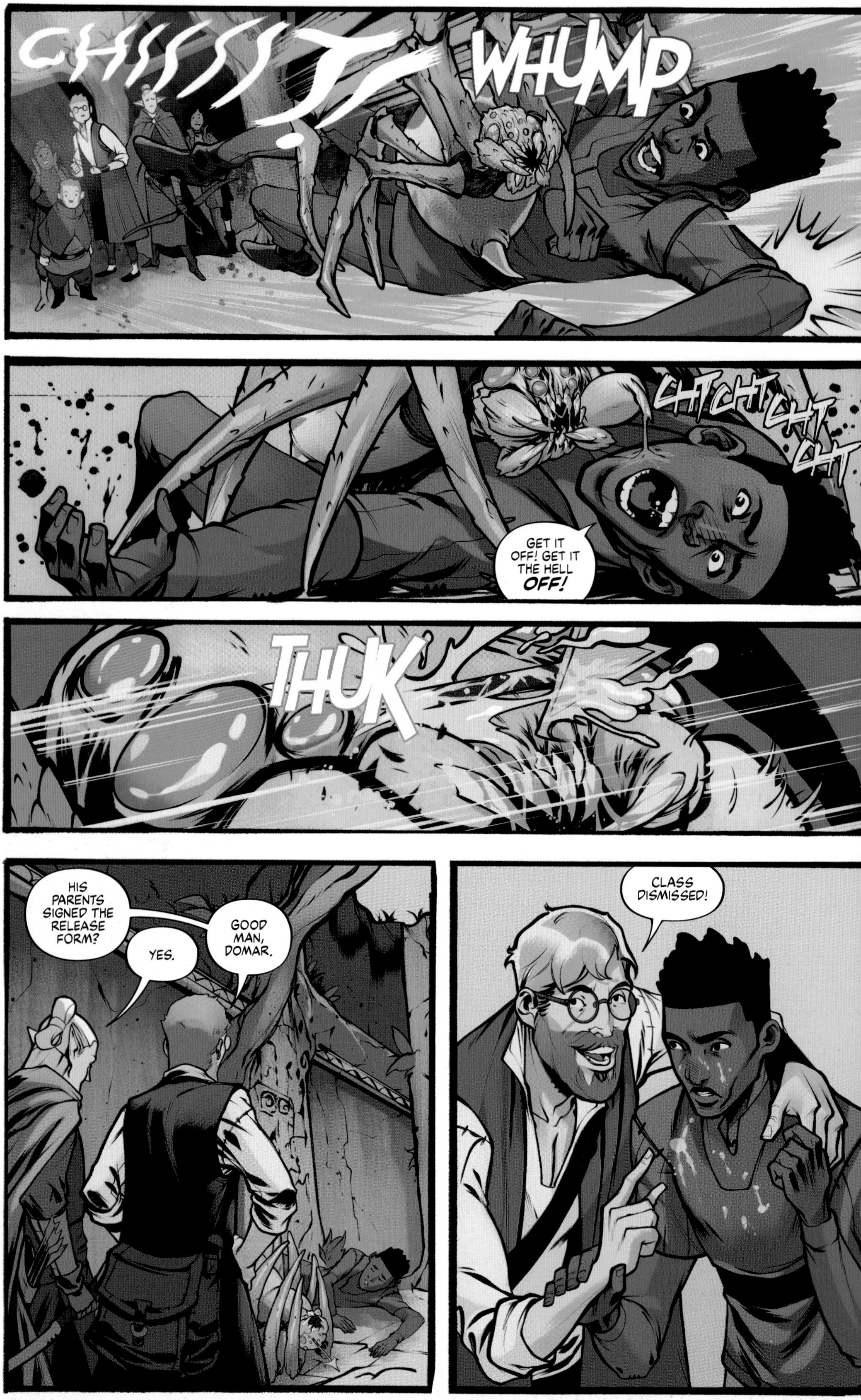
CHISSST
WHUMP
CHTCHTCHT CHT
GET IT OFF! GET IT THE HELL OFF!
THUK
HIS PARENTS SIGNED THE RELEASE FORM?
YES.
GOOD MAN, DOMAR.
CLASS DISMISSED!

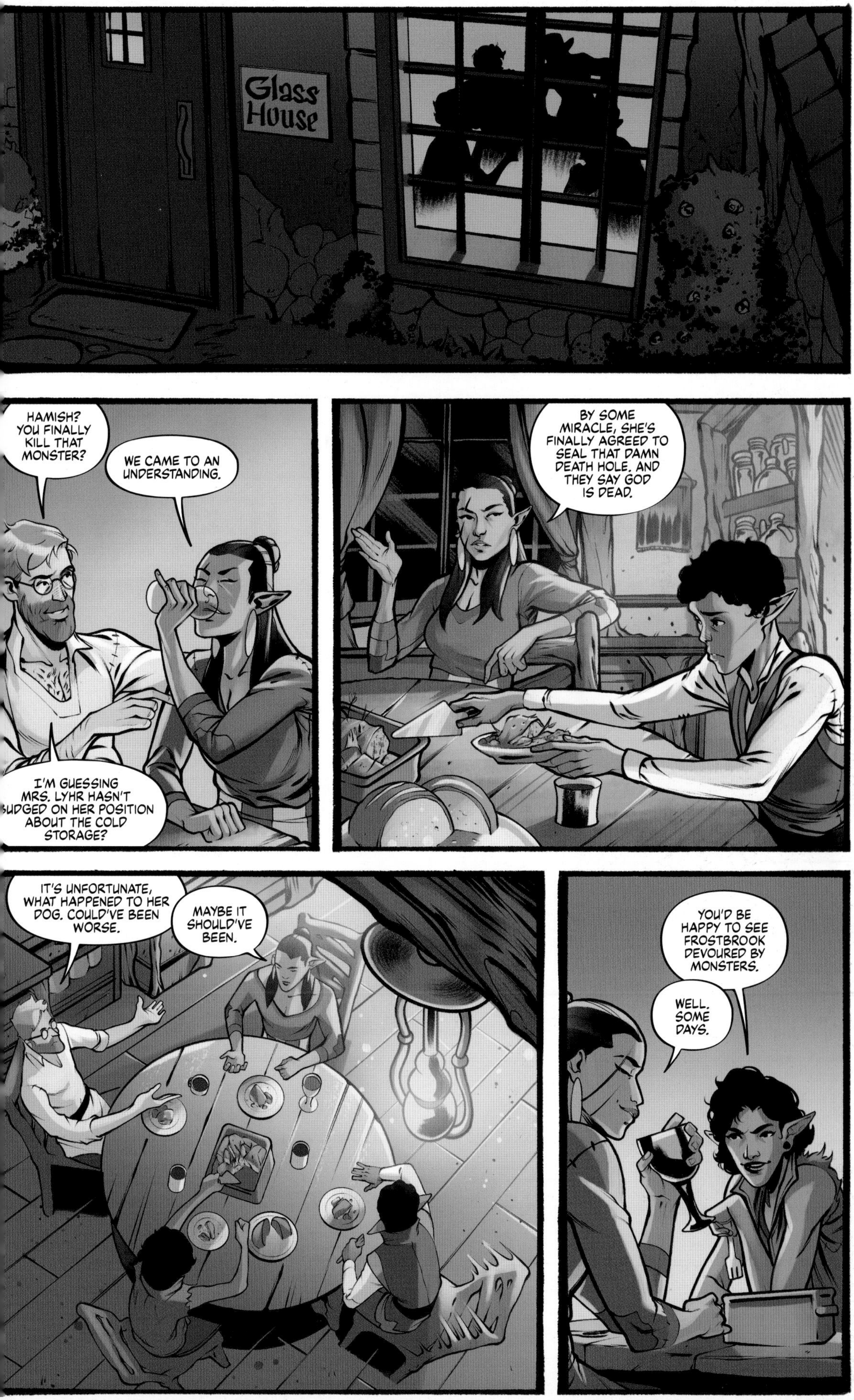
Glass House
HAMISH? YOU FINALLY KILL THAT MONSTER?
WE CAME TO AN UNDERSTANDING.
I'M GUESSING MRS. LYHR HASN'T BUDGED ON HER POSITION ABOUT THE COLD STORAGE?
BY SOME MIRACLE, SHE'S FINALLY AGREED TO SEAL THAT DAMN DEATH HOLE. AND THEY SAY GOD IS DEAD.
IT'S UNFORTUNATE, WHAT HAPPENED TO HER DOG. COULD'VE BEEN WORSE.
MAYBE IT SHOULD'VE BEEN.
YOU'D BE HAPPY TO SEE FROSTBROOK DEVOURED BY MONSTERS.
WELL. SOME DAYS.

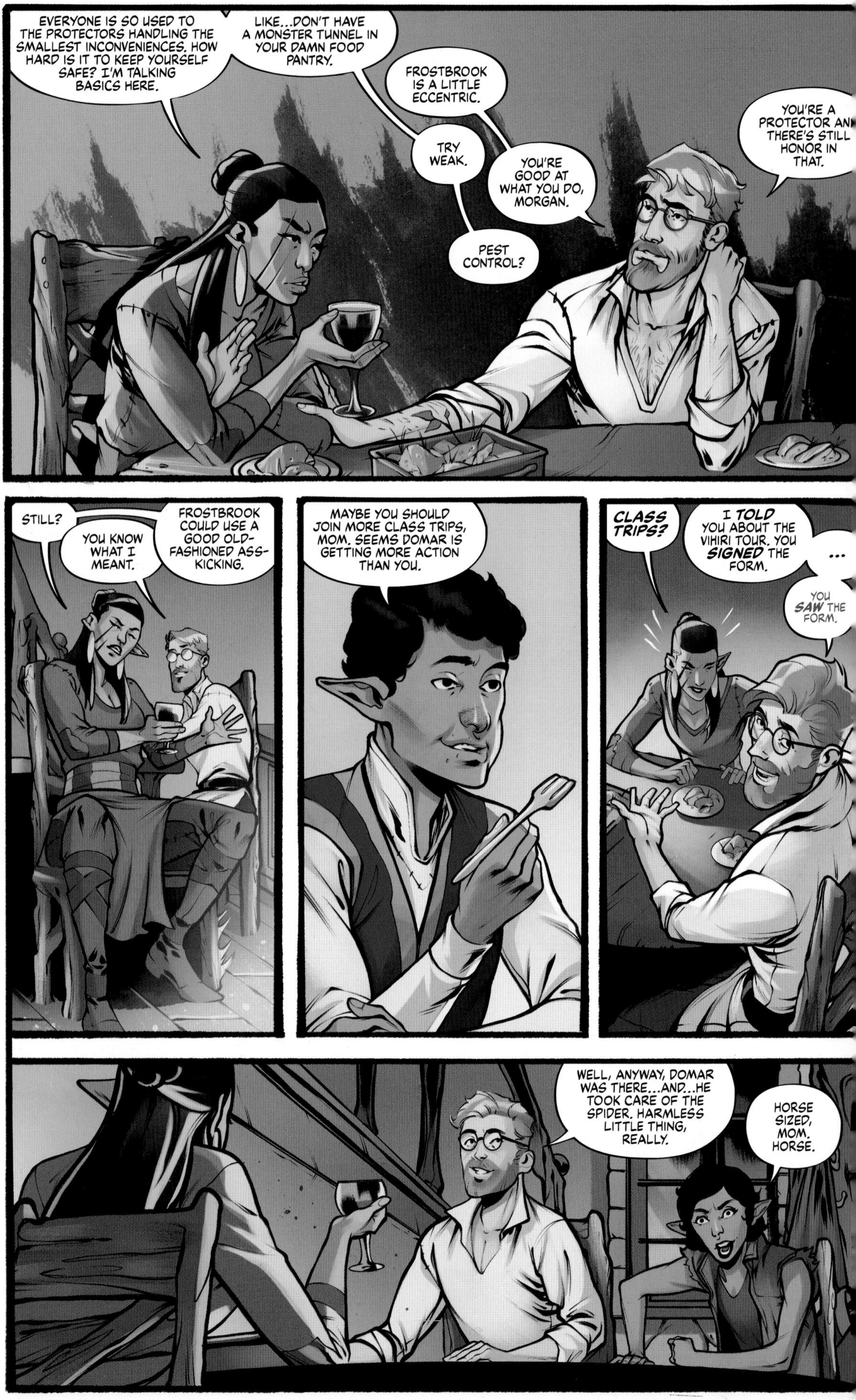

EVERYONE IS SO USED TO THE PROTECTORS HANDLING THE SMALLEST INCONVENIENCES. HOW HARD IS IT TO KEEP YOURSELF SAFE? I'M TALKING BASICS HERE.
LIKE...DON'T HAVE A MONSTER TUNNEL IN YOUR DAMN FOOD PANTRY.
FROSTBROOK IS A LITTLE ECCENTRIC.
TRY WEAK.
YOU'RE GOOD AT WHAT YOU DO, MORGAN.
PEST CONTROL?
YOU'RE A PROTECTOR AN THERE'S STILL HONOR IN THAT.
STILL?
YOU KNOW WHAT I MEANT.
FROSTBROOK COULD USE A GOOD OLD-FASHIONED ASS-KICKING.
MAYBE YOU SHOULD JOIN MORE CLASS TRIPS, MOM. SEEMS DOMAR IS GETTING MORE ACTION THAN YOU.
CLASS TRIPS?
I TOLD YOU ABOUT THE VIHIRI TOUR. YOU SIGNED THE FORM.
...
YOU SAW THE FORM.
WELL, ANYWAY, DOMAR WAS THERE...AND...HE TOOK CARE OF THE SPIDER. HARMLESS LITTLE THING, REALLY.
HORSE SIZED, MOM. HORSE.

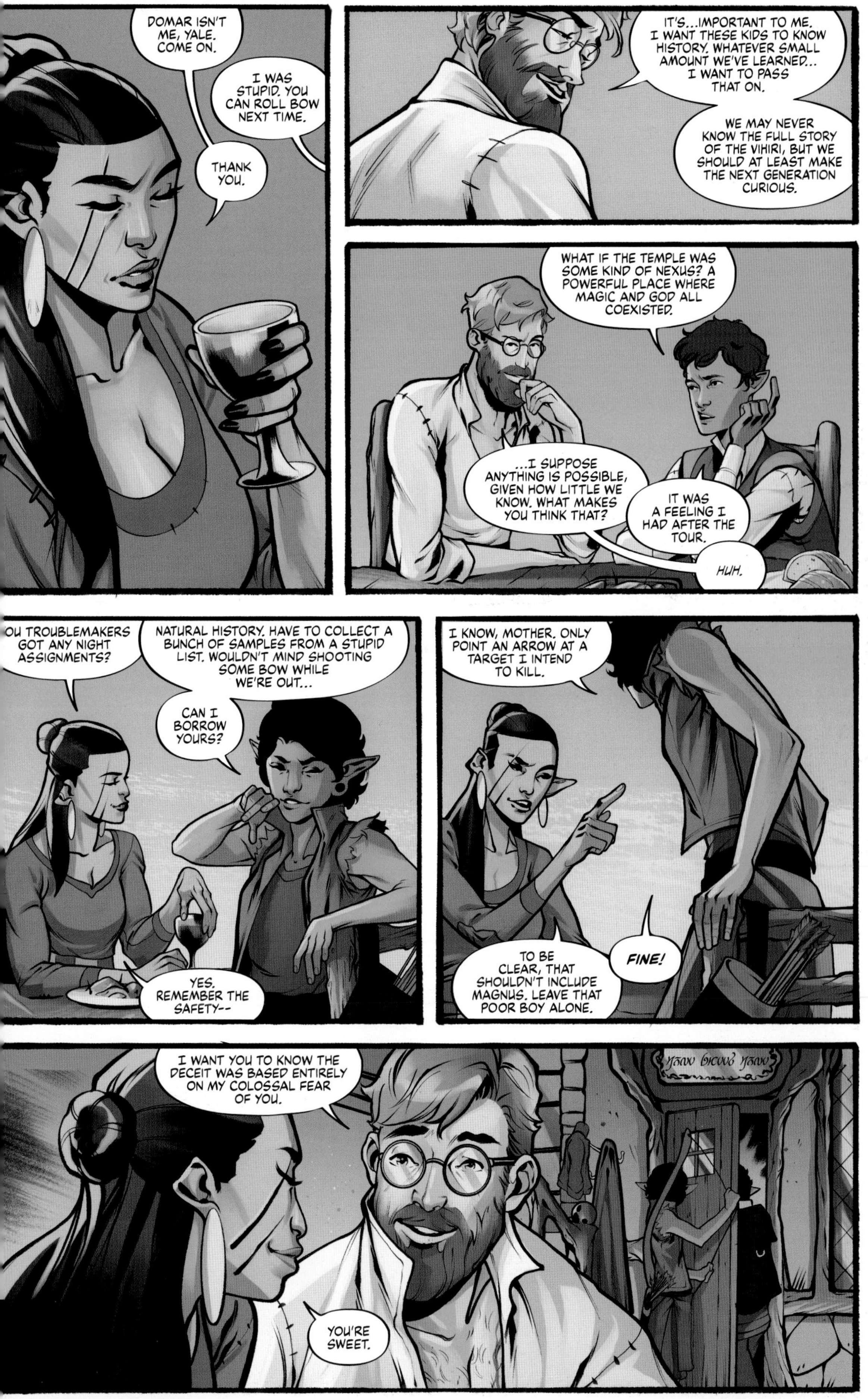
DOMAR ISN'T ME, YALE. COME ON.
I WAS STUPID. YOU CAN ROLL BOW NEXT TIME.
THANK YOU.
IT'S...IMPORTANT TO ME. I WANT THESE KIDS TO KNOW HISTORY. WHATEVER SMALL AMOUNT WE'VE LEARNED... I WANT TO PASS THAT ON.
WE MAY NEVER KNOW THE FULL STORY OF THE VIHIRI, BUT WE SHOULD AT LEAST MAKE THE NEXT GENERATION CURIOUS.
WHAT IF THE TEMPLE WAS SOME KIND OF NEXUS? A POWERFUL PLACE WHERE MAGIC AND GOD ALL COEXISTED.
...I SUPPOSE ANYTHING IS POSSIBLE, GIVEN HOW LITTLE WE KNOW. WHAT MAKES YOU THINK THAT?
IT WAS A FEELING I HAD AFTER THE TOUR.
HUH.
OU TROUBLEMAKERS GOT ANY NIGHT ASSIGNMENTS?
NATURAL HISTORY. HAVE TO COLLECT A BUNCH OF SAMPLES FROM A STUPID LIST. WOULDN'T MIND SHOOTING SOME BOW WHILE WE'RE OUT...
CAN I BORROW YOURS?
YES. REMEMBER THE SAFETY--
I KNOW, MOTHER. ONLY POINT AN ARROW AT A TARGET I INTEND TO KILL.
TO BE CLEAR, THAT SHOULDN'T INCLUDE MAGNUS. LEAVE THAT POOR BOY ALONE.
FINE!
I WANT YOU TO KNOW THE DECEIT WAS BASED ENTIRELY ON MY COLOSSAL FEAR OF YOU.
YOU'RE SWEET.

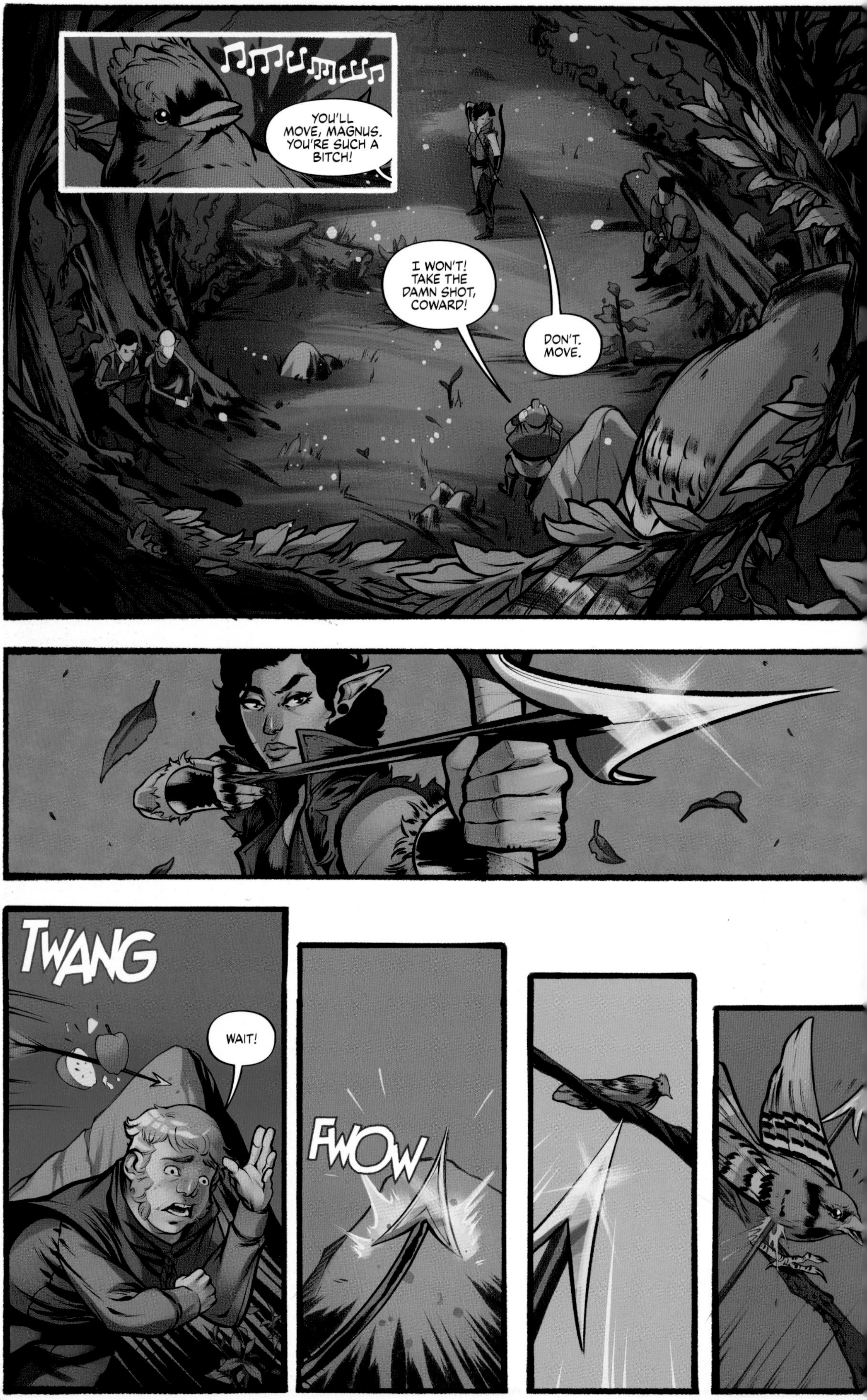
YOU'LL MOVE, MAGNUS. YOU'RE SUCH A BITCH!
I WON'T! TAKE THE DAMN SHOT, COWARD!
DON'T. MOVE.
TWANG
WAIT!
FWOW

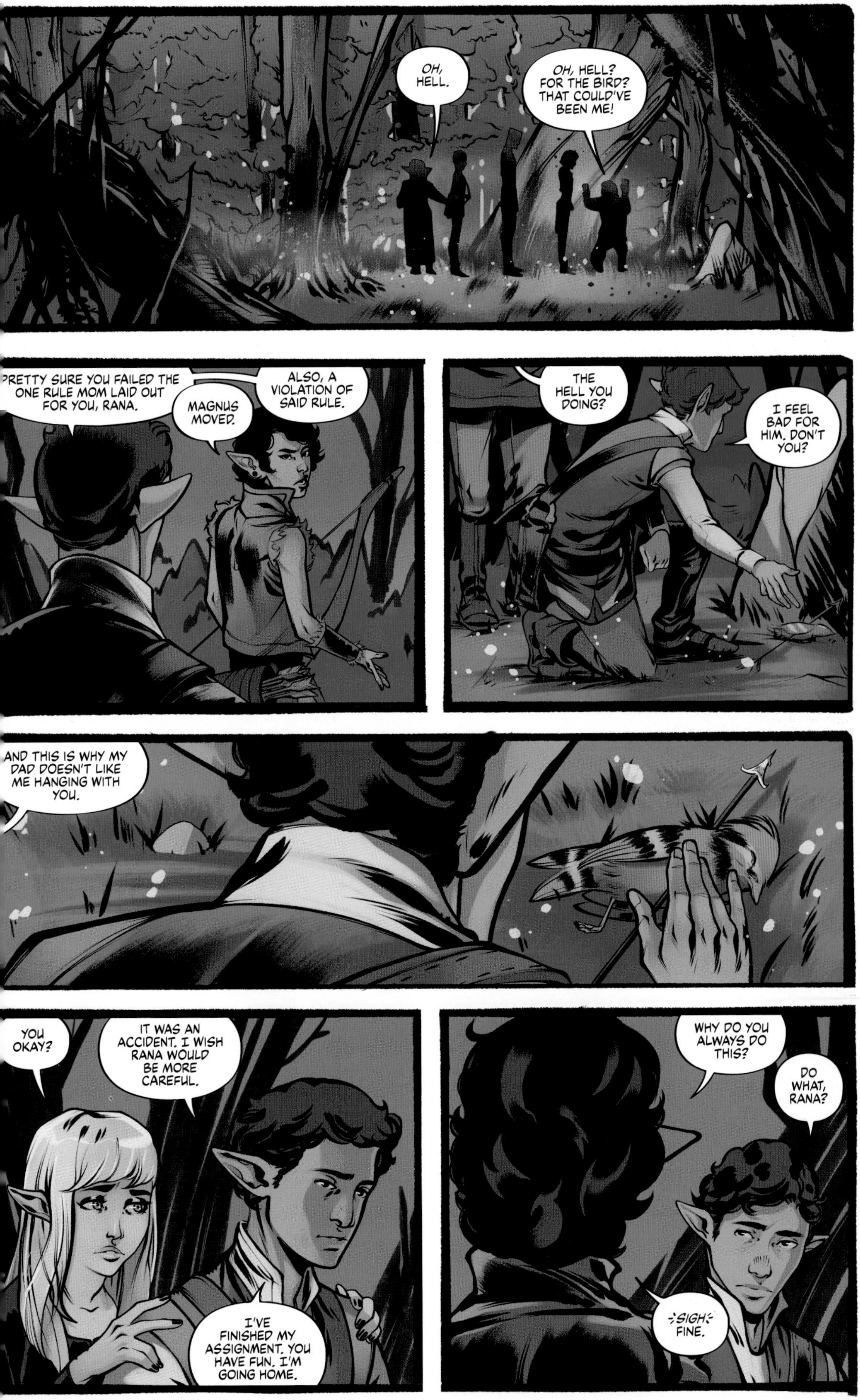
OH, HELL.
OH, HELL? FOR THE BIRD? THAT COULD'VE BEEN ME!
PRETTY SURE YOU FAILED THE ONE RULE MOM LAID OUT FOR YOU, RANA.
MAGNUS MOVED.
ALSO, A VIOLATION OF SAID RULE.
THE HELL YOU DOING?
I FEEL BAD FOR HIM. DON'T YOU?
AND THIS IS WHY MY DAD DOESN'T LIKE ME HANGING WITH YOU.
YOU OKAY?
IT WAS AN ACCIDENT. I WISH RANA WOULD BE MORE CAREFUL.
I'VE FINISHED MY ASSIGNMENT. YOU HAVE FUN. I'M GOING HOME.
WHY DO YOU ALWAYS DO THIS?
DO WHAT, RANA?
SIGH FINE.

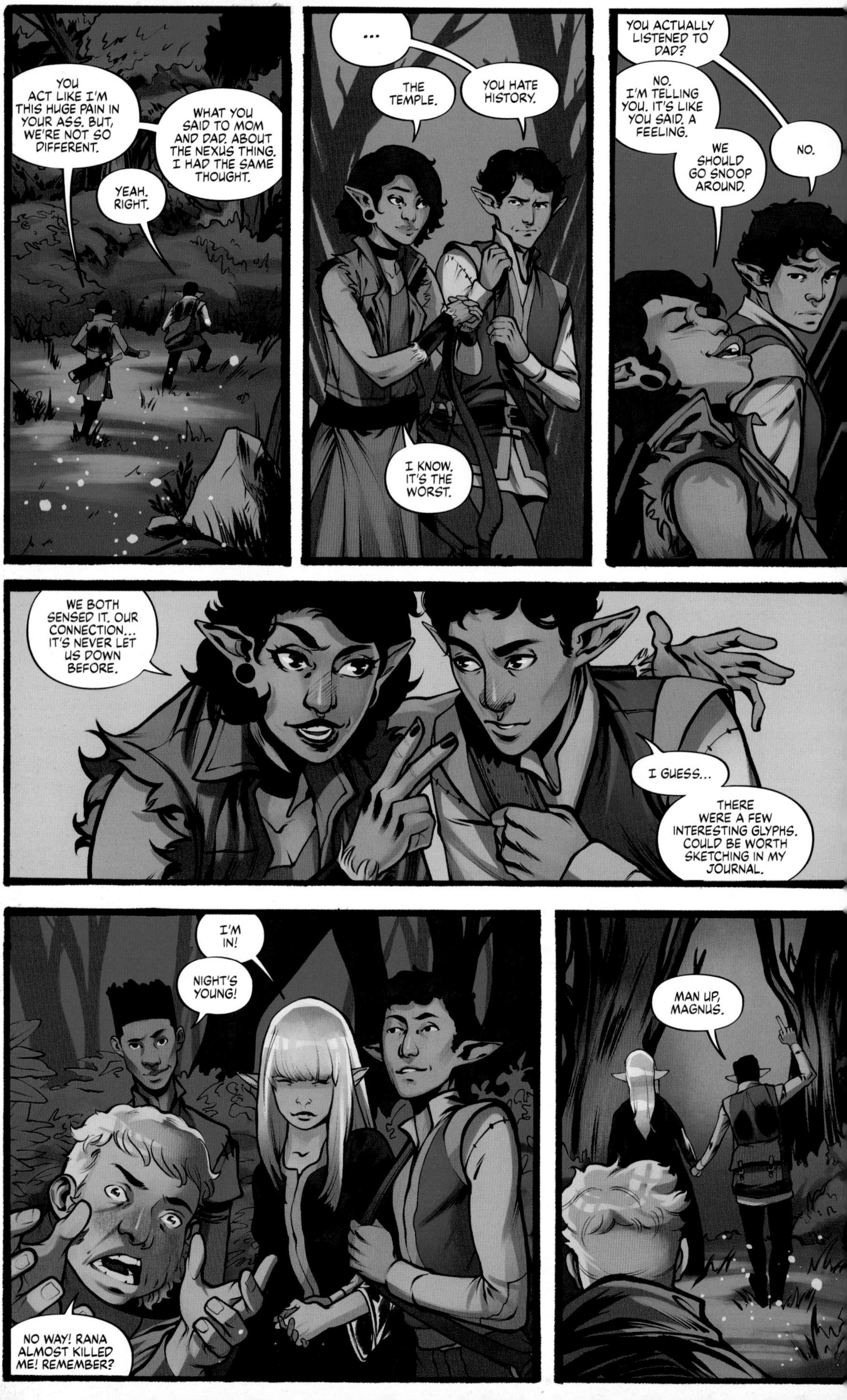
YOU ACT LIKE I'M THIS HUGE PAIN IN YOUR ASS. BUT, WE'RE NOT SO DIFFERENT.
WHAT YOU SAID TO MOM AND DAD. ABOUT THE NEXUS THING. I HAD THE SAME THOUGHT.
YEAH. RIGHT.
...
THE TEMPLE.
YOU HATE HISTORY.
I KNOW. IT'S THE WORST.
YOU ACTUALLY LISTENED TO DAD?
NO. I'M TELLING YOU. IT'S LIKE YOU SAID. A FEELING.
WE SHOULD GO SNOOP AROUND.
NO.
WE BOTH SENSED IT. OUR CONNECTION... IT'S NEVER LET US DOWN BEFORE.
I GUESS...
THERE WERE A FEW INTERESTING GLYPHS. COULD BE WORTH SKETCHING IN MY JOURNAL.
I'M IN!
NIGHT'S YOUNG!
NO WAY! RANA ALMOST KILLED ME! REMEMBER?
MAN UP, MAGNUS.

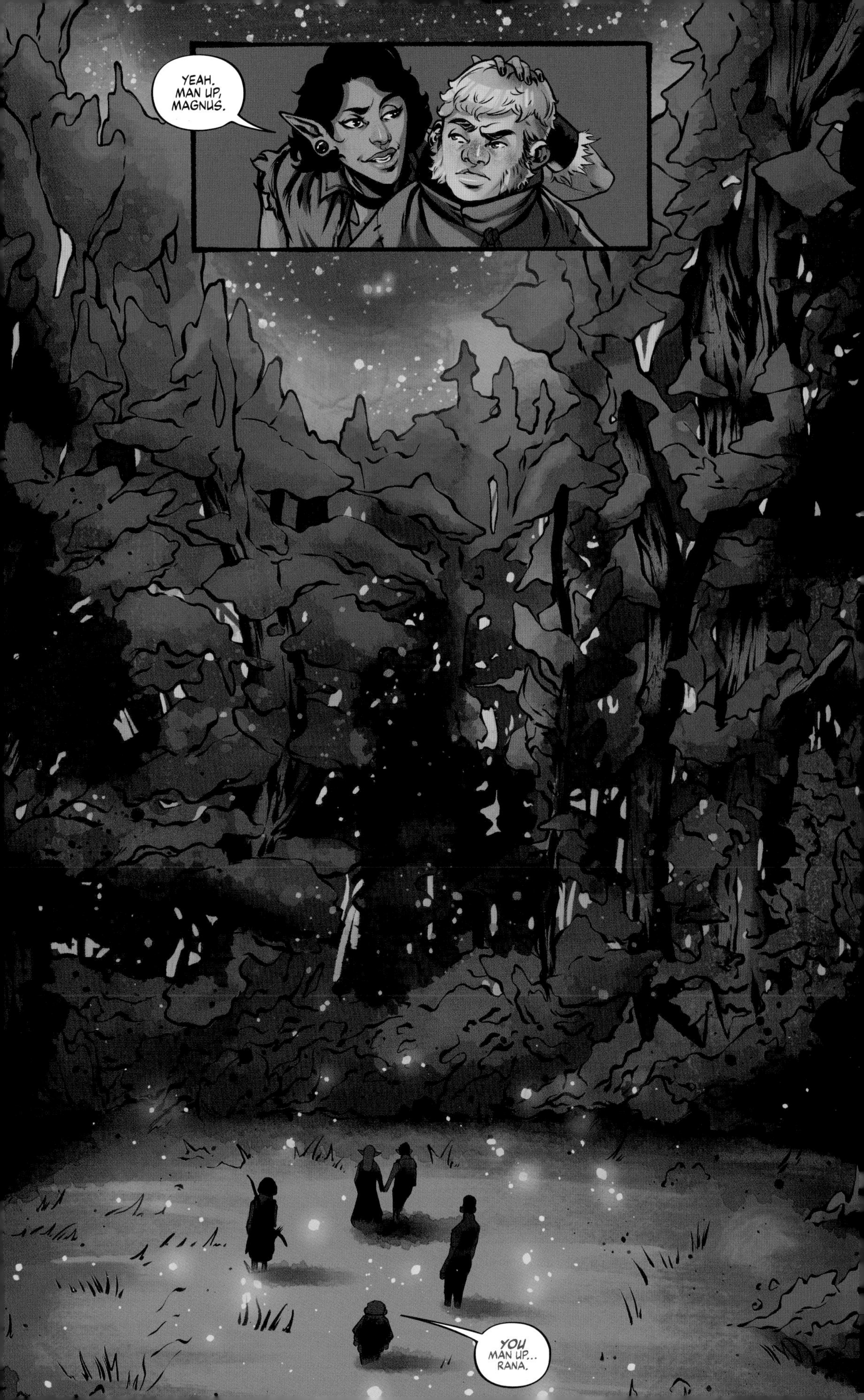
YEAH. MAN UP, MAGNUS.
YOU MAN UP... RANA.

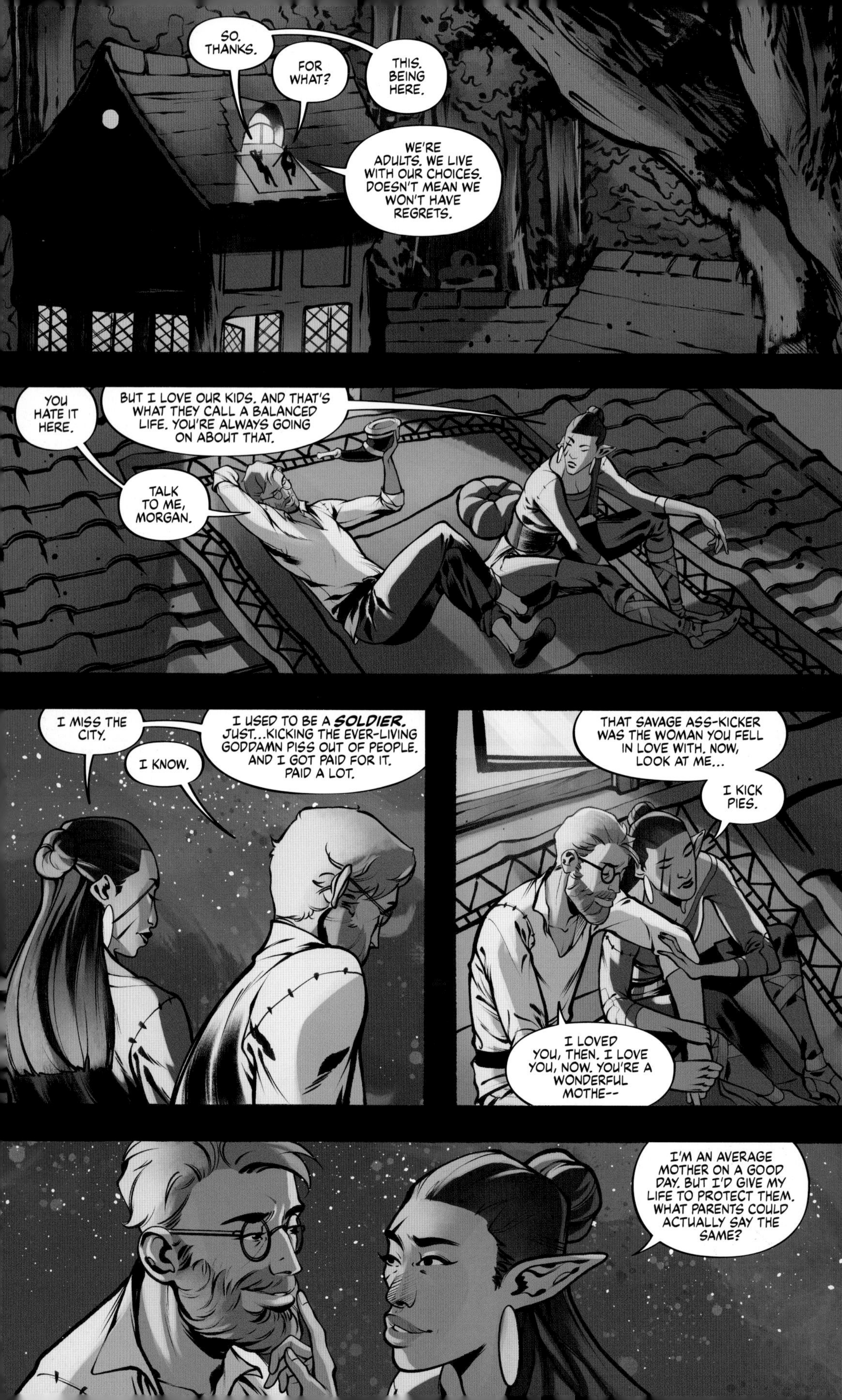
SO. THANKS.
FOR WHAT?
THIS. BEING HERE.
WE'RE ADULTS. WE LIVE WITH OUR CHOICES. DOESN'T MEAN WE WON'T HAVE REGRETS.
YOU HATE IT HERE.
BUT I LOVE OUR KIDS. AND THAT'S WHAT THEY CALL A BALANCED LIFE. YOU'RE ALWAYS GOING ON ABOUT THAT.
TALK TO ME, MORGAN.
I MISS THE CITY.
I KNOW.
I USED TO BE A SOLDIER. JUST...KICKING THE EVER-LIVING GODDAMN PISS OUT OF PEOPLE. AND I GOT PAID FOR IT. PAID A LOT.
THAT SAVAGE ASS-KICKER WAS THE WOMAN YOU FELL IN LOVE WITH. NOW, LOOK AT ME...
I KICK PIES.
I LOVED YOU, THEN. I LOVE YOU, NOW. YOU'RE A WONDERFUL MOTHE--
I'M AN AVERAGE MOTHER ON A GOOD DAY. BUT I'D GIVE MY LIFE TO PROTECT THEM. WHAT PARENTS COULD ACTUALLY SAY THE SAME?

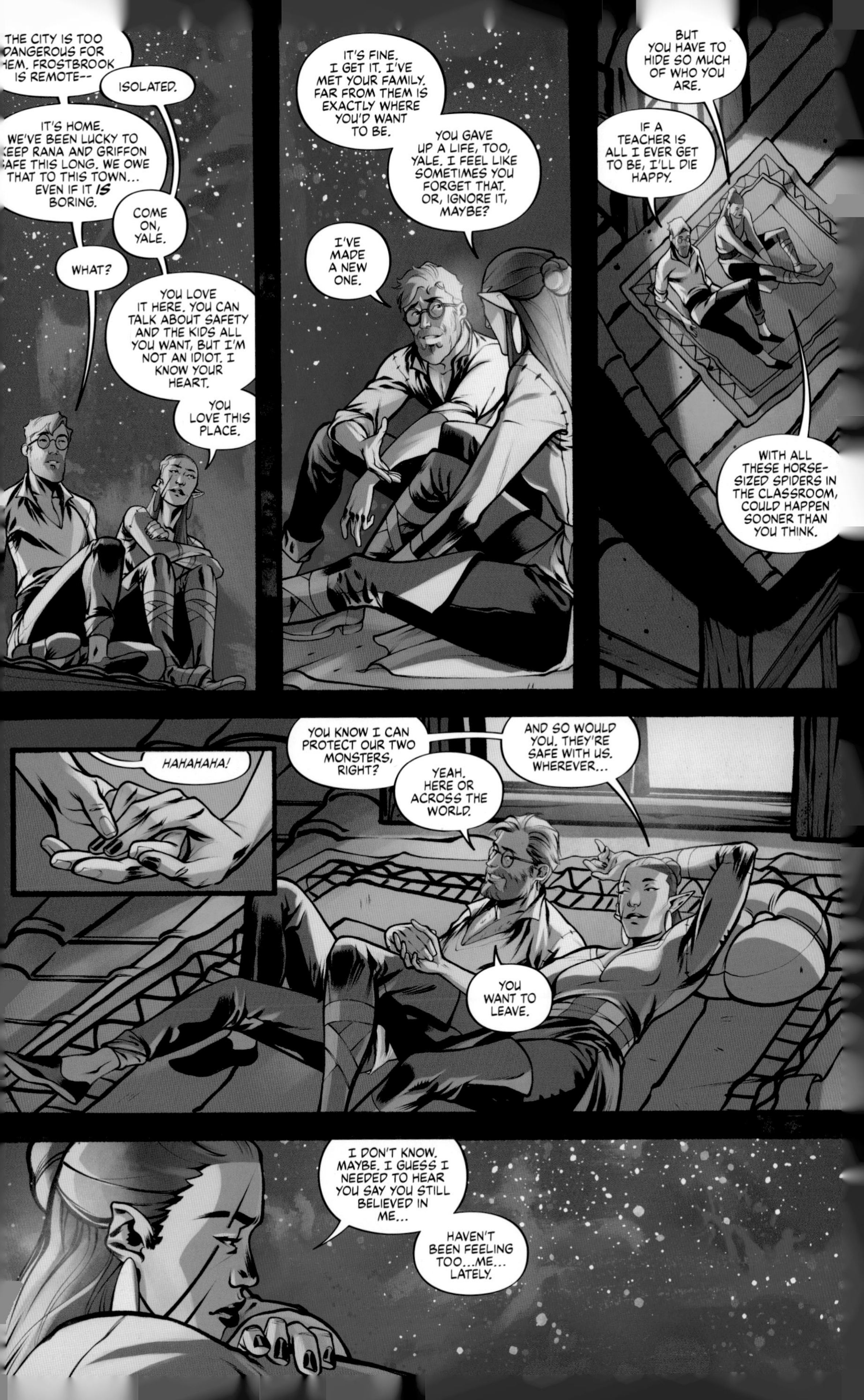
THE CITY IS TOO DANGEROUS FOR THEM. FROSTBROOK IS REMOTE--
ISOLATED.
IT'S HOME. WE'VE BEEN LUCKY TO KEEP RANA AND GRIFFON SAFE THIS LONG. WE OWE THAT TO THIS TOWN... EVEN IF IT IS BORING.
COME ON, YALE.
WHAT?
YOU LOVE IT HERE. YOU CAN TALK ABOUT SAFETY AND THE KIDS ALL YOU WANT, BUT I'M NOT AN IDIOT. I KNOW YOUR HEART.
YOU LOVE THIS PLACE.
IT'S FINE. I GET IT. I'VE MET YOUR FAMILY. FAR FROM THEM IS EXACTLY WHERE YOU'D WANT TO BE.
YOU GAVE UP A LIFE, TOO, YALE. I FEEL LIKE SOMETIMES YOU FORGET THAT. OR, IGNORE IT, MAYBE?
I'VE MADE A NEW ONE.
BUT YOU HAVE TO HIDE SO MUCH OF WHO YOU ARE.
IF A TEACHER IS ALL I EVER GET TO BE, I'LL DIE HAPPY.
WITH ALL THESE HORSE-SIZED SPIDERS IN THE CLASSROOM, COULD HAPPEN SOONER THAN YOU THINK.
HAHAHAHA!
YOU KNOW I CAN PROTECT OUR TWO MONSTERS, RIGHT?
AND SO WOULD YOU. THEY'RE SAFE WITH US. WHEREVER...
YEAH. HERE OR ACROSS THE WORLD.
YOU WANT TO LEAVE.
I DON'T KNOW. MAYBE. I GUESS I NEEDED TO HEAR YOU SAY YOU STILL BELIEVED IN ME...
HAVEN'T BEEN FEELING TOO...ME... LATELY.

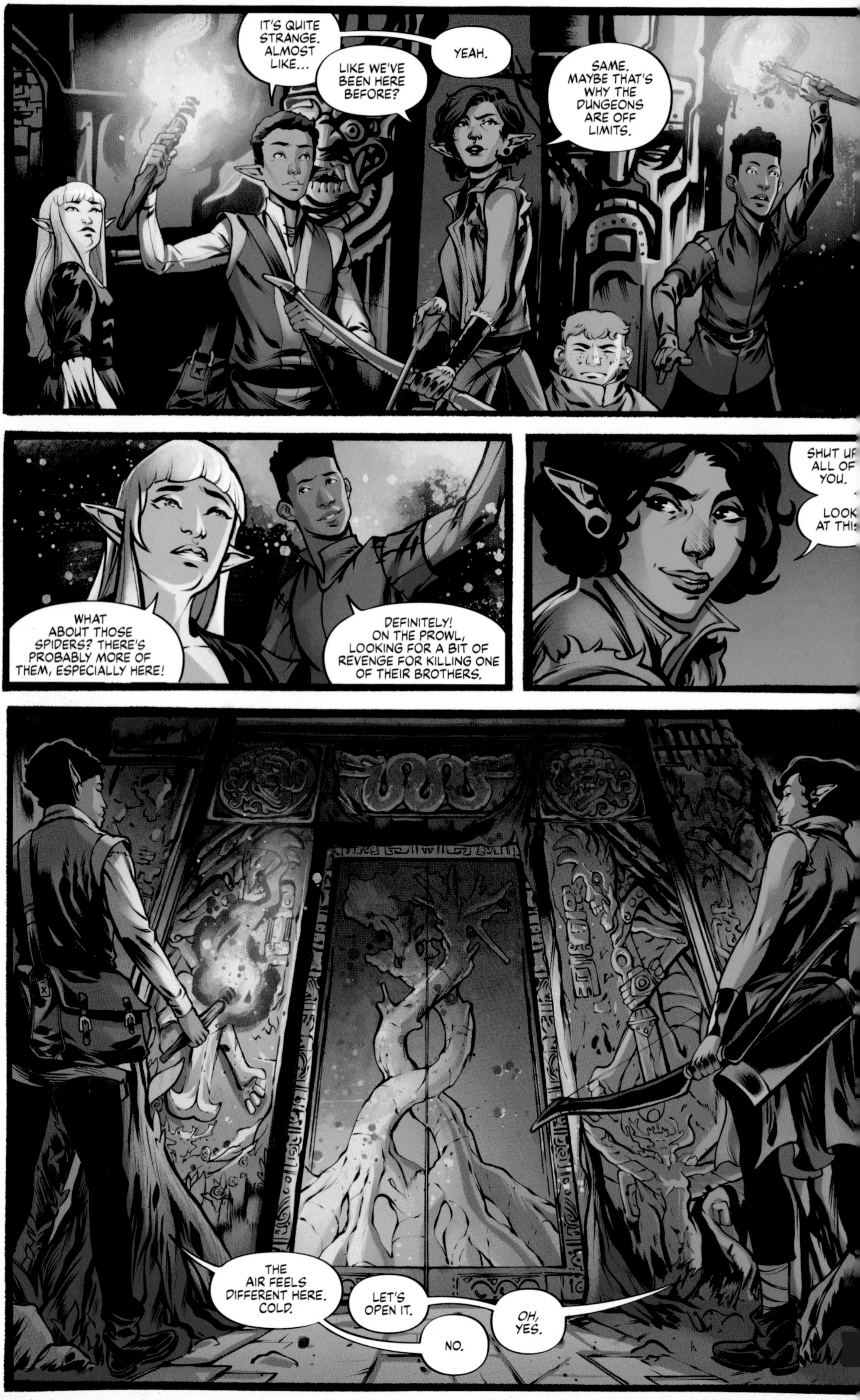
IT'S QUITE STRANGE. ALMOST LIKE...
LIKE WE'VE BEEN HERE BEFORE?
YEAH.
SAME. MAYBE THAT'S WHY THE DUNGEONS ARE OFF LIMITS.
WHAT ABOUT THOSE SPIDERS? THERE'S PROBABLY MORE OF THEM, ESPECIALLY HERE!
DEFINITELY! ON THE PROWL, LOOKING FOR A BIT OF REVENGE FOR KILLING ONE OF THEIR BROTHERS.
SHUT U
ALL OF
YOU.
LOOK
AT THI
THE AIR FEELS DIFFERENT HERE. COLD.
LET'S OPEN IT.
NO.
OH, YES.

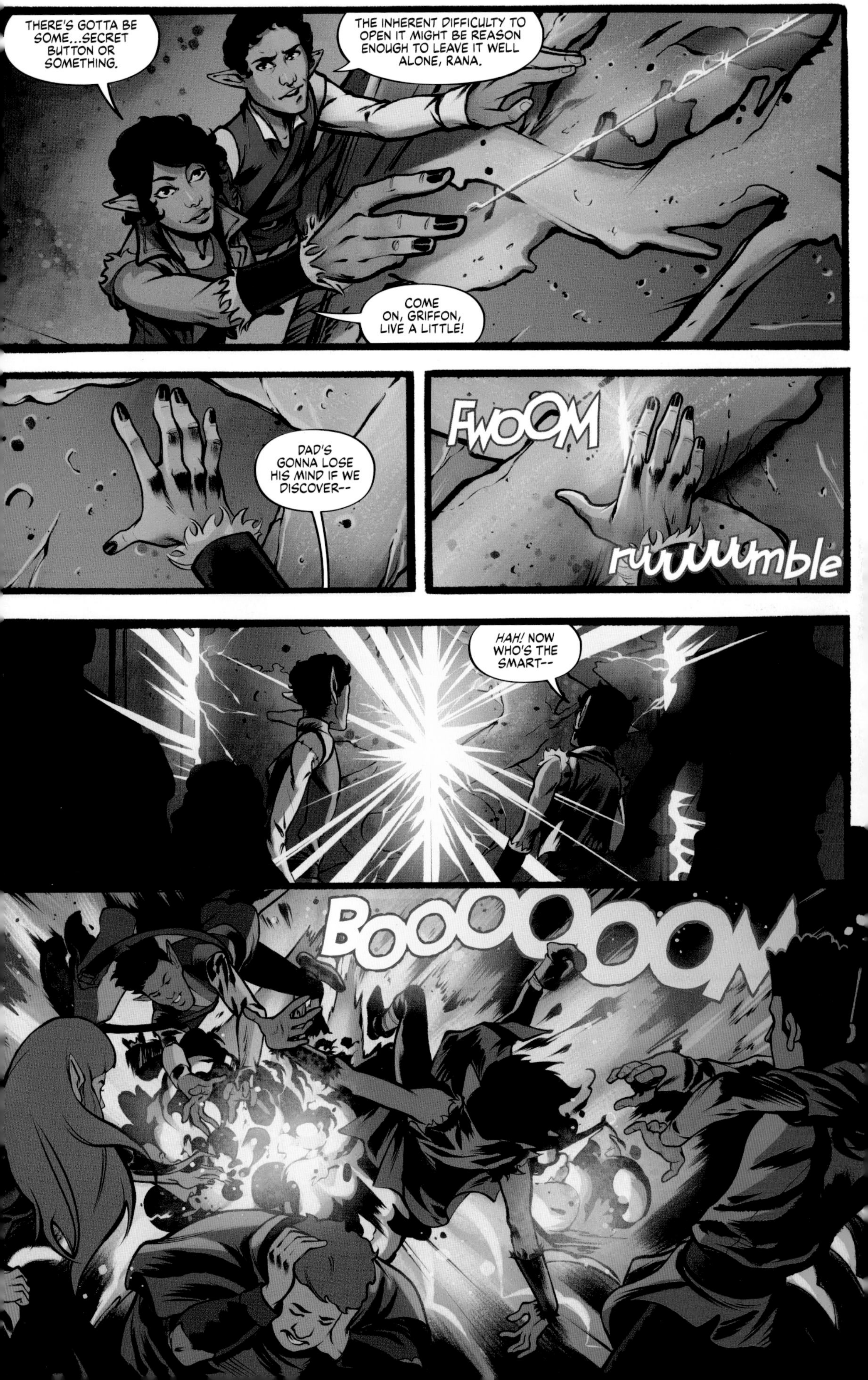
THERE'S GOTTA BE SOME...SECRET BUTTON OR SOMETHING.
THE INHERENT DIFFICULTY TO OPEN IT MIGHT BE REASON ENOUGH TO LEAVE IT WELL ALONE, RANA.
COME ON, GRIFFON, LIVE A LITTLE!
DAD'S GONNA LOSE HIS MIND IF WE DISCOVER--
FWOOM
ruuuumble
HAH! NOW WHO'S THE SMART--
BOOOOOOOM

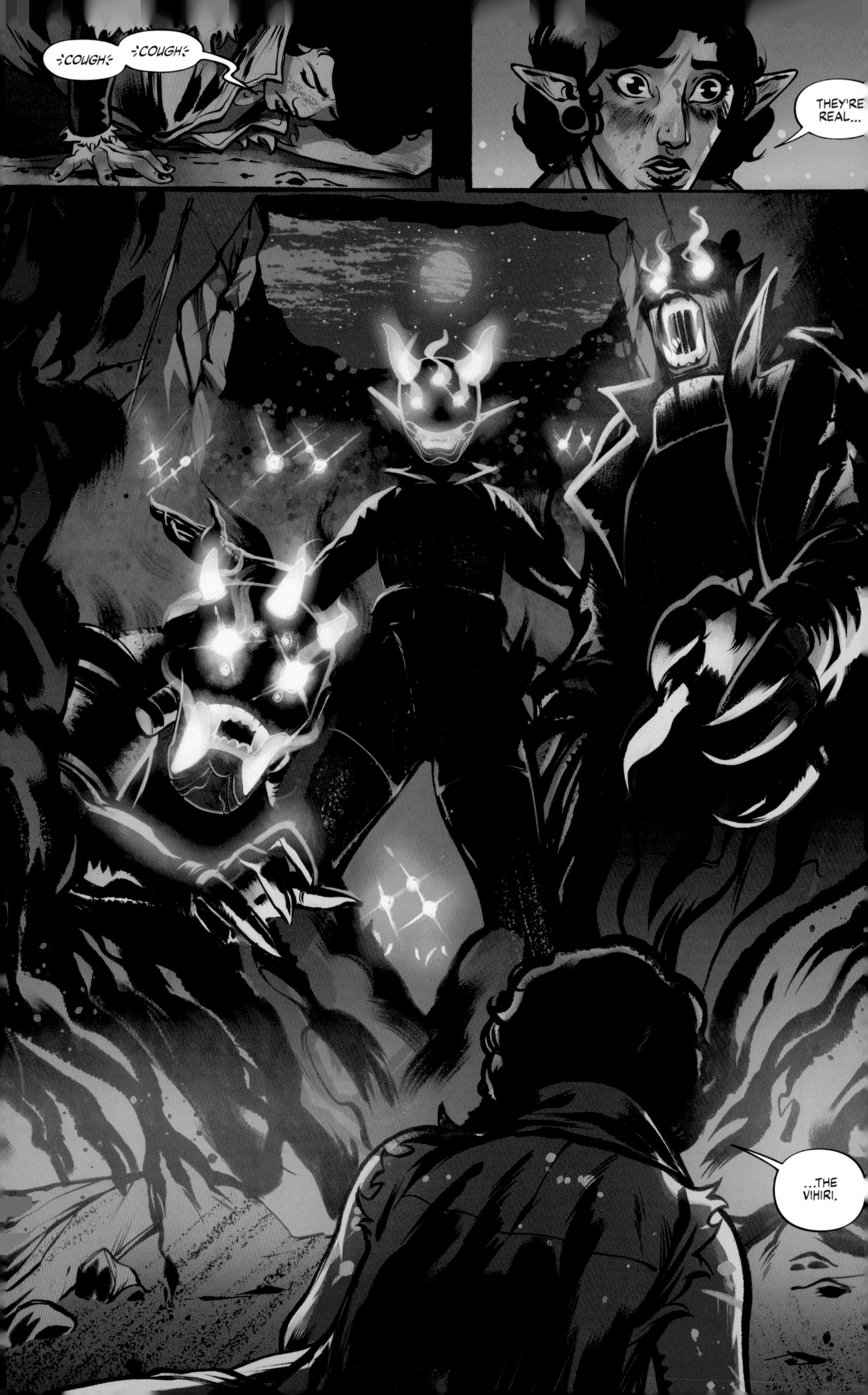
-COUGH- -COUGH-
THEY'RE REAL...
...THE VIHIRI.

CHAPTER TWO

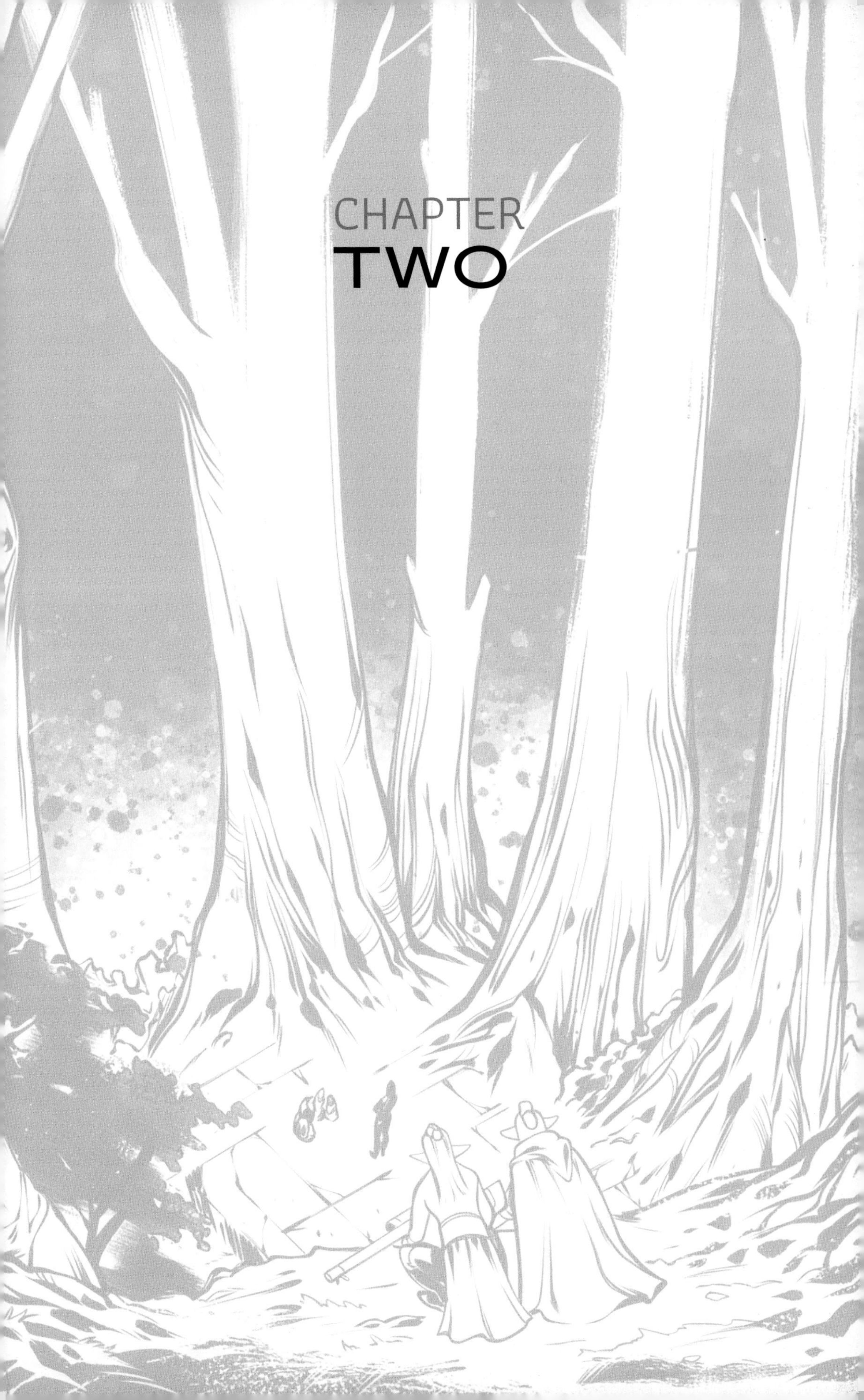

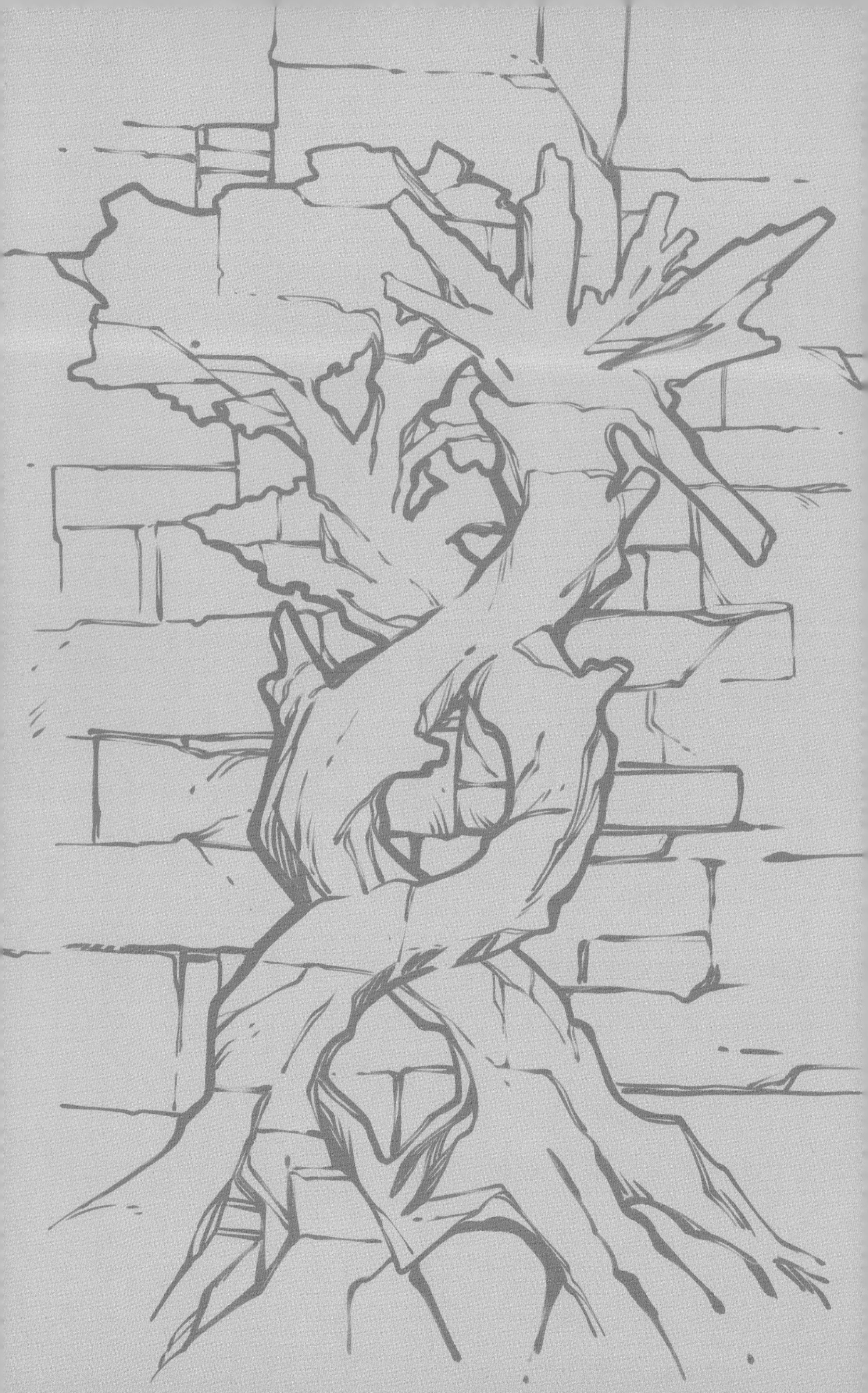

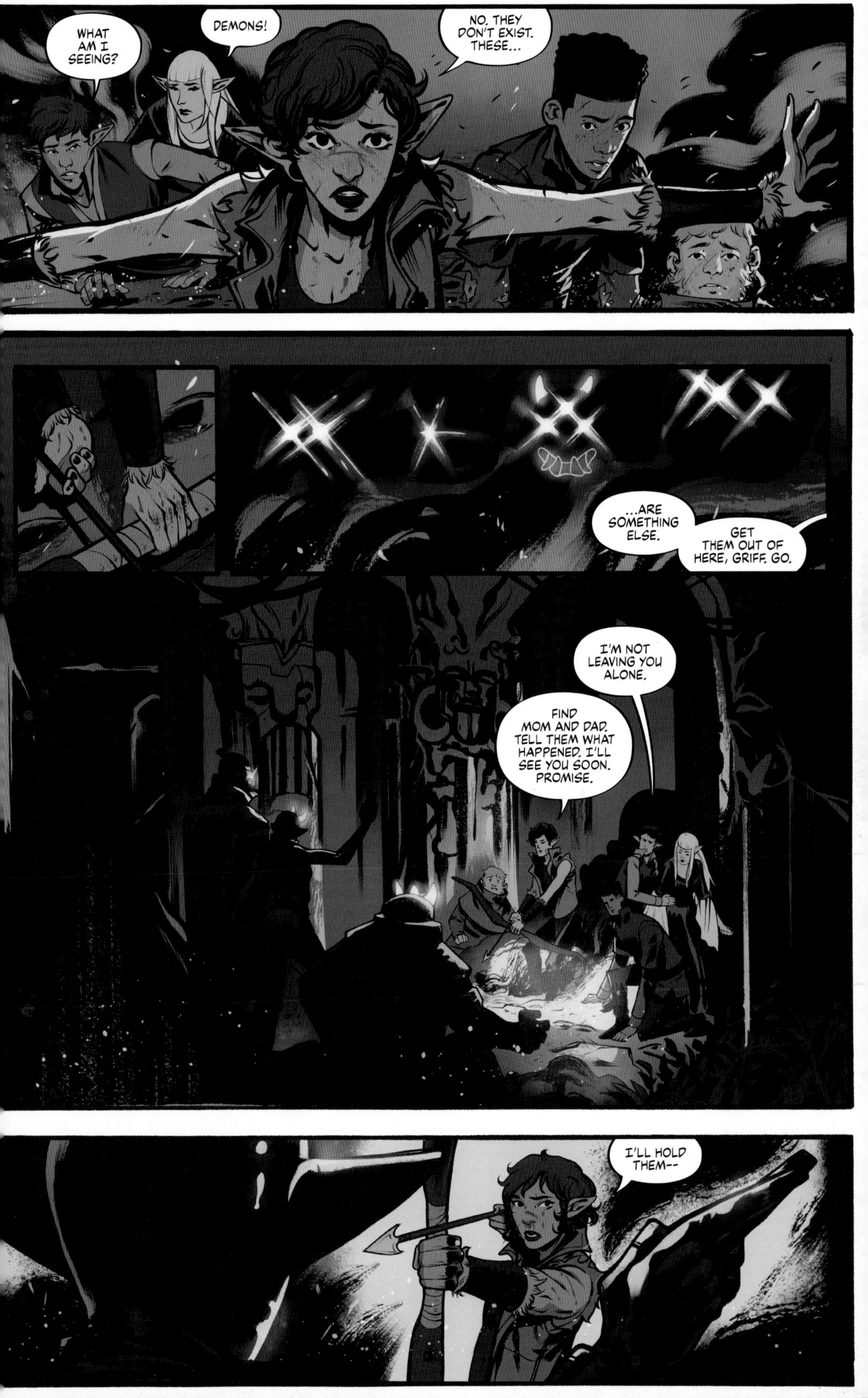
WHAT AM I SEEING?
DEMONS!
NO. THEY DON'T EXIST. THESE...
...ARE SOMETHING ELSE.
GET THEM OUT OF HERE, GRIFF. GO.
I'M NOT LEAVING YOU ALONE.
FIND MOM AND DAD. TELL THEM WHAT HAPPENED. I'LL SEE YOU SOON. PROMISE.
I'LL HOLD THEM--

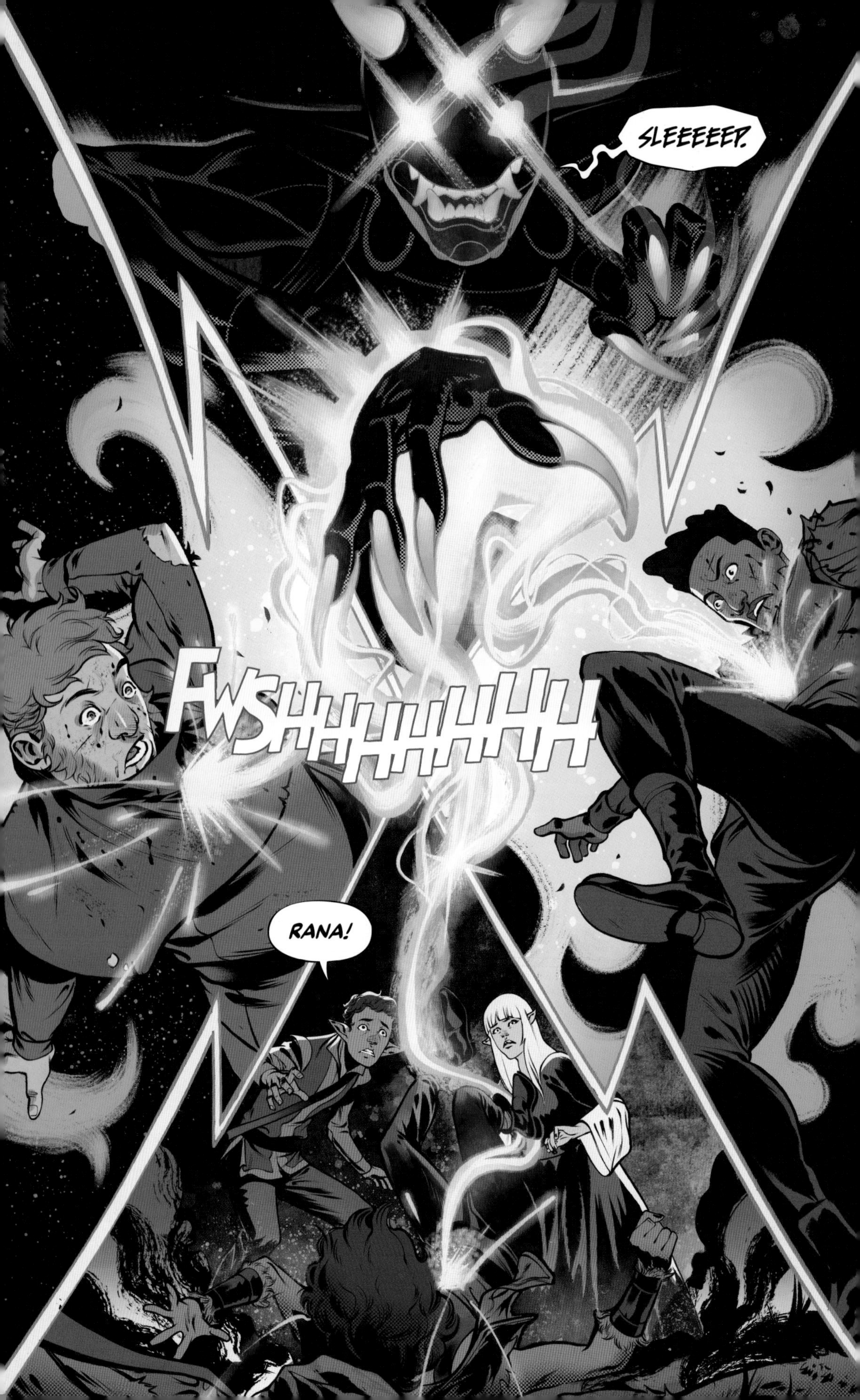
SLEEEEEP.
FWSHHHHHHHHH
RANA!

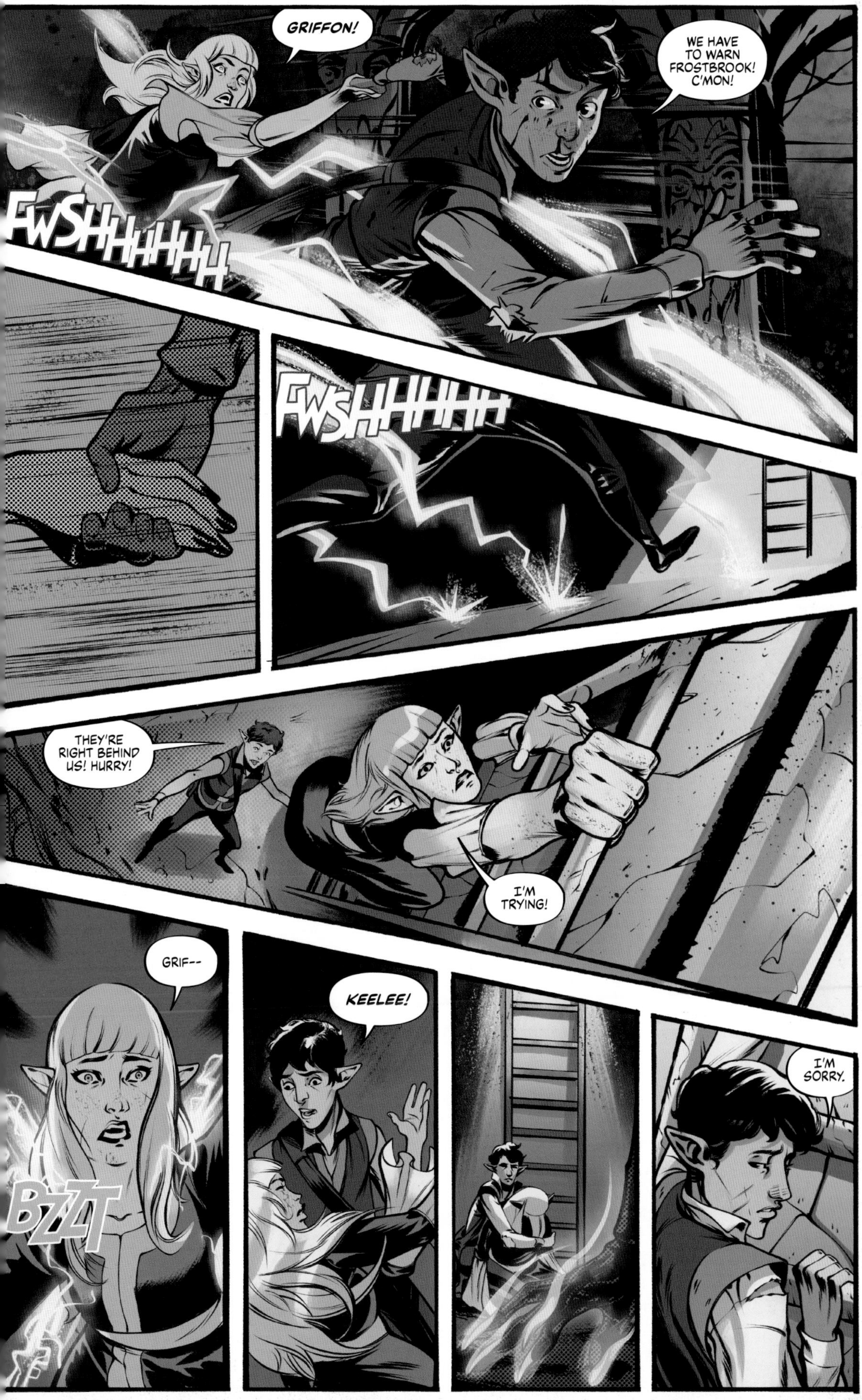
GRIFFON!
WE HAVE TO WARN FROSTBROOK! C'MON!
FWSHHHHHHH
FWSHHHHHH
THEY'RE RIGHT BEHIND US! HURRY!
I'M TRYING!
GRIF--
BZZT
KEELEE!
I'M SORRY.

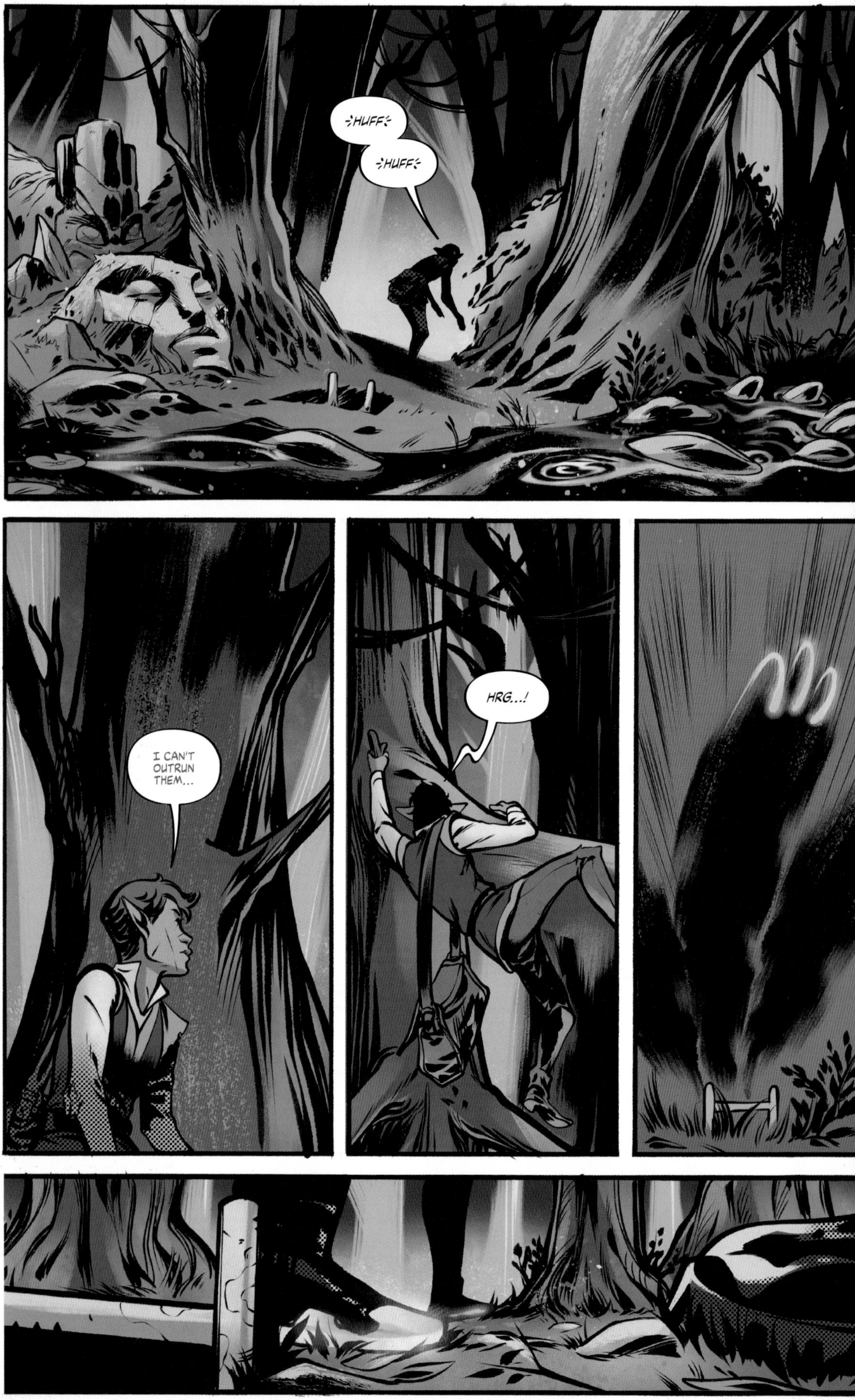
HUFF
HUFF
I CAN'T OUTRUN THEM...
HRG...!

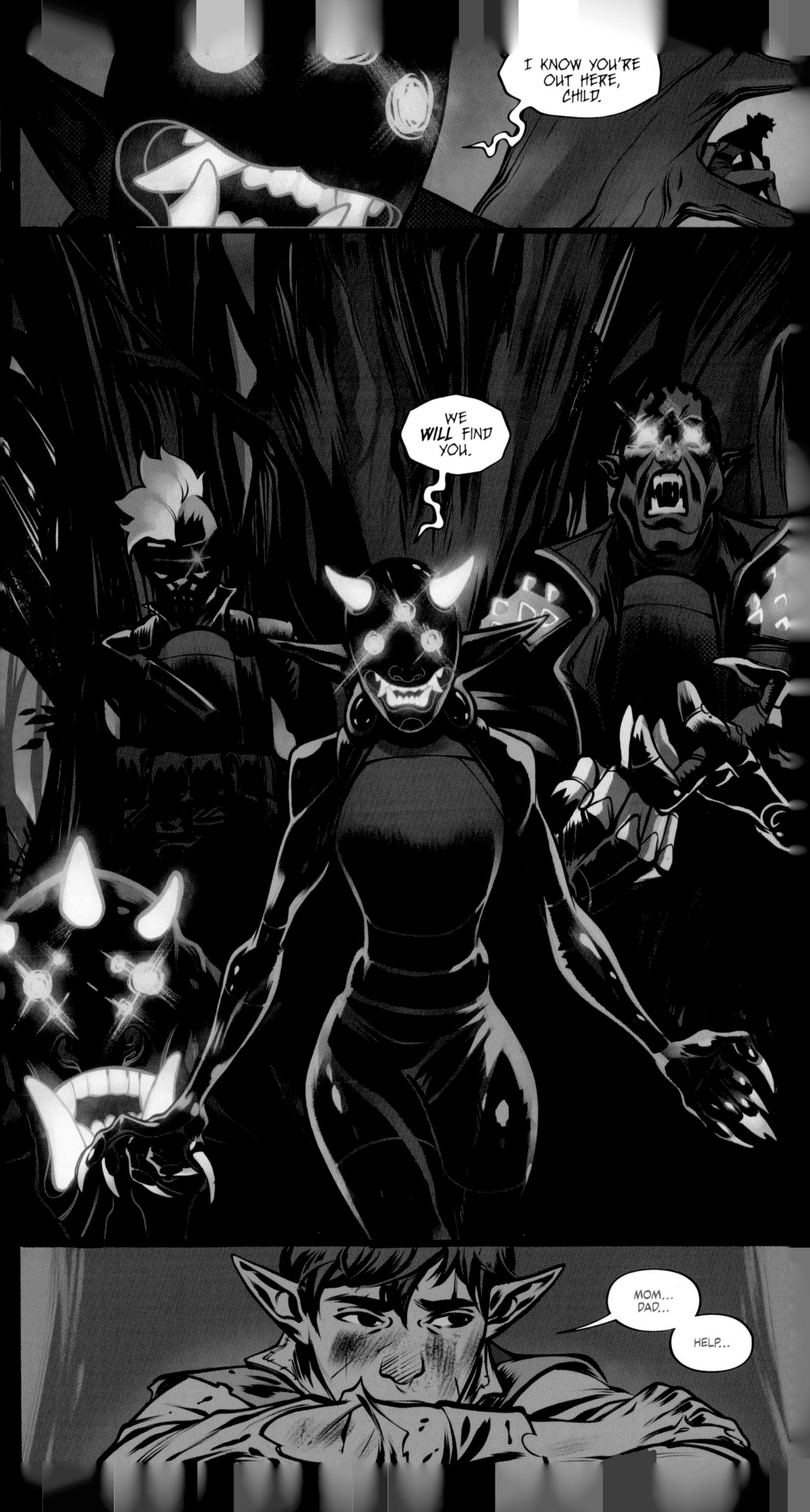
I KNOW YOU'RE OUT HERE, CHILD.
WE WILL FIND YOU.
MOM... DAD...
HELP...

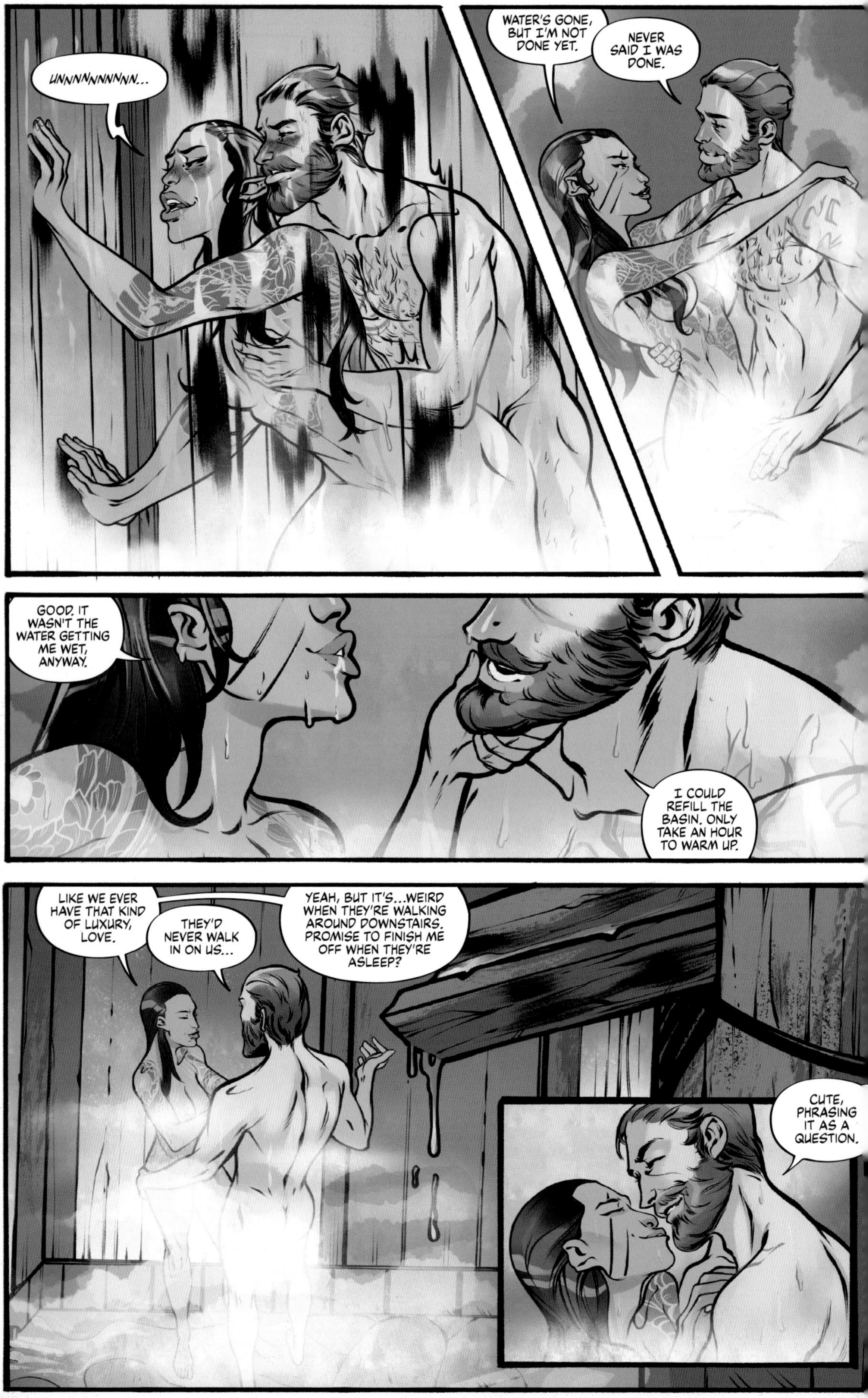
UNNNNNNNNNN...
WATER'S GONE, BUT I'M NOT DONE YET.
NEVER SAID I WAS DONE.
GOOD. IT WASN'T THE WATER GETTING ME WET, ANYWAY.
I COULD REFILL THE BASIN. ONLY TAKE AN HOUR TO WARM UP.
LIKE WE EVER HAVE THAT KIND OF LUXURY, LOVE.
THEY'D NEVER WALK IN ON US...
YEAH, BUT IT'S...WEIRD WHEN THEY'RE WALKING AROUND DOWNSTAIRS. PROMISE TO FINISH ME OFF WHEN THEY'RE ASLEEP?
CUTE, PHRASING IT AS A QUESTION.

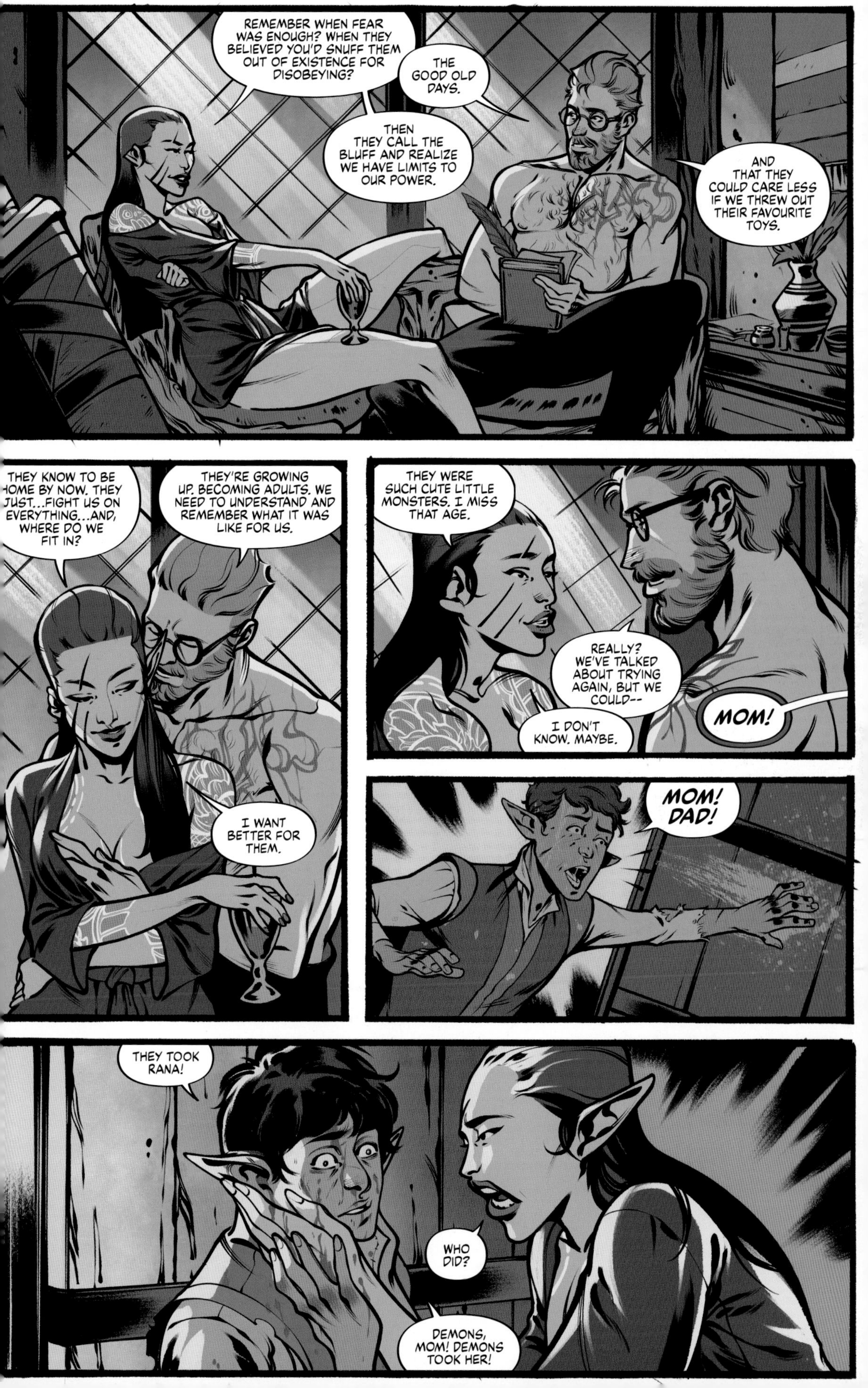
REMEMBER WHEN FEAR WAS ENOUGH? WHEN THEY BELIEVED YOU'D SNUFF THEM OUT OF EXISTENCE FOR DISOBEYING?
THE GOOD OLD DAYS.
THEN THEY CALL THE BLUFF AND REALIZE WE HAVE LIMITS TO OUR POWER.
AND THAT THEY COULD CARE LESS IF WE THREW OUT THEIR FAVOURITE TOYS.
THEY KNOW TO BE HOME BY NOW. THEY JUST...FIGHT US ON EVERYTHING...AND, WHERE DO WE FIT IN?
THEY'RE GROWING UP. BECOMING ADULTS. WE NEED TO UNDERSTAND AND REMEMBER WHAT IT WAS LIKE FOR US.
I WANT BETTER FOR THEM.
THEY WERE SUCH CUTE LITTLE MONSTERS. I MISS THAT AGE.
REALLY? WE'VE TALKED ABOUT TRYING AGAIN, BUT WE COULD--
I DON'T KNOW. MAYBE.
MOM!
MOM! DAD!
THEY TOOK RANA!
WHO DID?
DEMONS, MOM! DEMONS TOOK HER!

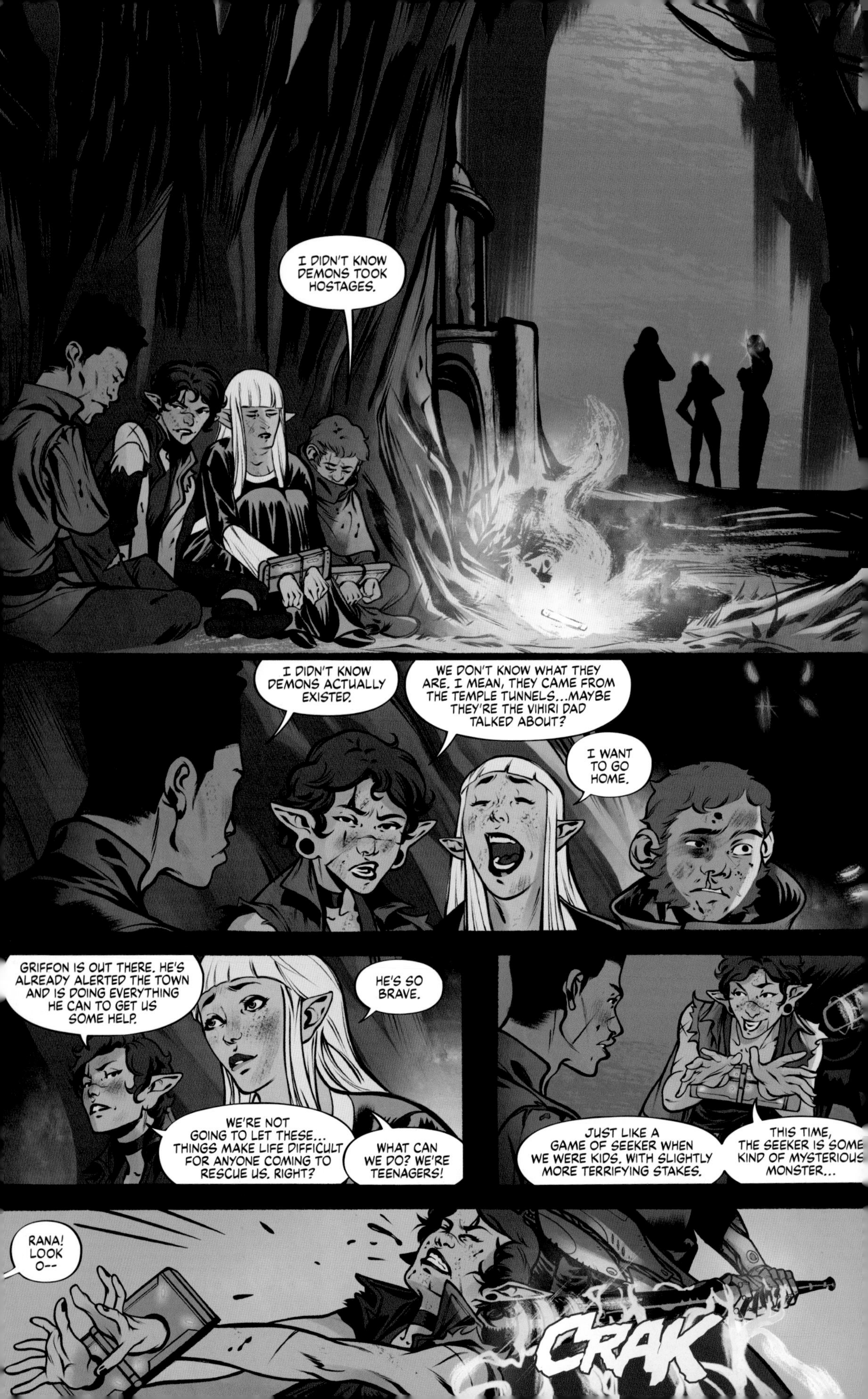
I DIDN'T KNOW DEMONS TOOK HOSTAGES.
I DIDN'T KNOW DEMONS ACTUALLY EXISTED.
WE DON'T KNOW WHAT THEY ARE. I MEAN, THEY CAME FROM THE TEMPLE TUNNELS...MAYBE THEY'RE THE VIHIRI DAD TALKED ABOUT?
I WANT TO GO HOME.
GRIFFON IS OUT THERE. HE'S ALREADY ALERTED THE TOWN AND IS DOING EVERYTHING HE CAN TO GET US SOME HELP.
HE'S SO BRAVE.
WE'RE NOT GOING TO LET THESE... THINGS MAKE LIFE DIFFICULT FOR ANYONE COMING TO RESCUE US. RIGHT?
WHAT CAN WE DO? WE'RE TEENAGERS!
JUST LIKE A GAME OF SEEKER WHEN WE WERE KIDS. WITH SLIGHTLY MORE TERRIFYING STAKES.
THIS TIME, THE SEEKER IS SOME KIND OF MYSTERIOUS MONSTER...
RANA! LOOK O--
CRAK

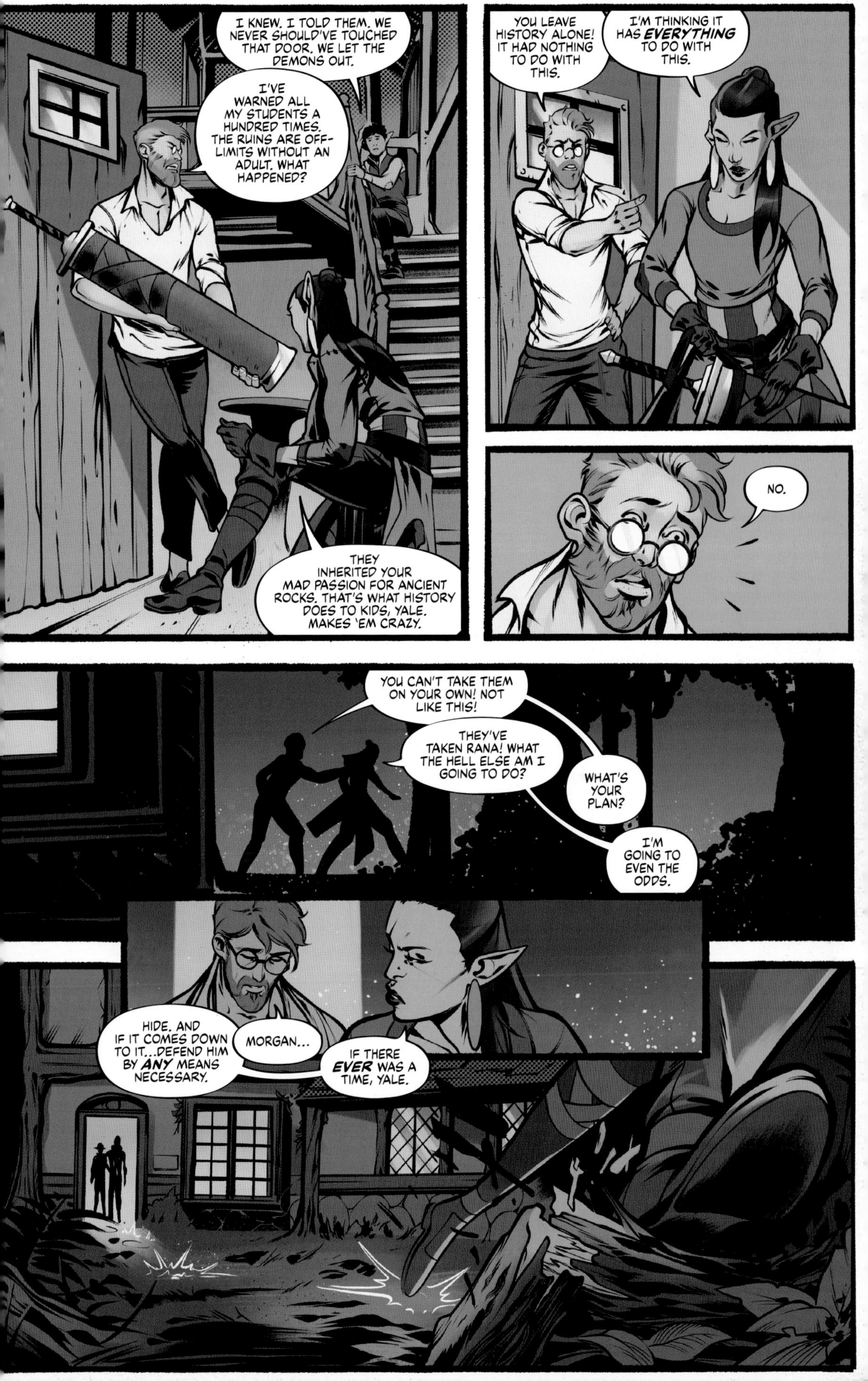
I KNEW. I TOLD THEM. WE NEVER SHOULD'VE TOUCHED THAT DOOR. WE LET THE DEMONS OUT.
I'VE WARNED ALL MY STUDENTS A HUNDRED TIMES. THE RUINS ARE OFF-LIMITS WITHOUT AN ADULT. WHAT HAPPENED?
THEY INHERITED YOUR MAD PASSION FOR ANCIENT ROCKS. THAT'S WHAT HISTORY DOES TO KIDS, YALE. MAKES 'EM CRAZY.
YOU LEAVE HISTORY ALONE! IT HAD NOTHING TO DO WITH THIS.
I'M THINKING IT HAS EVERYTHING TO DO WITH THIS.
NO.
YOU CAN'T TAKE THEM ON YOUR OWN! NOT LIKE THIS!
THEY'VE TAKEN RANA! WHAT THE HELL ELSE AM I GOING TO DO?
WHAT'S YOUR PLAN?
I'M GOING TO EVEN THE ODDS.
HIDE. AND IF IT COMES DOWN TO IT...DEFEND HIM BY ANY MEANS NECESSARY.
MORGAN...
IF THERE EVER WAS A TIME, YALE.

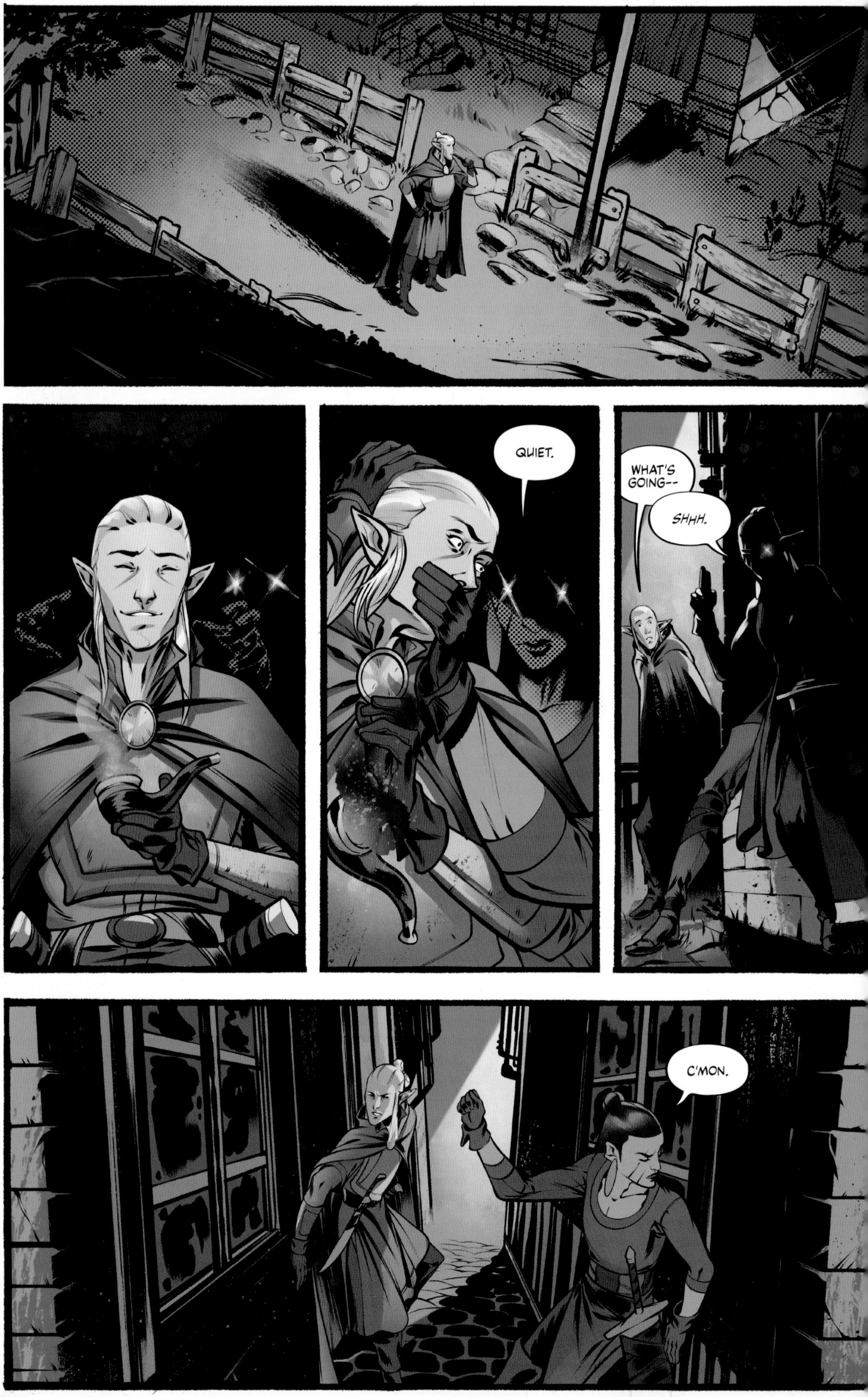
QUIET.
WHAT'S GOING--
SHHH.
C'MON.

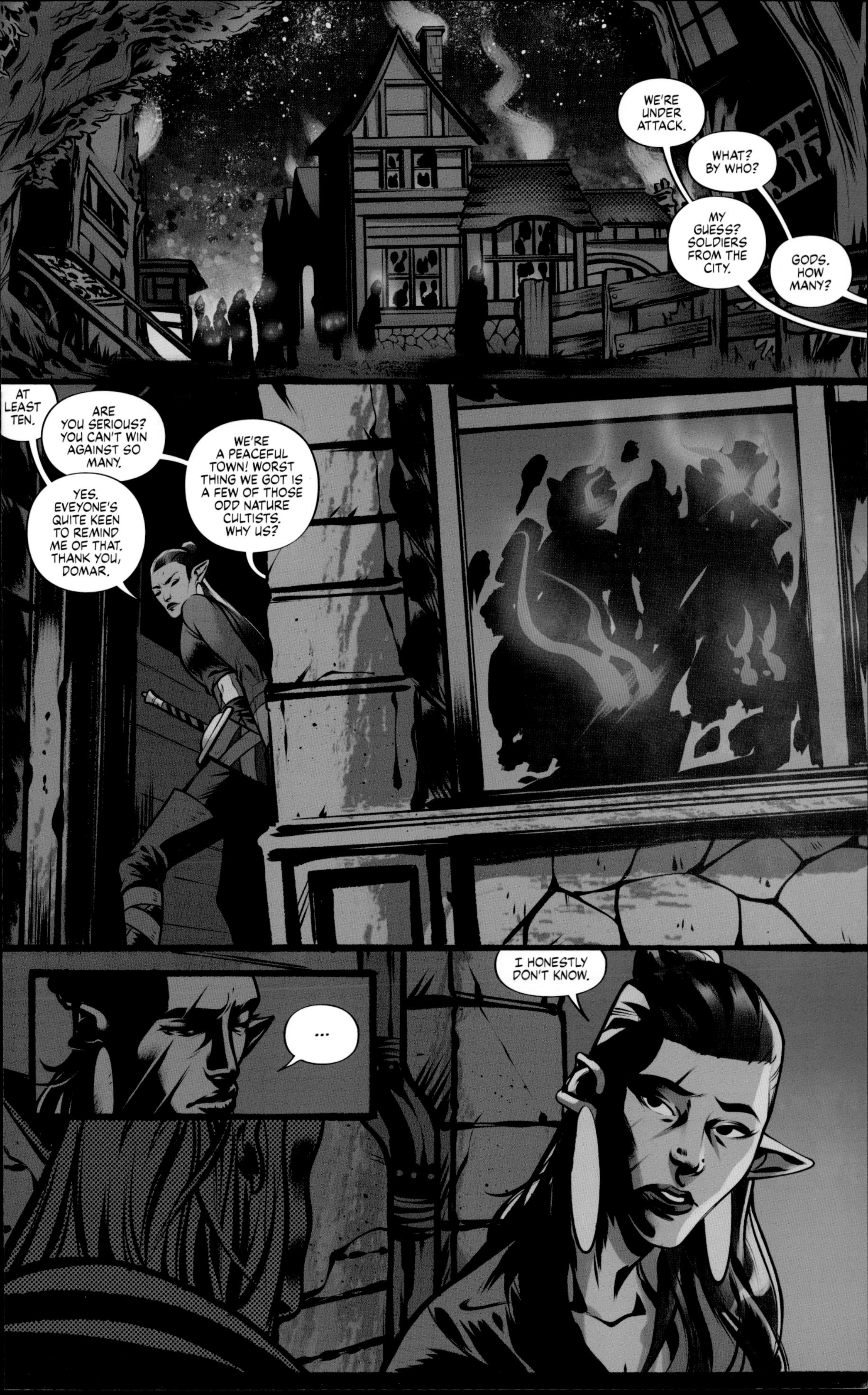
WE'RE UNDER ATTACK.
WHAT? BY WHO?
MY GUESS? SOLDIERS FROM THE CITY.
GODS. HOW MANY?
AT LEAST TEN.
ARE YOU SERIOUS? YOU CAN'T WIN AGAINST SO MANY.
YES. EVEYONE'S QUITE KEEN TO REMIND ME OF THAT. THANK YOU, DOMAR.
WE'RE A PEACEFUL TOWN! WORST THING WE GOT IS A FEW OF THOSE ODD NATURE CULTISTS. WHY US?
...
I HONESTLY DON'T KNOW.

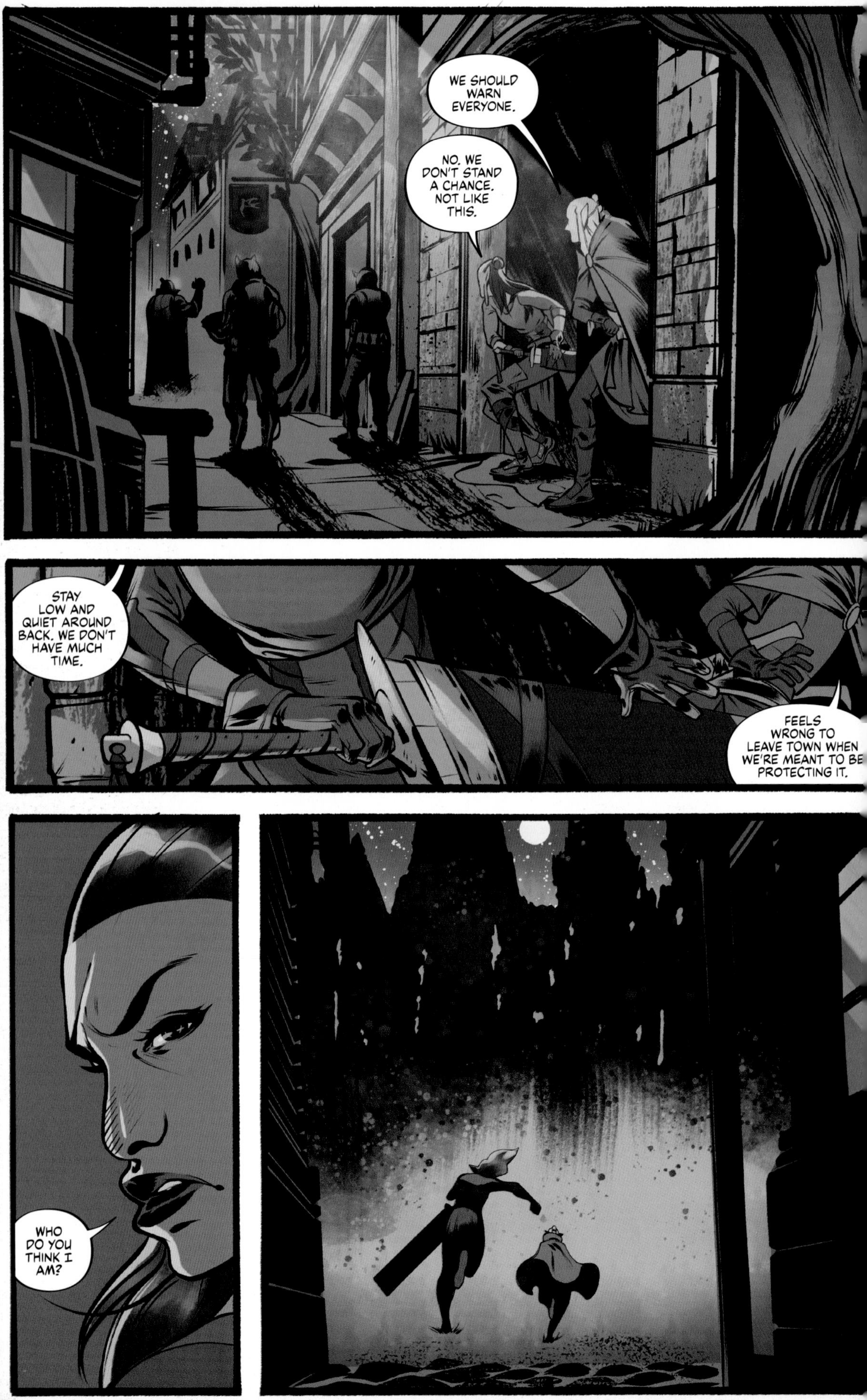
WE SHOULD WARN EVERYONE.
NO. WE DON'T STAND A CHANCE. NOT LIKE THIS.
STAY LOW AND QUIET AROUND BACK. WE DON'T HAVE MUCH TIME.
FEELS WRONG TO LEAVE TOWN WHEN WE'RE MEANT TO BE PROTECTING IT.
WHO DO YOU THINK I AM?

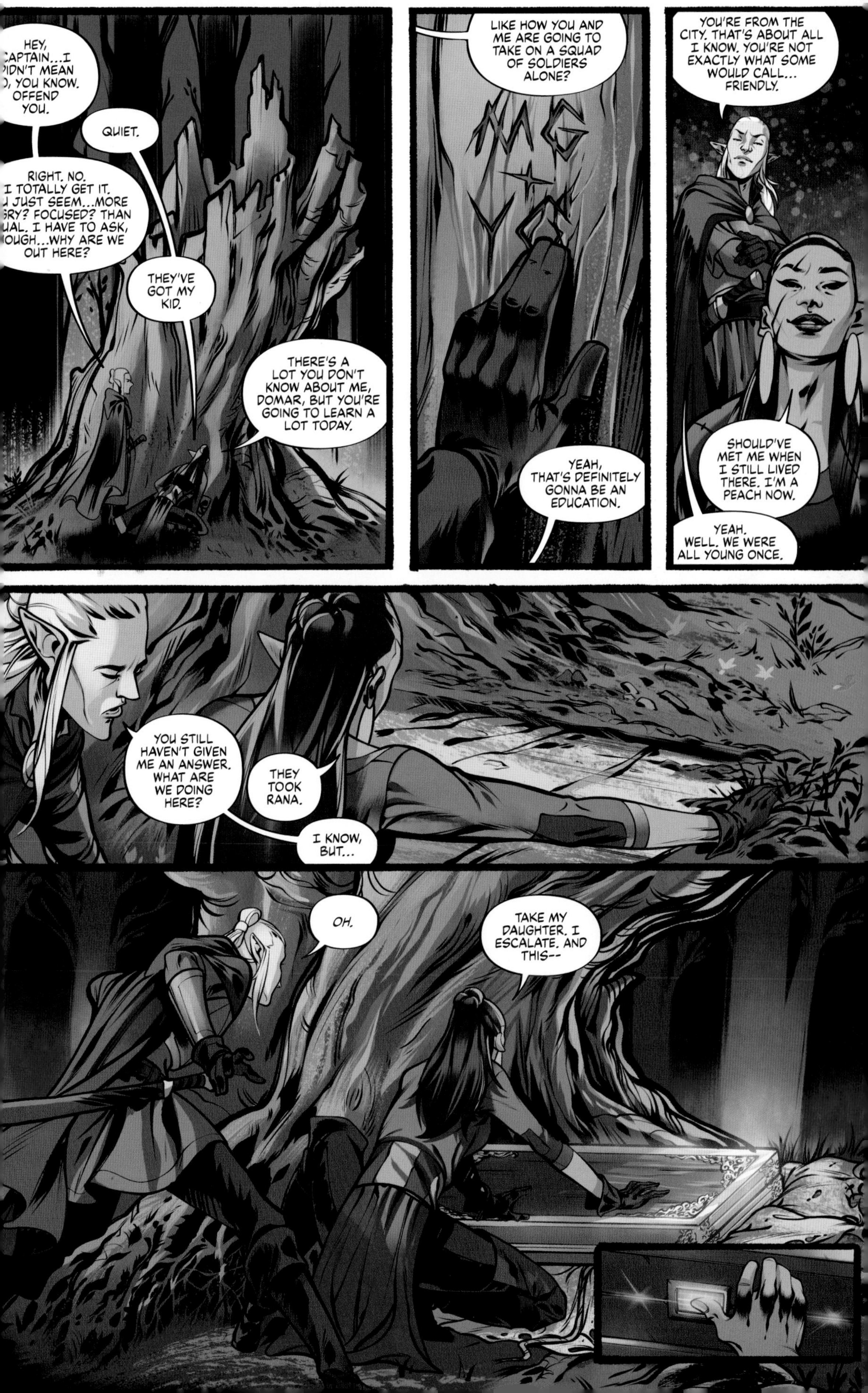
HEY, CAPTAIN...I DIDN'T MEAN , YOU KNOW. OFFEND YOU.
QUIET.
RIGHT. NO. I TOTALLY GET IT. U JUST SEEM...MORE GRY? FOCUSED? THAN UAL. I HAVE TO ASK, OUGH...WHY ARE WE OUT HERE?
THEY'VE GOT MY KID.
THERE'S A LOT YOU DON'T KNOW ABOUT ME, DOMAR, BUT YOU'RE GOING TO LEARN A LOT TODAY.
LIKE HOW YOU AND ME ARE GOING TO TAKE ON A SQUAD OF SOLDIERS ALONE?
YEAH, THAT'S DEFINITELY GONNA BE AN EDUCATION.
YOU'RE FROM THE CITY. THAT'S ABOUT ALL I KNOW. YOU'RE NOT EXACTLY WHAT SOME WOULD CALL... FRIENDLY.
SHOULD'VE MET ME WHEN I STILL LIVED THERE. I'M A PEACH NOW.
YEAH. WELL. WE WERE ALL YOUNG ONCE.
YOU STILL HAVEN'T GIVEN ME AN ANSWER. WHAT ARE WE DOING HERE?
THEY TOOK RANA.
I KNOW, BUT...
OH.
TAKE MY DAUGHTER. I ESCALATE. AND THIS--

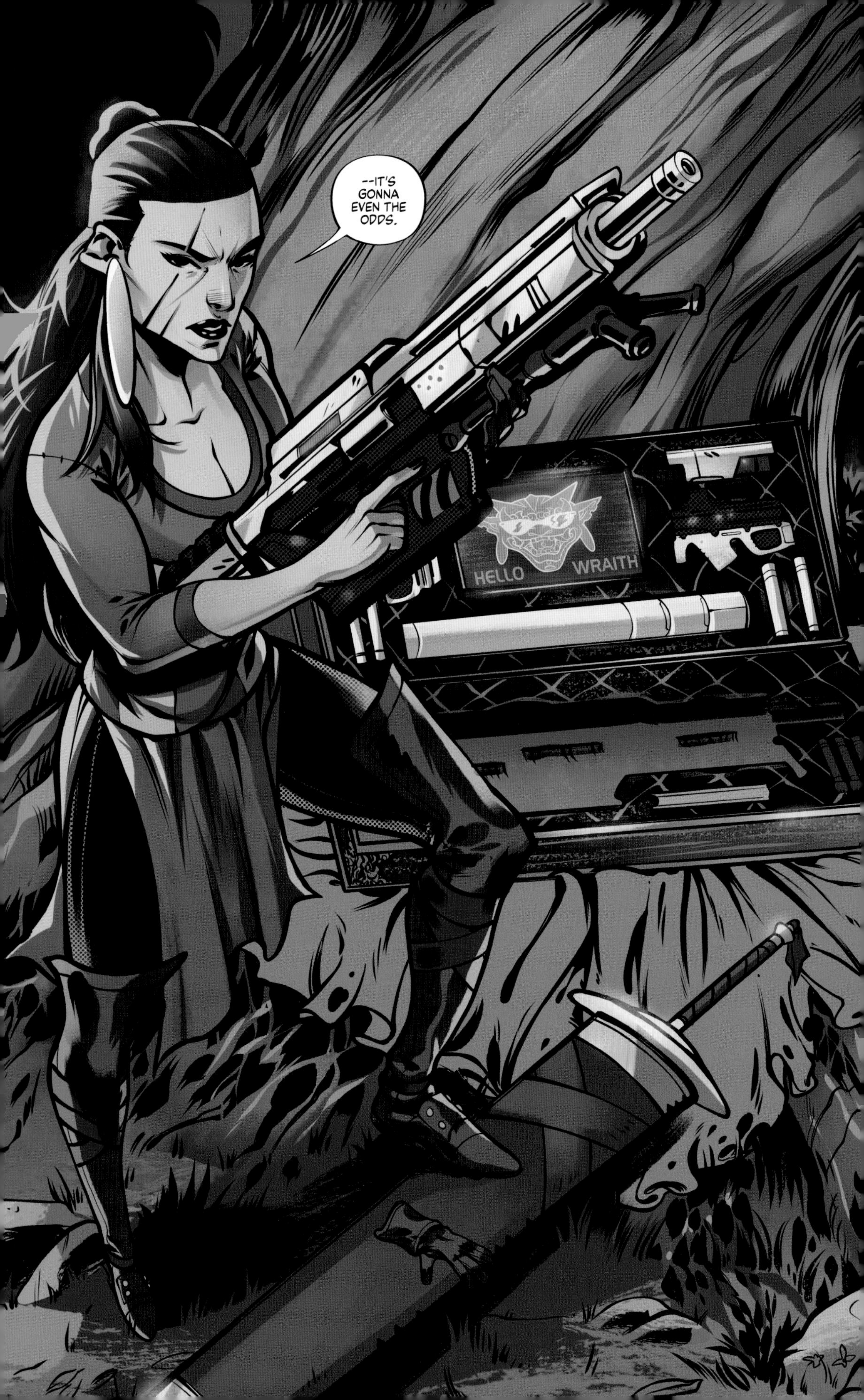
--IT'S GONNA EVEN THE ODDS.
HELLO WRAITH

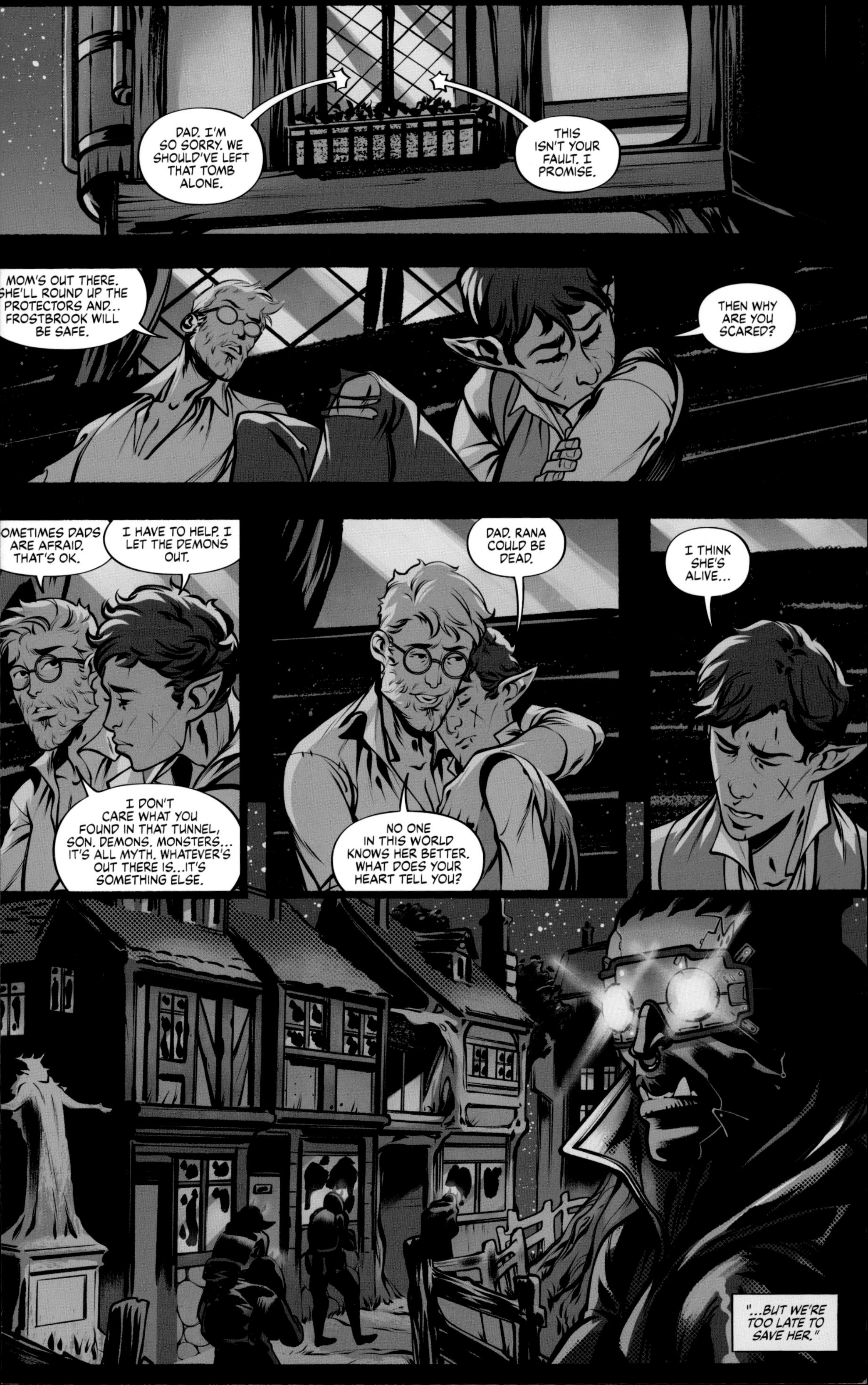
DAD. I'M SO SORRY. WE SHOULD'VE LEFT THAT TOMB ALONE.
THIS ISN'T YOUR FAULT. I PROMISE.
MOM'S OUT THERE. SHE'LL ROUND UP THE PROTECTORS AND... FROSTBROOK WILL BE SAFE.
THEN WHY ARE YOU SCARED?
SOMETIMES DADS ARE AFRAID. THAT'S OK.
I HAVE TO HELP. I LET THE DEMONS OUT.
I DON'T CARE WHAT YOU FOUND IN THAT TUNNEL, SON. DEMONS. MONSTERS... IT'S ALL MYTH. WHATEVER'S OUT THERE IS...IT'S SOMETHING ELSE.
DAD. RANA COULD BE DEAD.
NO ONE IN THIS WORLD KNOWS HER BETTER. WHAT DOES YOUR HEART TELL YOU?
I THINK SHE'S ALIVE...
"...BUT WE'RE TOO LATE TO SAVE HER."

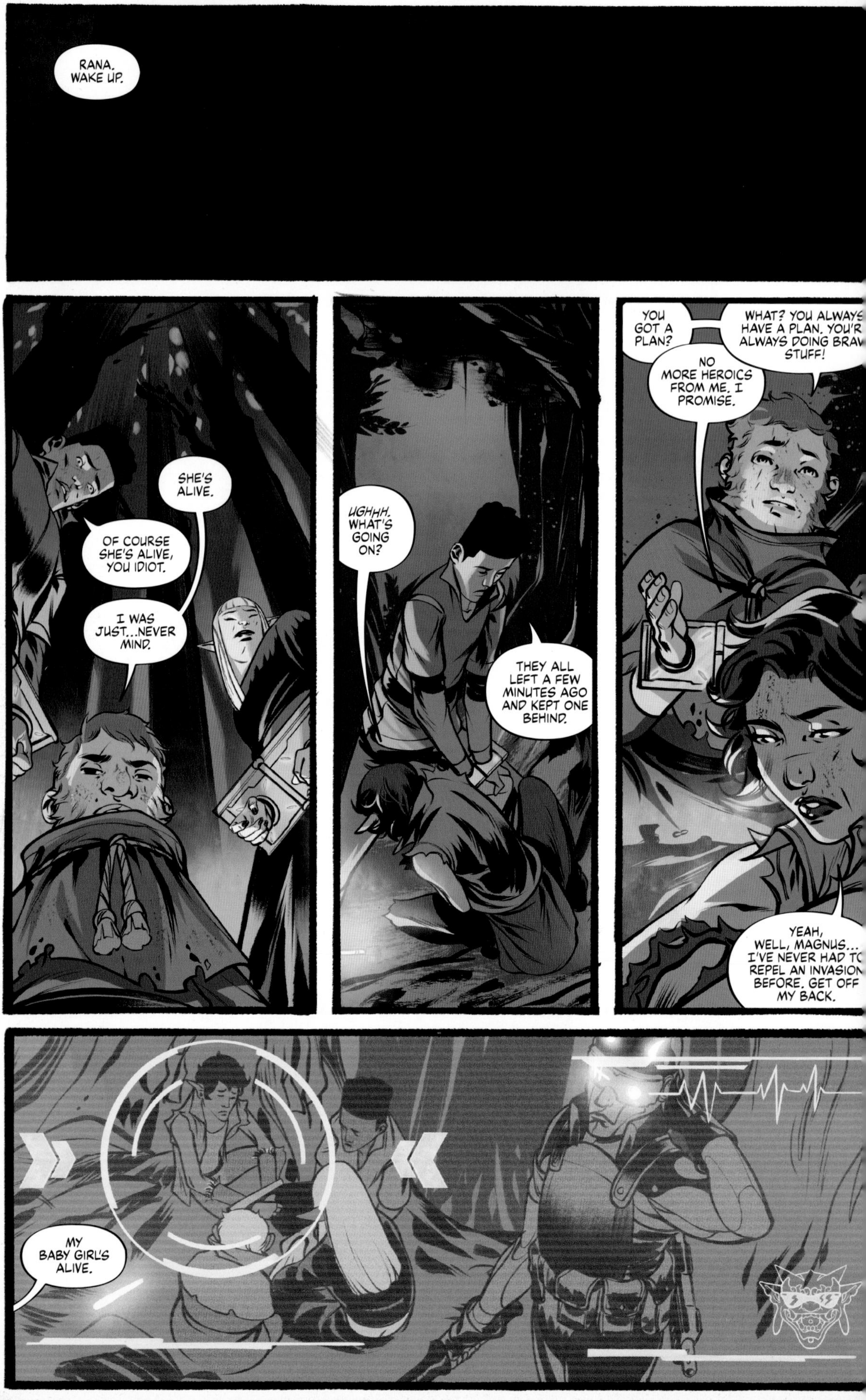
RANA. WAKE UP.
SHE'S ALIVE.
OF COURSE SHE'S ALIVE, YOU IDIOT.
I WAS JUST...NEVER MIND.
UGHHH. WHAT'S GOING ON?
THEY ALL LEFT A FEW MINUTES AGO AND KEPT ONE BEHIND.
YOU GOT A PLAN?
WHAT? YOU ALWAYS HAVE A PLAN. YOU'R ALWAYS DOING BRAV STUFF!
NO MORE HEROICS FROM ME. I PROMISE.
YEAH, WELL, MAGNUS... I'VE NEVER HAD TO REPEL AN INVASION BEFORE. GET OFF MY BACK.
MY BABY GIRL'S ALIVE.

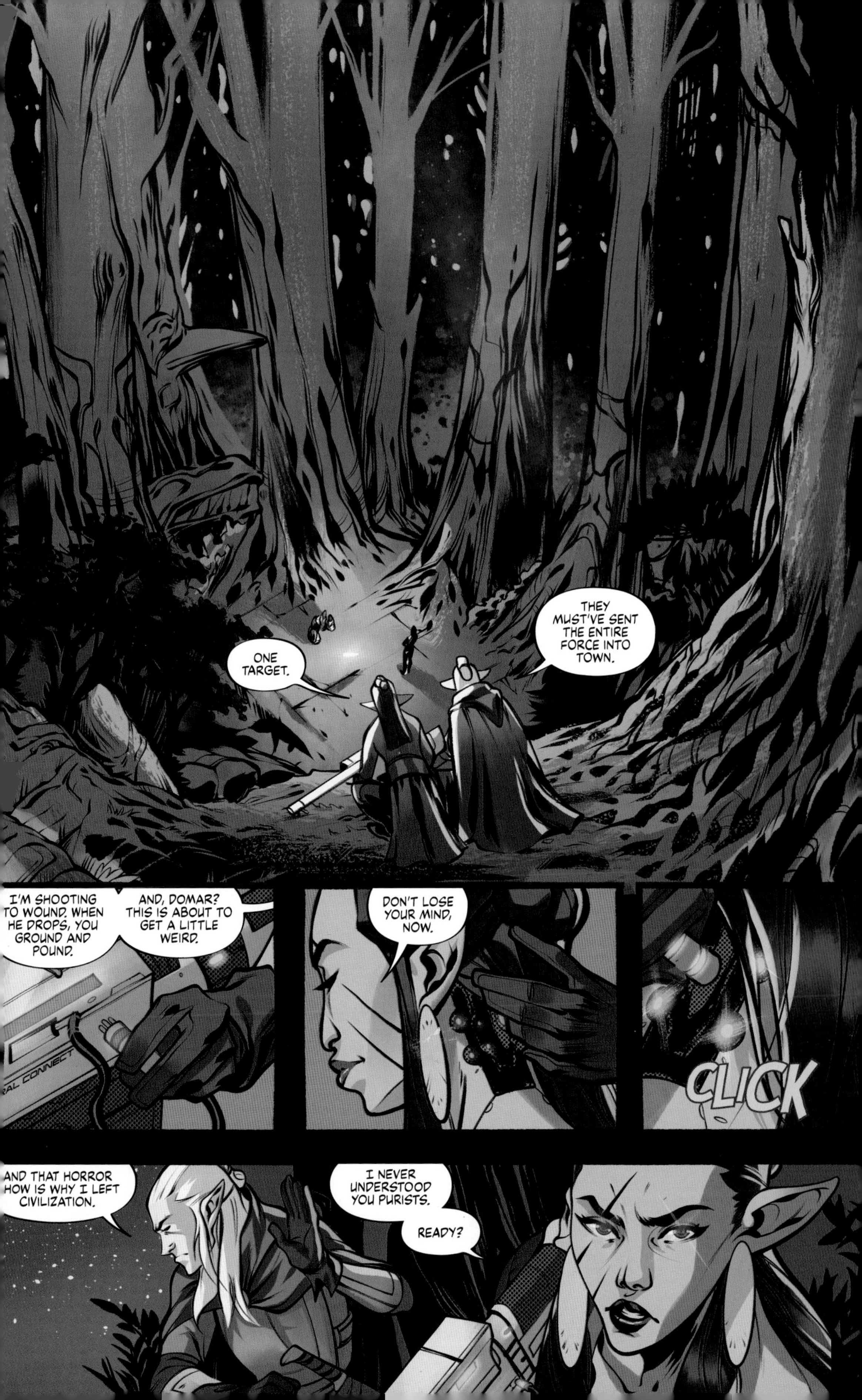
ONE TARGET.
THEY MUST'VE SENT THE ENTIRE FORCE INTO TOWN.
I'M SHOOTING TO WOUND. WHEN HE DROPS, YOU GROUND AND POUND.
AND, DOMAR? THIS IS ABOUT TO GET A LITTLE WEIRD.
DON'T LOSE YOUR MIND, NOW.
CLICK
AND THAT HORROR HOW IS WHY I LEFT CIVILIZATION.
I NEVER UNDERSTOOD YOU PURISTS.
READY?

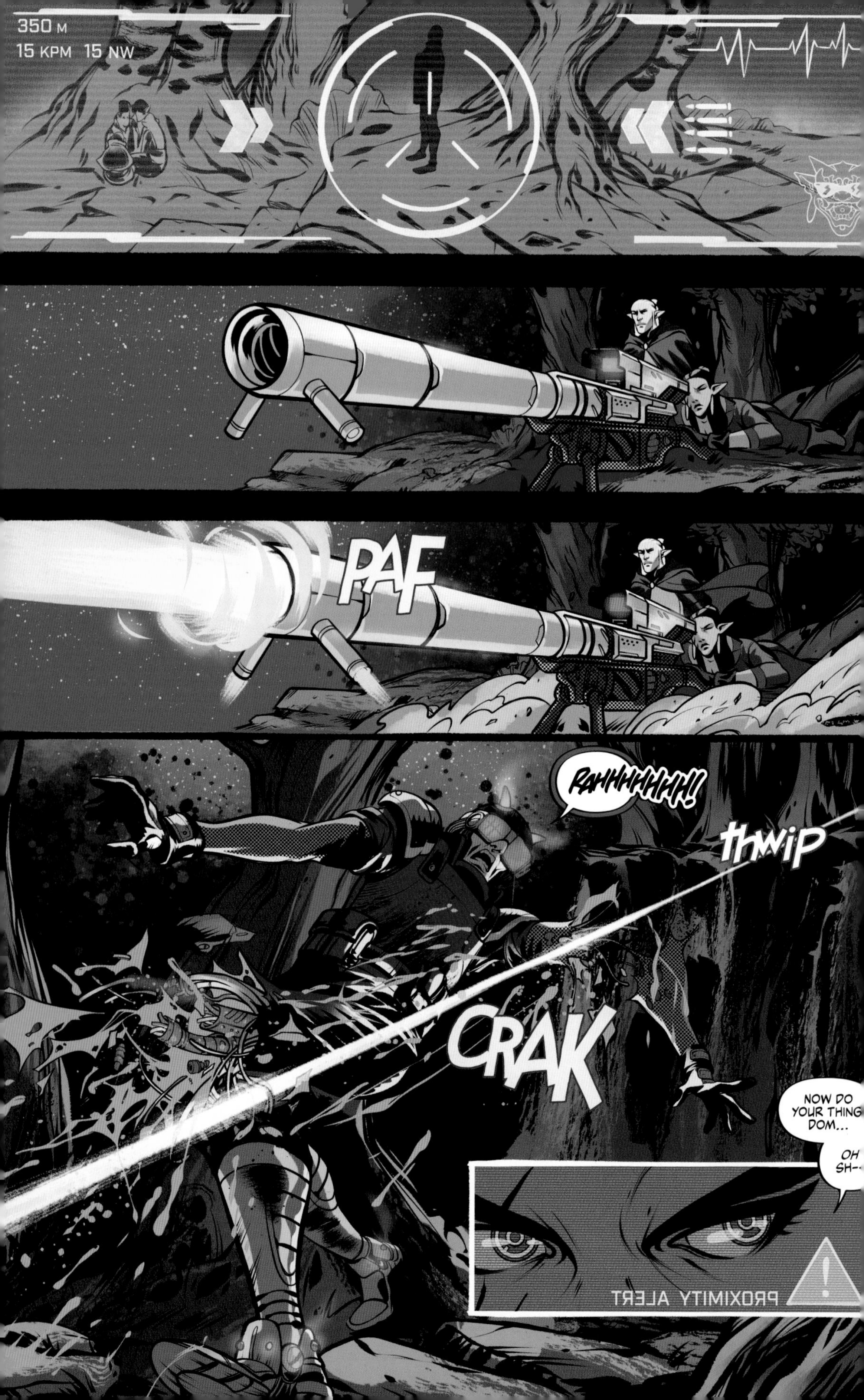

350 M
15 KPM 15 NW
PAF
RAHHHHHHH!
THWIP
CRAK
NOW DO YOUR THING DOM...
OH SH--
PROXIMITY ALERT

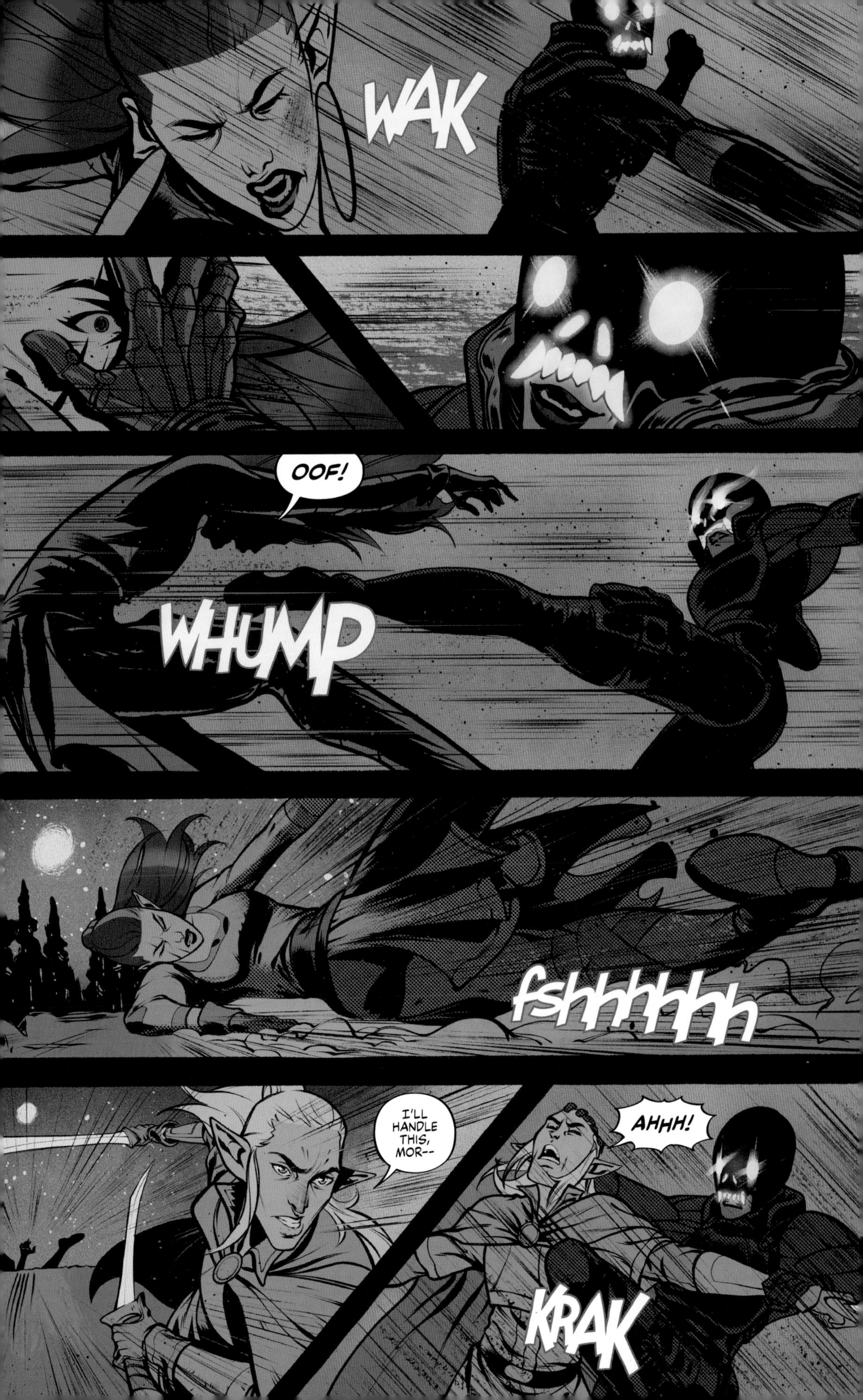
WAK
OOF!
WHUMP
fshhhhhh
I'LL HANDLE THIS, MOR--
AHHH!
KRAK

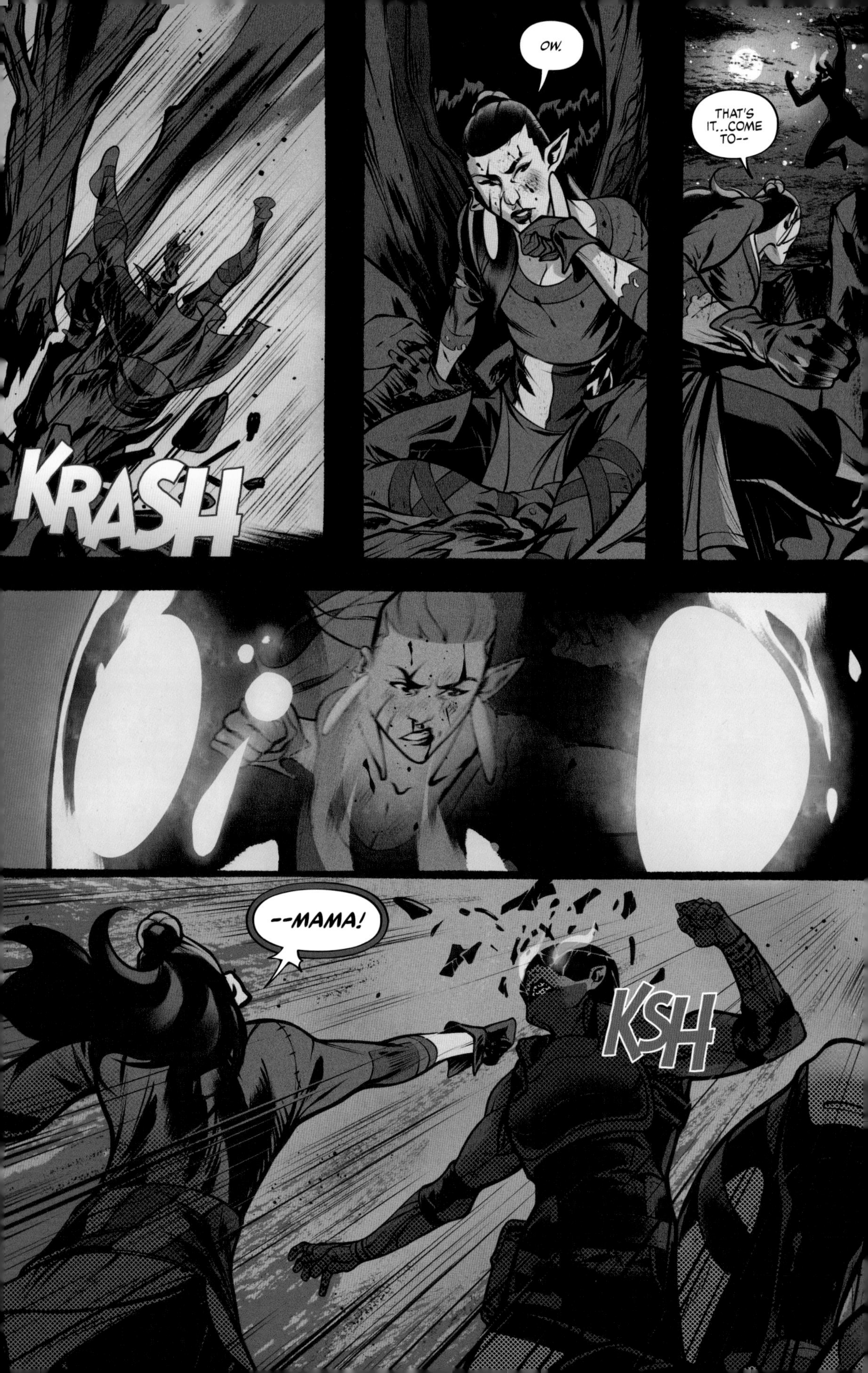
KRASH
OW.
THAT'S IT...COME TO--
--MAMA!
KSH

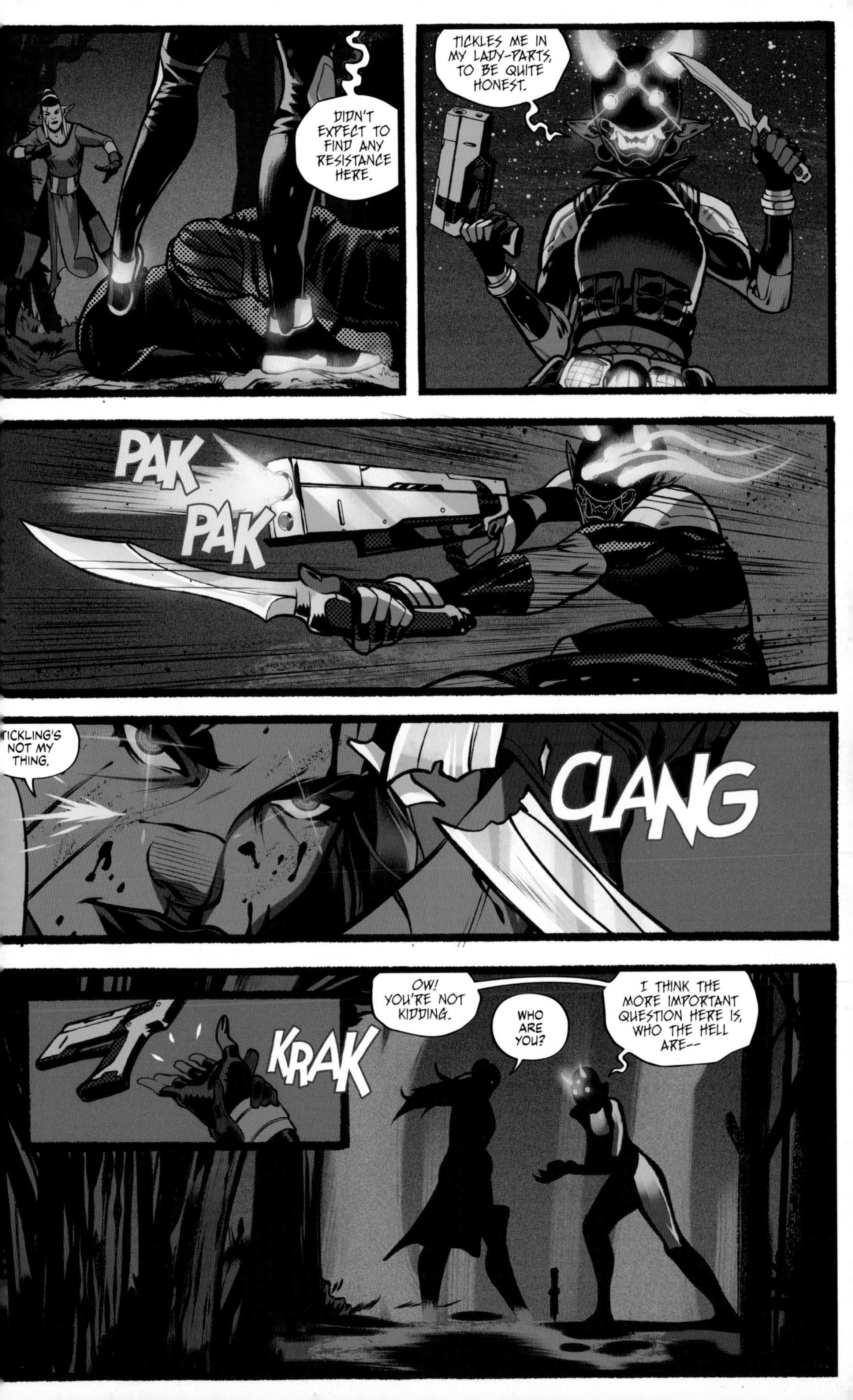
DIDN'T EXPECT TO FIND ANY RESISTANCE HERE.
TICKLES ME IN MY LADY-PARTS, TO BE QUITE HONEST.
PAK
PAK
TICKLING'S NOT MY THING.
CLANG
KRAK
OW! YOU'RE NOT KIDDING.
WHO ARE YOU?
I THINK THE MORE IMPORTANT QUESTION HERE IS, WHO THE HELL ARE--

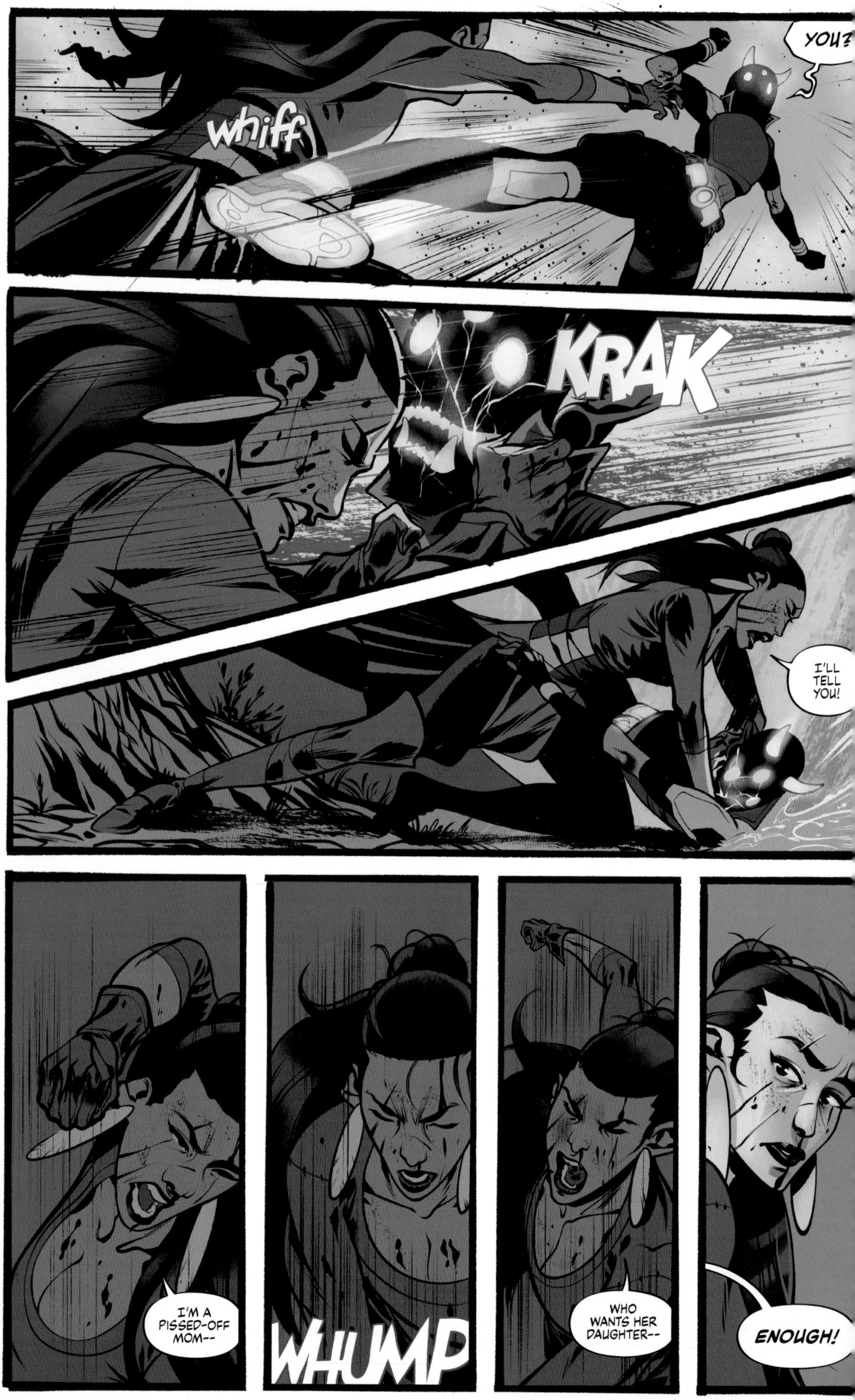
YOU?!
whiff
KRAK
I'LL TELL YOU!
I'M A PISSED-OFF MOM--
WHUMP
WHO WANTS HER DAUGHTER--
ENOUGH!

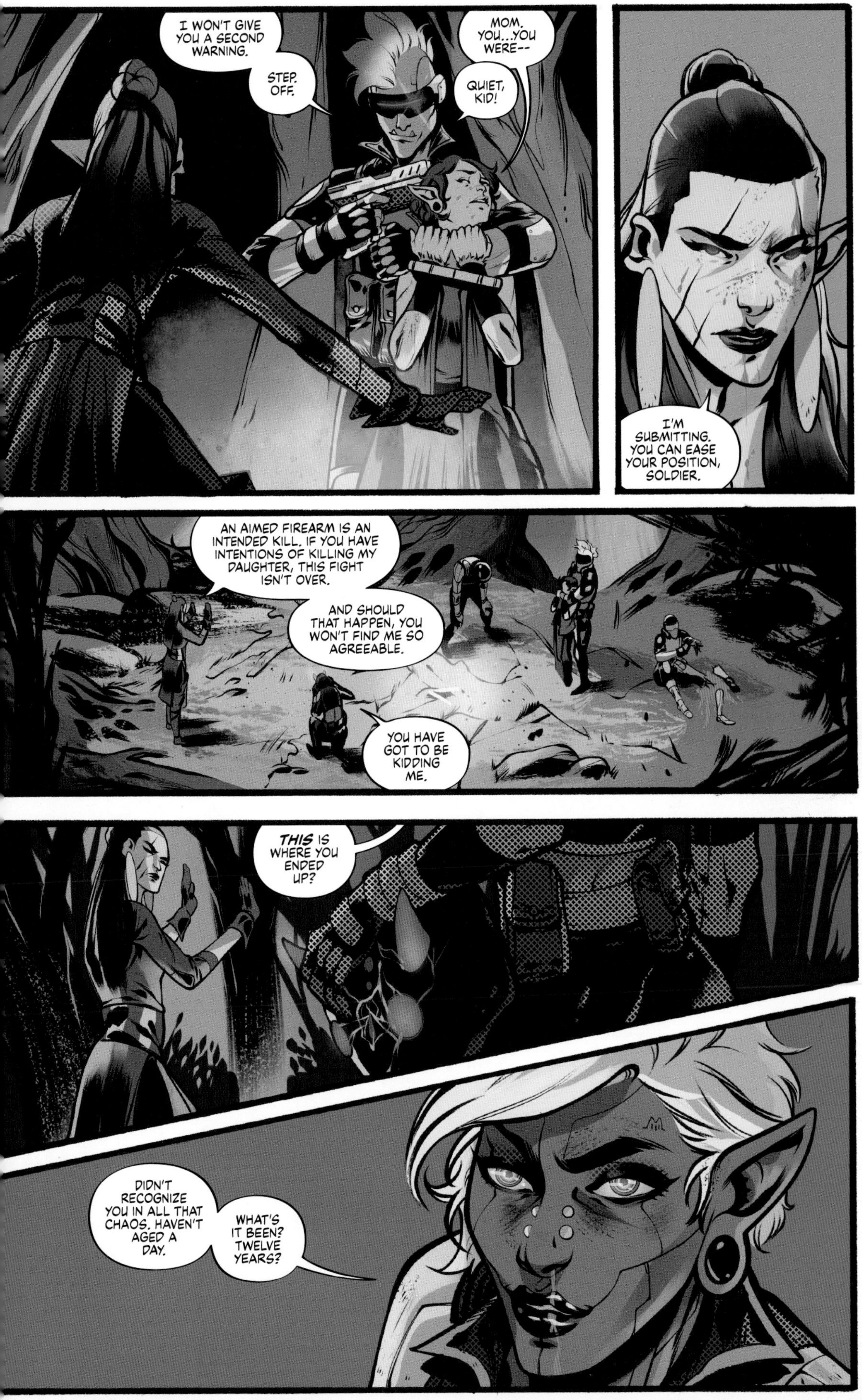
I WON'T GIVE YOU A SECOND WARNING.
STEP. OFF.
MOM. YOU...YOU WERE--
QUIET, KID!
I'M SUBMITTING. YOU CAN EASE YOUR POSITION, SOLDIER.
AN AIMED FIREARM IS AN INTENDED KILL. IF YOU HAVE INTENTIONS OF KILLING MY DAUGHTER, THIS FIGHT ISN'T OVER.
AND SHOULD THAT HAPPEN, YOU WON'T FIND ME SO AGREEABLE.
YOU HAVE GOT TO BE KIDDING ME.
THIS IS WHERE YOU ENDED UP?
DIDN'T RECOGNIZE YOU IN ALL THAT CHAOS. HAVEN'T AGED A DAY.
WHAT'S IT BEEN? TWELVE YEARS?

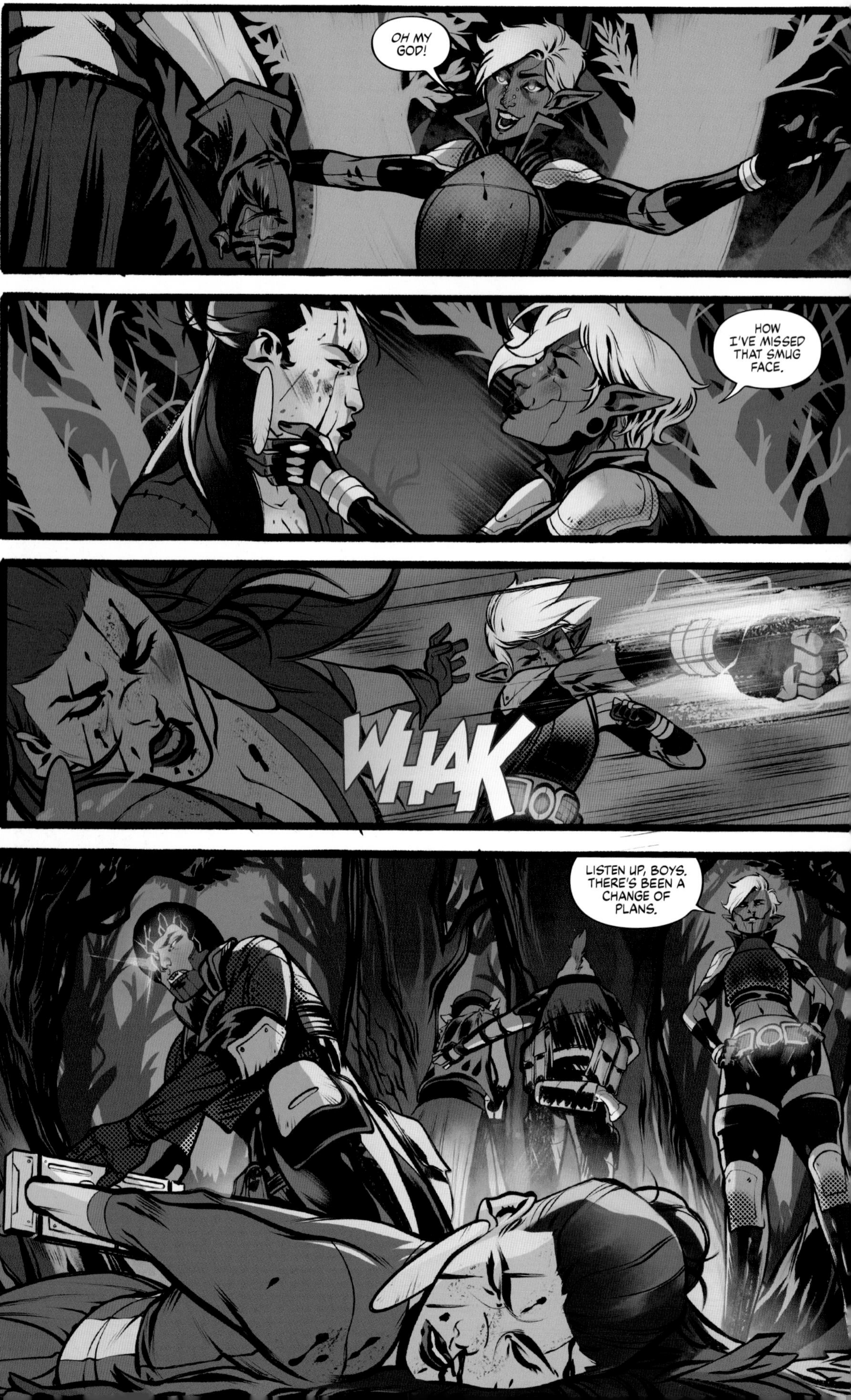
OH MY GOD!
HOW I'VE MISSED THAT SMUG FACE.
WHAK
LISTEN UP, BOYS. THERE'S BEEN A CHANGE OF PLANS.

CHAPTER THREE

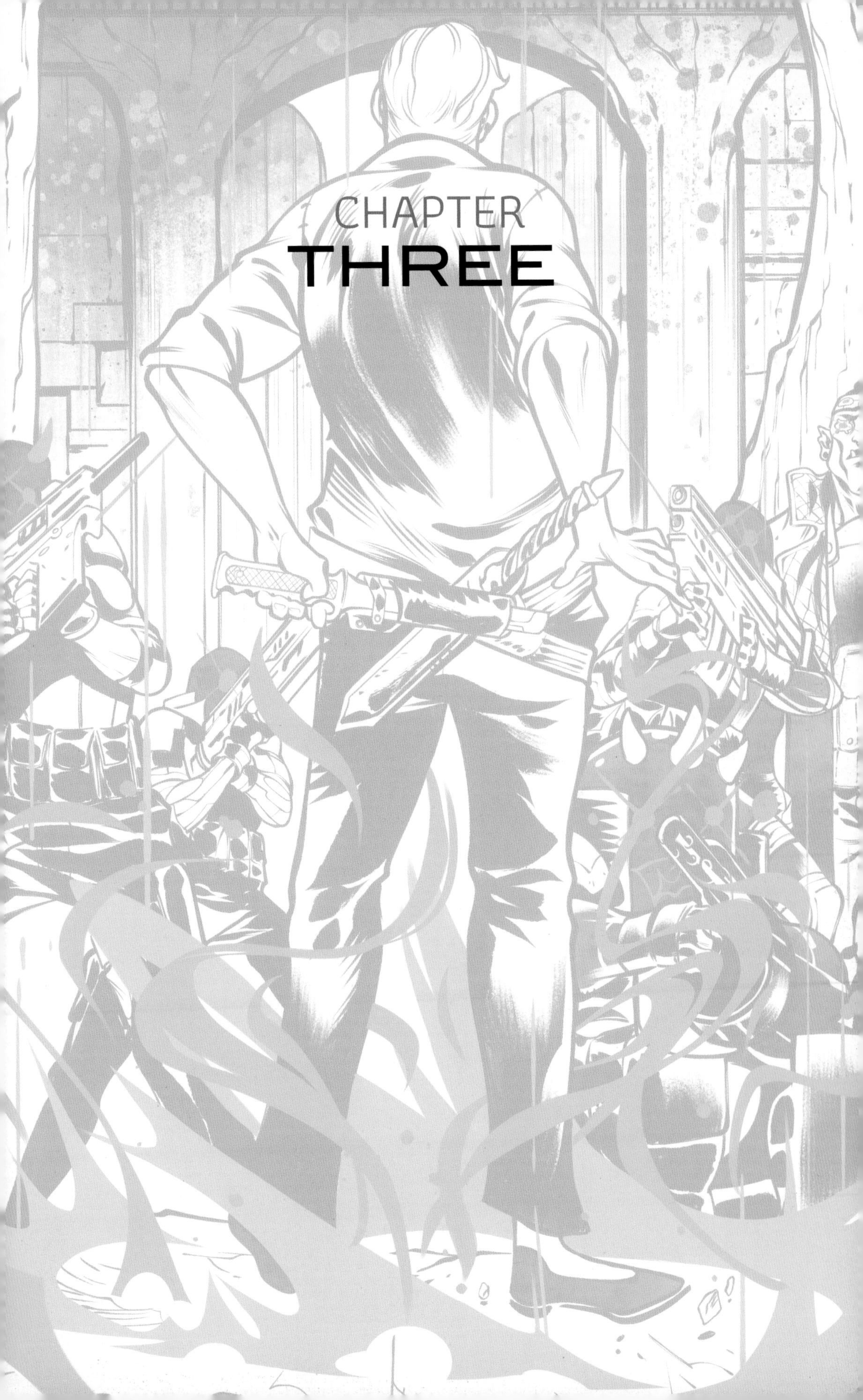

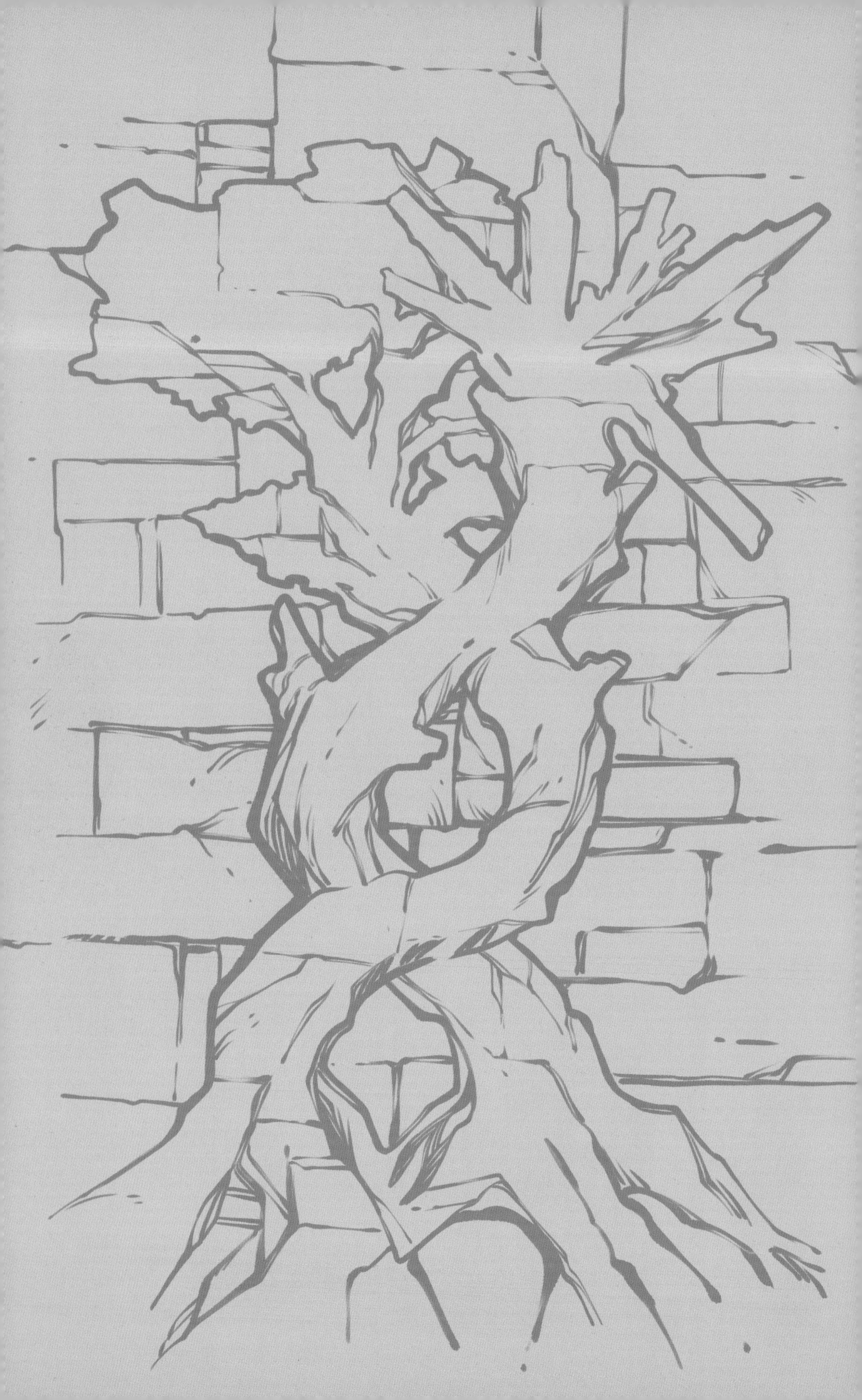

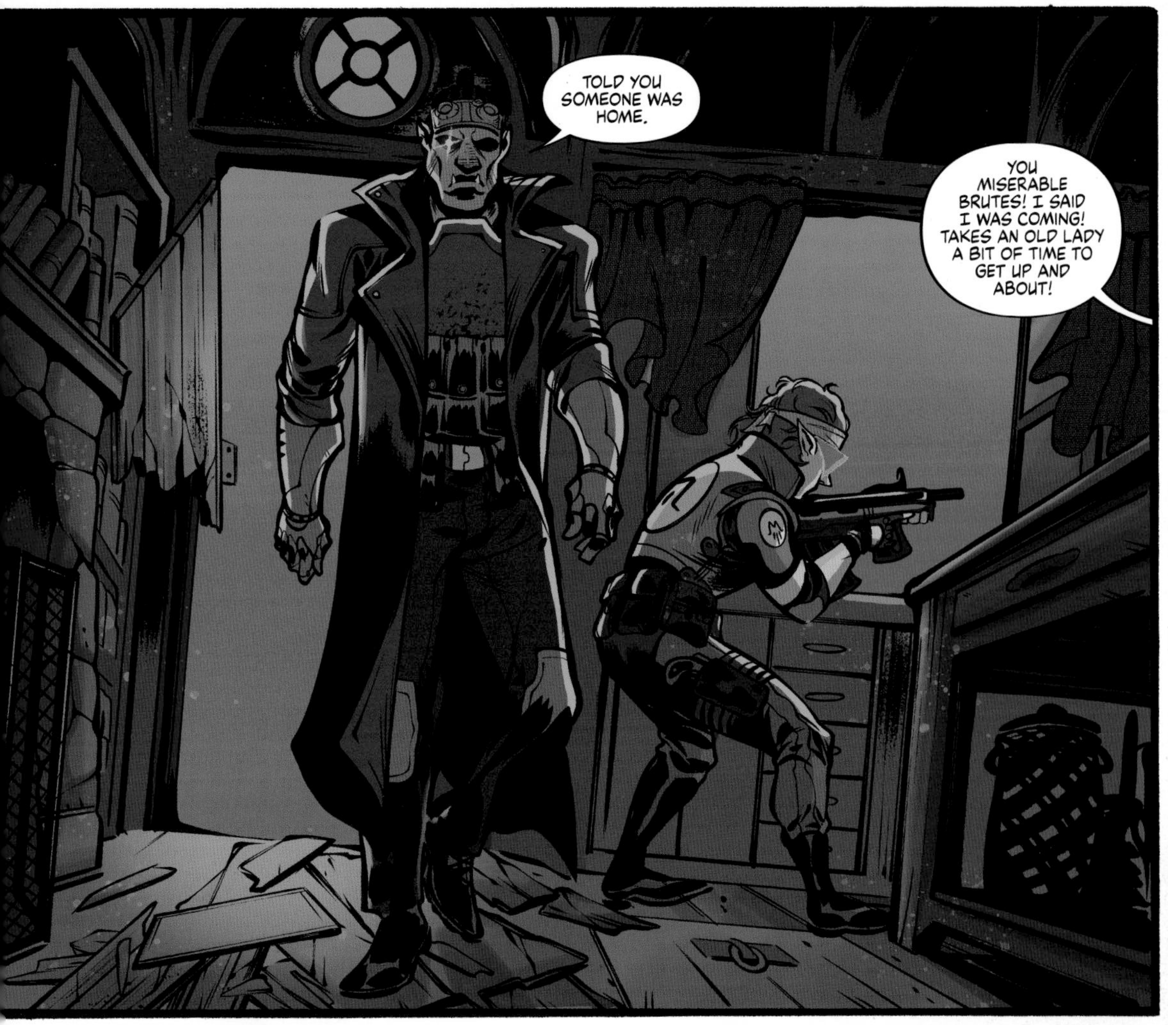
TOLD YOU SOMEONE WAS HOME.
YOU MISERABLE BRUTES! I SAID I WAS COMING! TAKES AN OLD LADY A BIT OF TIME TO GET UP AND ABOUT!

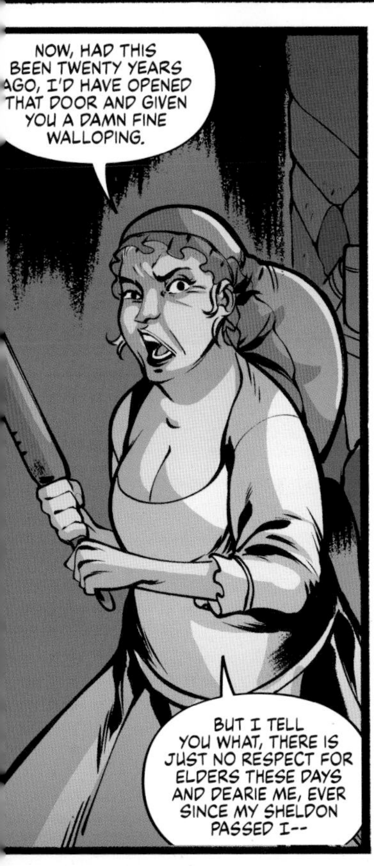
NOW, HAD THIS BEEN TWENTY YEARS AGO, I'D HAVE OPENED THAT DOOR AND GIVEN YOU A DAMN FINE WALLOPING.
BUT I TELL YOU WHAT, THERE IS JUST NO RESPECT FOR ELDERS THESE DAYS AND DEARIE ME, EVER SINCE MY SHELDON PASSED I--

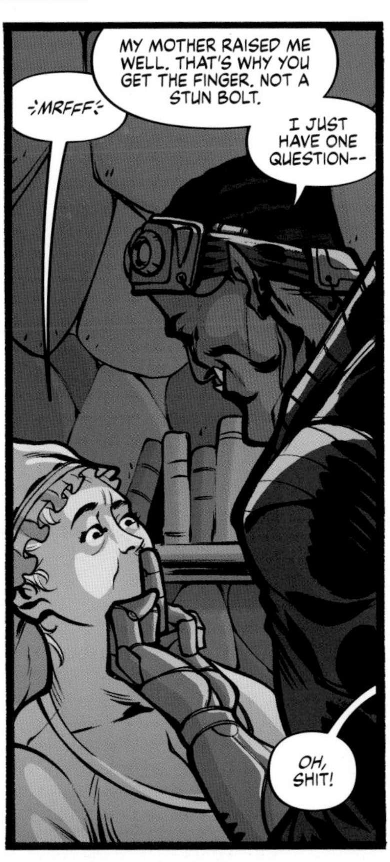
MRFFF
MY MOTHER RAISED ME WELL. THAT'S WHY YOU GET THE FINGER. NOT A STUN BOLT.
I JUST HAVE ONE QUESTION--
OH, SHIT!

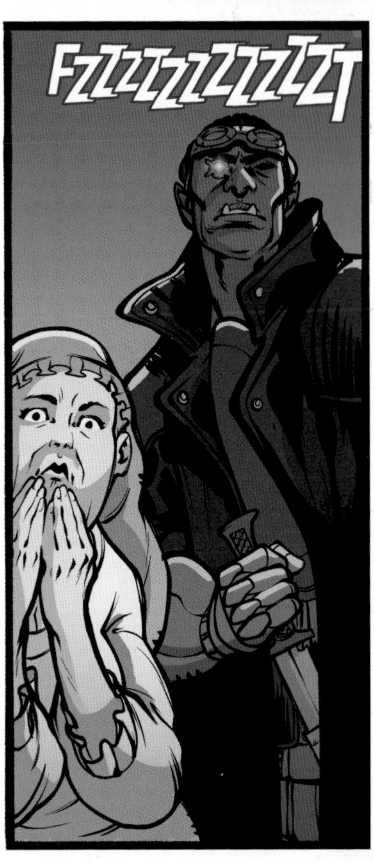
FZZZZZZZZZZZT

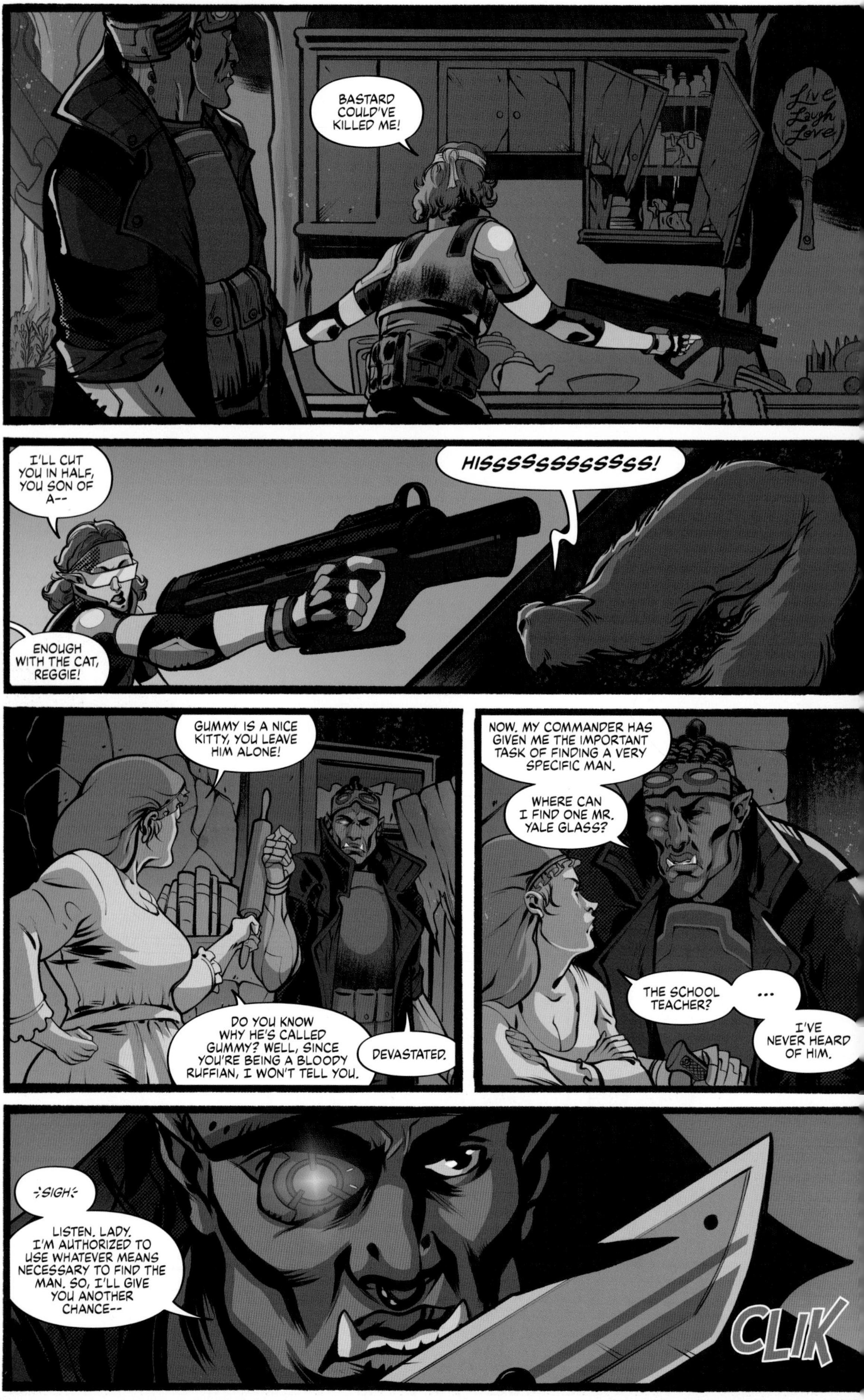
BASTARD COULD'VE KILLED ME!
Live Laugh Love
I'LL CUT YOU IN HALF, YOU SON OF A--
HISSSSSSSSSSSSS!
ENOUGH WITH THE CAT, REGGIE!
GUMMY IS A NICE KITTY, YOU LEAVE HIM ALONE!
DO YOU KNOW WHY HE'S CALLED GUMMY? WELL, SINCE YOU'RE BEING A BLOODY RUFFIAN, I WON'T TELL YOU.
DEVASTATED.
NOW. MY COMMANDER HAS GIVEN ME THE IMPORTANT TASK OF FINDING A VERY SPECIFIC MAN.
WHERE CAN I FIND ONE MR. YALE GLASS?
THE SCHOOL TEACHER?
...
I'VE NEVER HEARD OF HIM.
SIGH
LISTEN. LADY. I'M AUTHORIZED TO USE WHATEVER MEANS NECESSARY TO FIND THE MAN. SO, I'LL GIVE YOU ANOTHER CHANCE--
CLIK

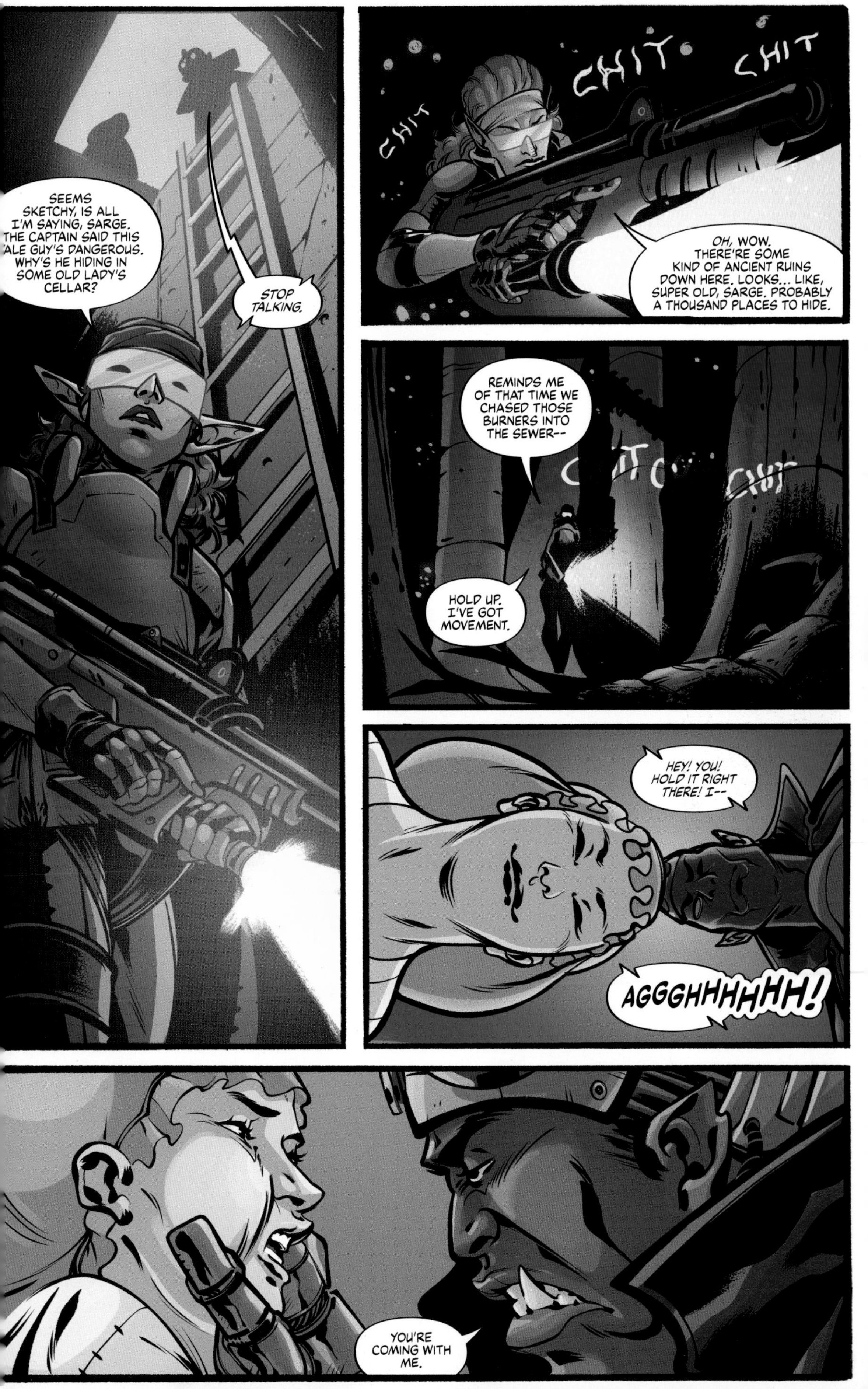

SEEMS SKETCHY, IS ALL I'M SAYING, SARGE. THE CAPTAIN SAID THIS ALE GUY'S DANGEROUS. WHY'S HE HIDING IN SOME OLD LADY'S CELLAR?
STOP TALKING.
CHIT CHIT CHIT CHIT
OH, WOW. THERE'RE SOME KIND OF ANCIENT RUINS DOWN HERE. LOOKS... LIKE, SUPER OLD, SARGE. PROBABLY A THOUSAND PLACES TO HIDE.
REMINDS ME OF THAT TIME WE CHASED THOSE BURNERS INTO THE SEWER--
HOLD UP. I'VE GOT MOVEMENT.
HEY! YOU! HOLD IT RIGHT THERE! I--
AGGGHHHHHH!
YOU'RE COMING WITH ME.

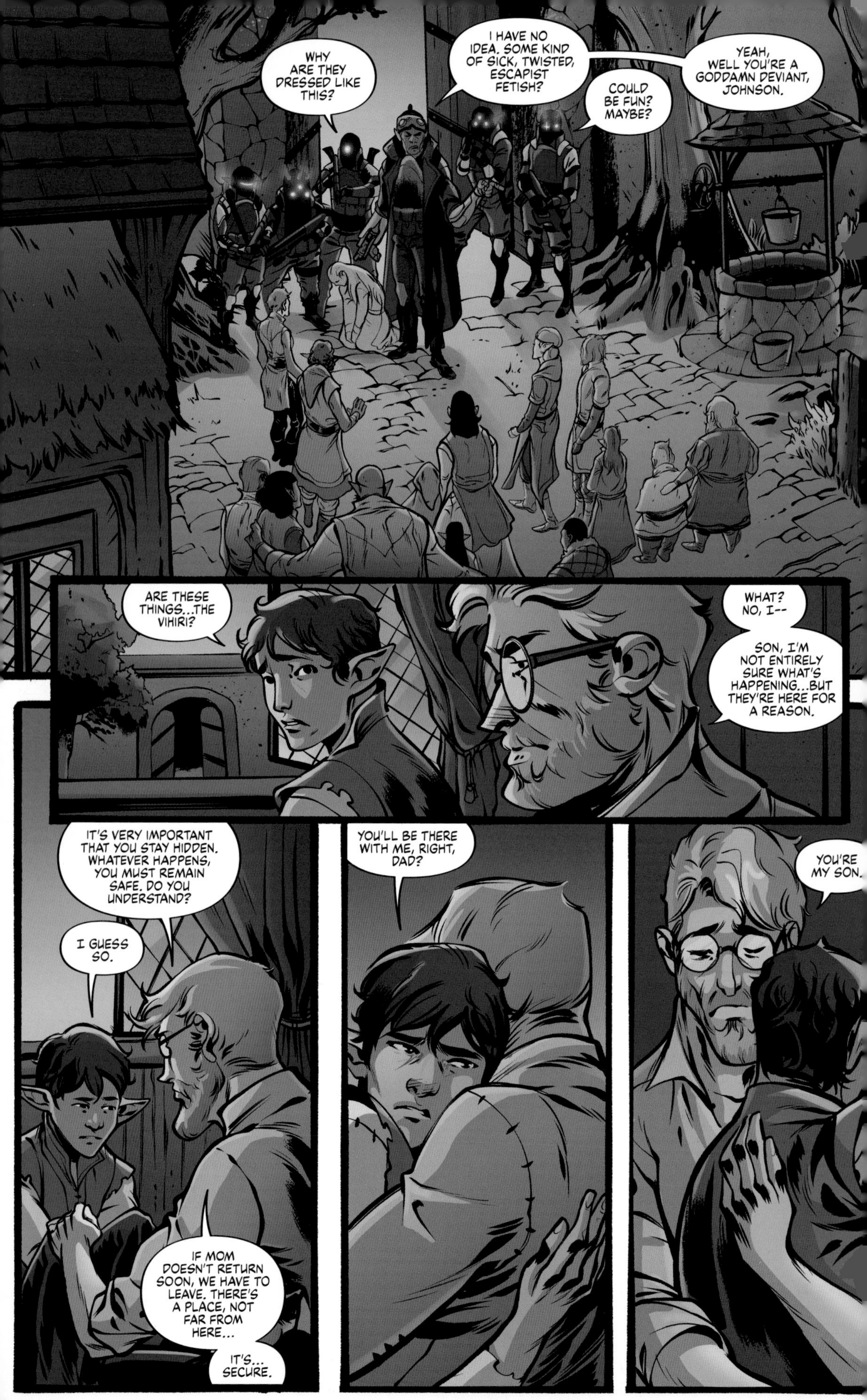
WHY ARE THEY DRESSED LIKE THIS?
I HAVE NO IDEA. SOME KIND OF SICK, TWISTED, ESCAPIST FETISH?
COULD BE FUN? MAYBE?
YEAH, WELL YOU'RE A GODDAMN DEVIANT, JOHNSON.
ARE THESE THINGS...THE VIHIRI?
WHAT? NO, I--
SON, I'M NOT ENTIRELY SURE WHAT'S HAPPENING...BUT THEY'RE HERE FOR A REASON.
IT'S VERY IMPORTANT THAT YOU STAY HIDDEN. WHATEVER HAPPENS, YOU MUST REMAIN SAFE. DO YOU UNDERSTAND?
I GUESS SO.
IF MOM DOESN'T RETURN SOON, WE HAVE TO LEAVE. THERE'S A PLACE, NOT FAR FROM HERE...
IT'S... SECURE.
YOU'LL BE THERE WITH ME, RIGHT, DAD?
YOU'RE MY SON.

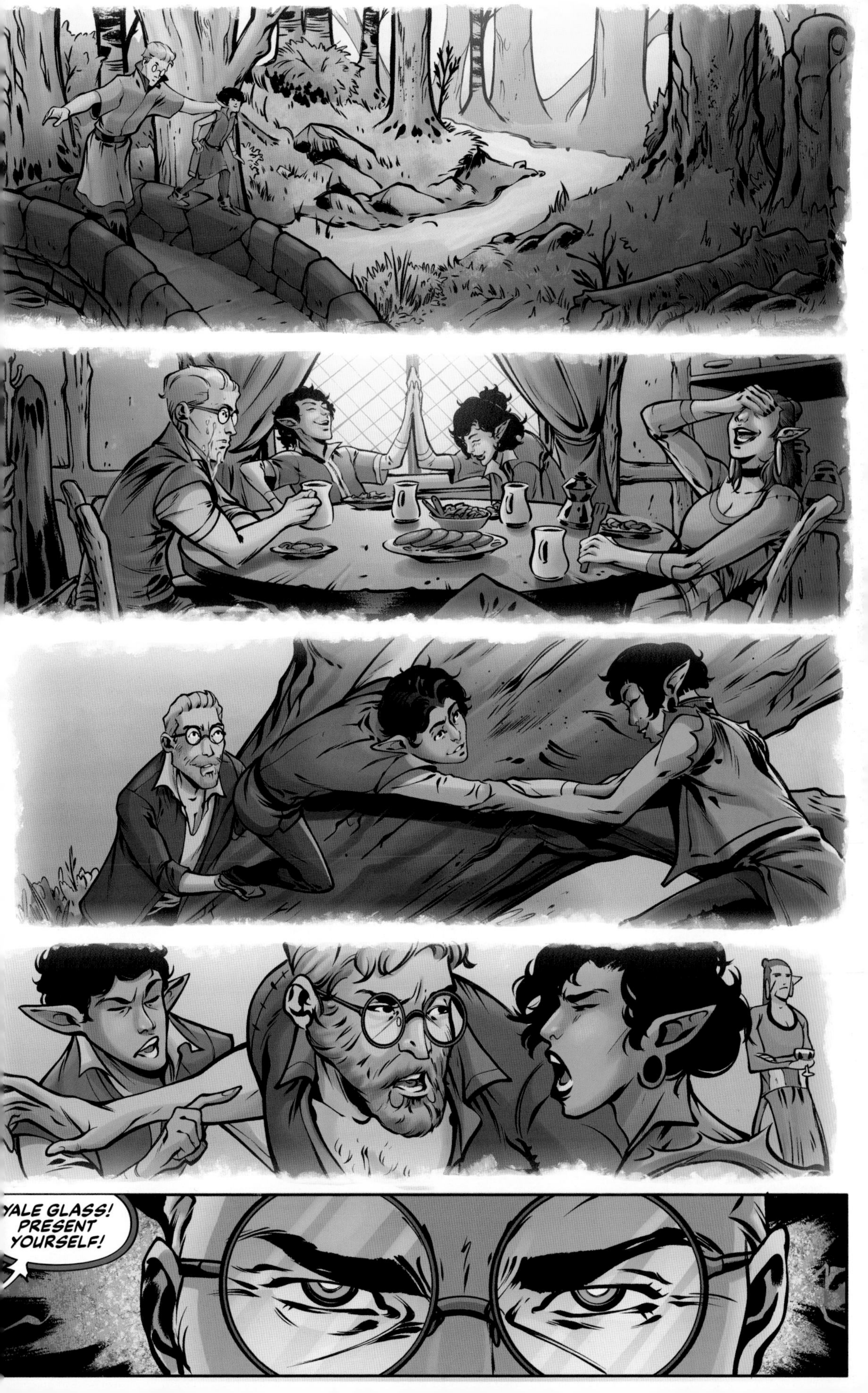
YALE GLASS! PRESENT YOURSELF!

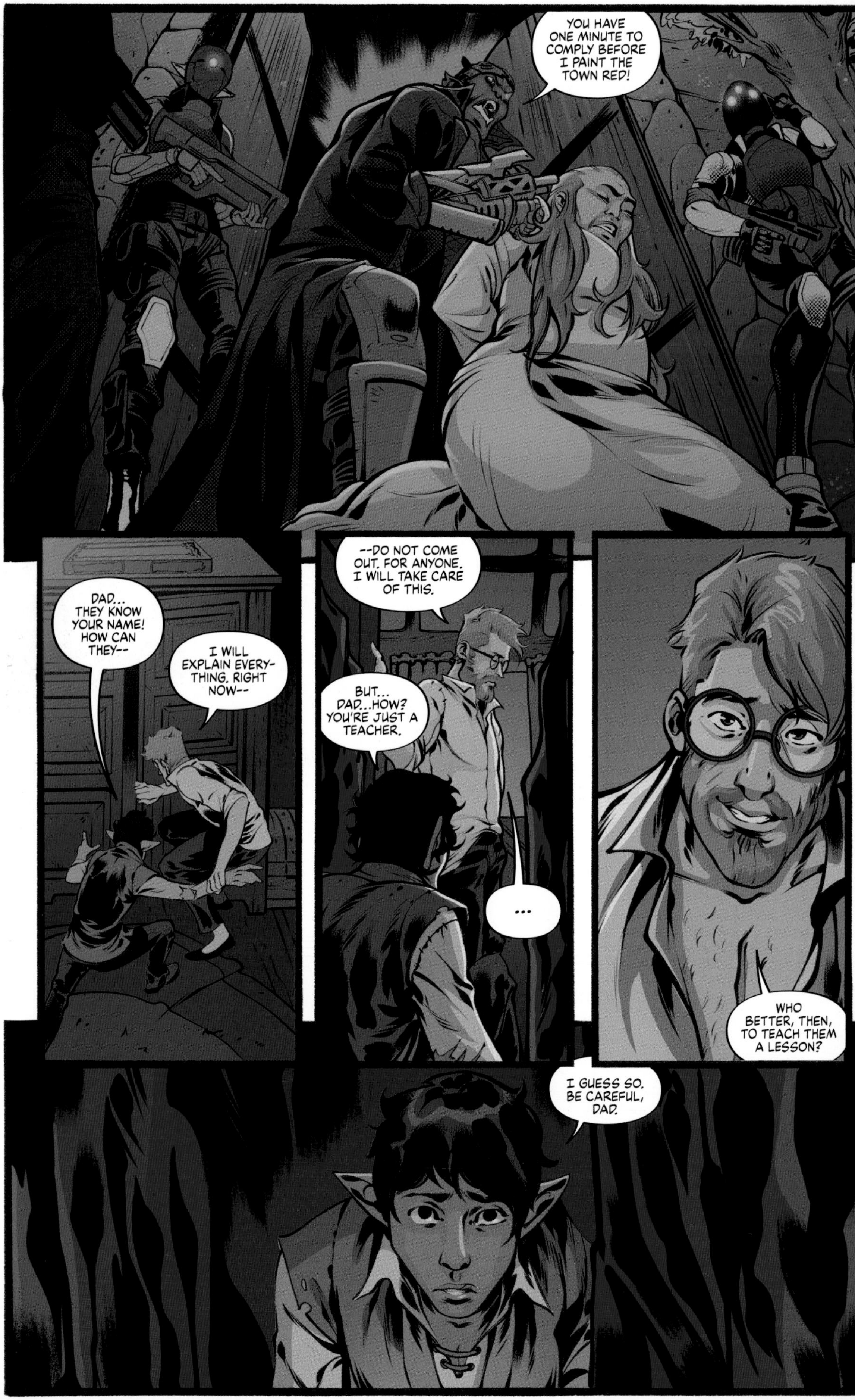
YOU HAVE ONE MINUTE TO COMPLY BEFORE I PAINT THE TOWN RED!
DAD... THEY KNOW YOUR NAME! HOW CAN THEY--
I WILL EXPLAIN EVERY-THING. RIGHT NOW--
--DO NOT COME OUT. FOR ANYONE. I WILL TAKE CARE OF THIS.
BUT... DAD...HOW? YOU'RE JUST A TEACHER.
...
WHO BETTER, THEN, TO TEACH THEM A LESSON?
I GUESS SO. BE CAREFUL, DAD.

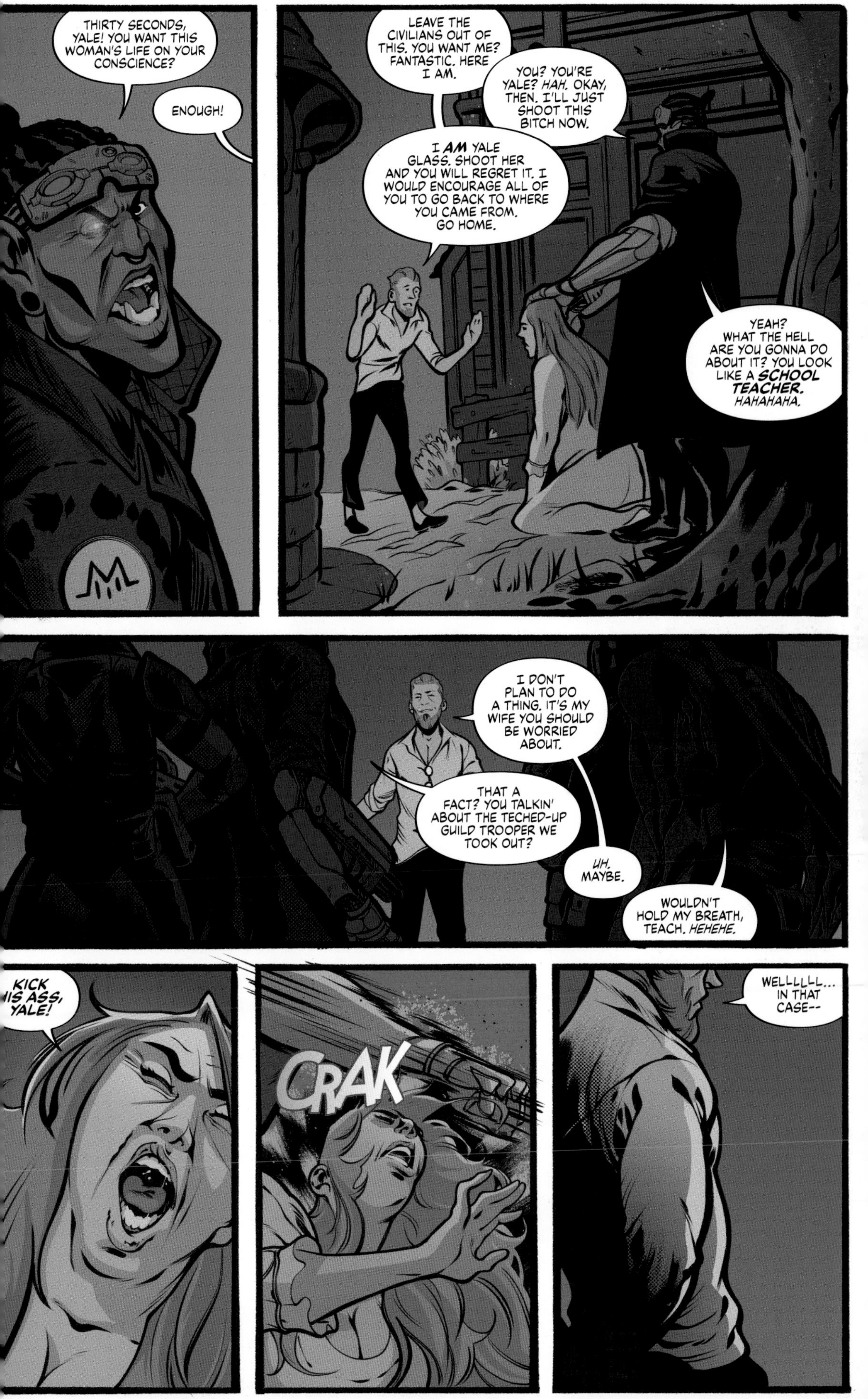
THIRTY SECONDS, YALE! YOU WANT THIS WOMAN'S LIFE ON YOUR CONSCIENCE?
ENOUGH!
LEAVE THE CIVILIANS OUT OF THIS. YOU WANT ME? FANTASTIC. HERE I AM.
YOU? YOU'RE YALE? *HAH.* OKAY, THEN. I'LL JUST SHOOT THIS BITCH NOW.
I **AM** YALE GLASS. SHOOT HER AND YOU WILL REGRET IT. I WOULD ENCOURAGE ALL OF YOU TO GO BACK TO WHERE YOU CAME FROM. GO HOME.
YEAH? WHAT THE HELL ARE YOU GONNA DO ABOUT IT? YOU LOOK LIKE A ***SCHOOL TEACHER.*** *HAHAHAHA.*
I DON'T PLAN TO DO A THING. IT'S MY WIFE YOU SHOULD BE WORRIED ABOUT.
THAT A FACT? YOU TALKIN' ABOUT THE TECHED-UP GUILD TROOPER WE TOOK OUT?
UH. MAYBE.
WOULDN'T HOLD MY BREATH, TEACH. *HEHEHE.*
KICK IS ASS, YALE!
CRAK
WELLLLLL... IN THAT CASE--

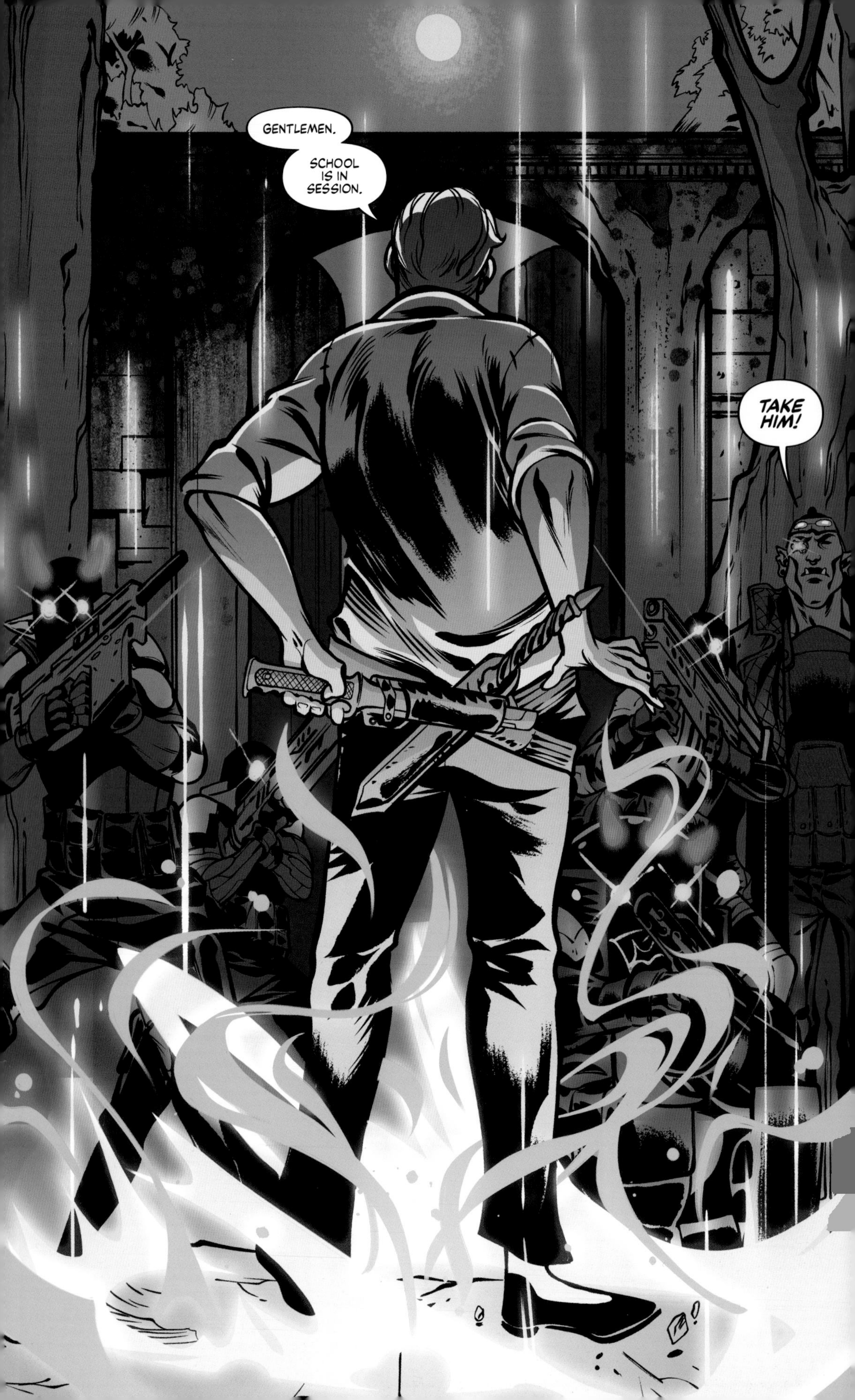
GENTLEMEN.
SCHOOL IS IN SESSION.
TAKE HIM!

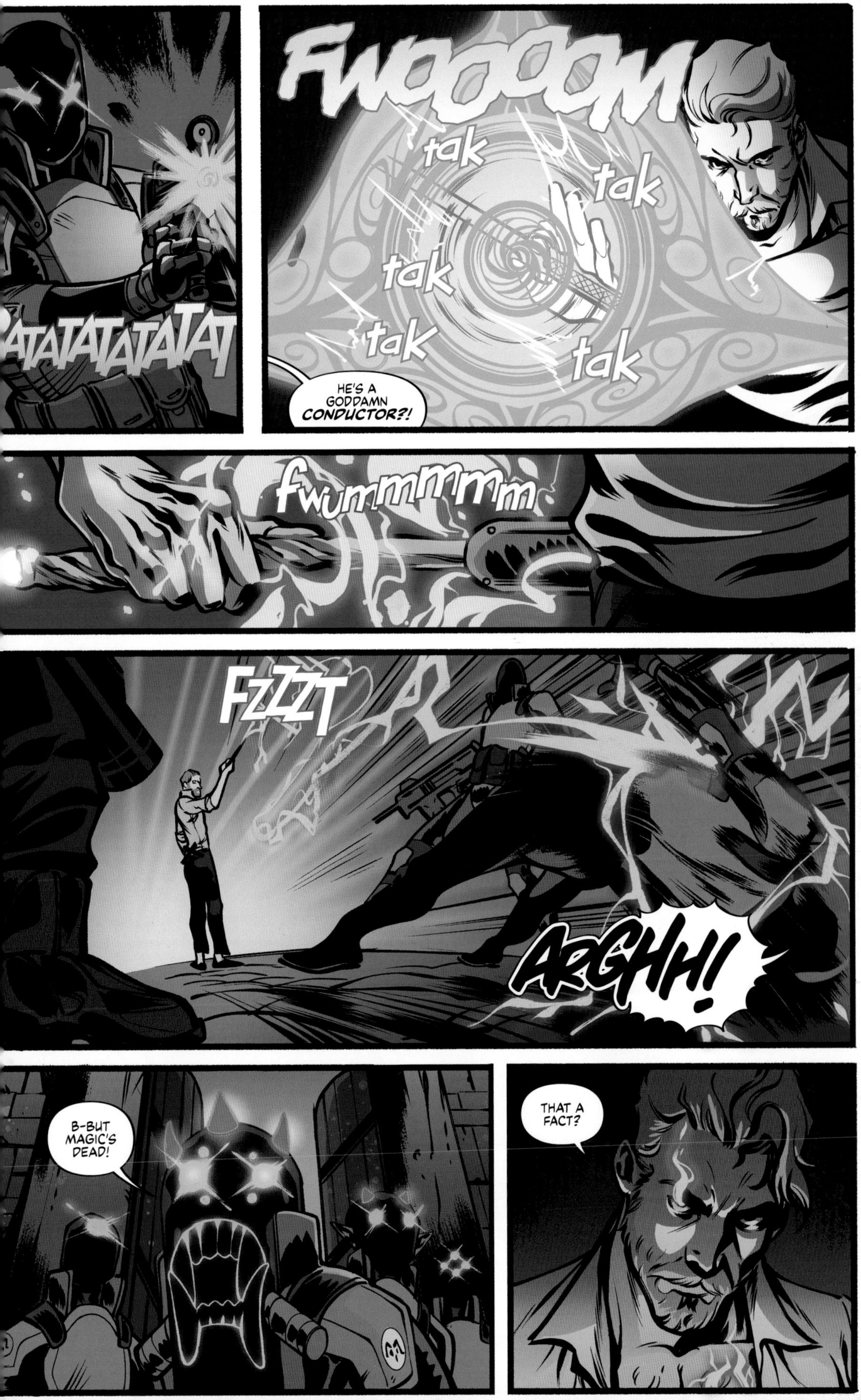
TATATATATATAT
FWOOOOM
tak
tak
tak
tak
tak
HE'S A GODDAMN CONDUCTOR?!
fwummmmm
FZZZT
ARGHH!
B-BUT MAGIC'S DEAD!
THAT A FACT?

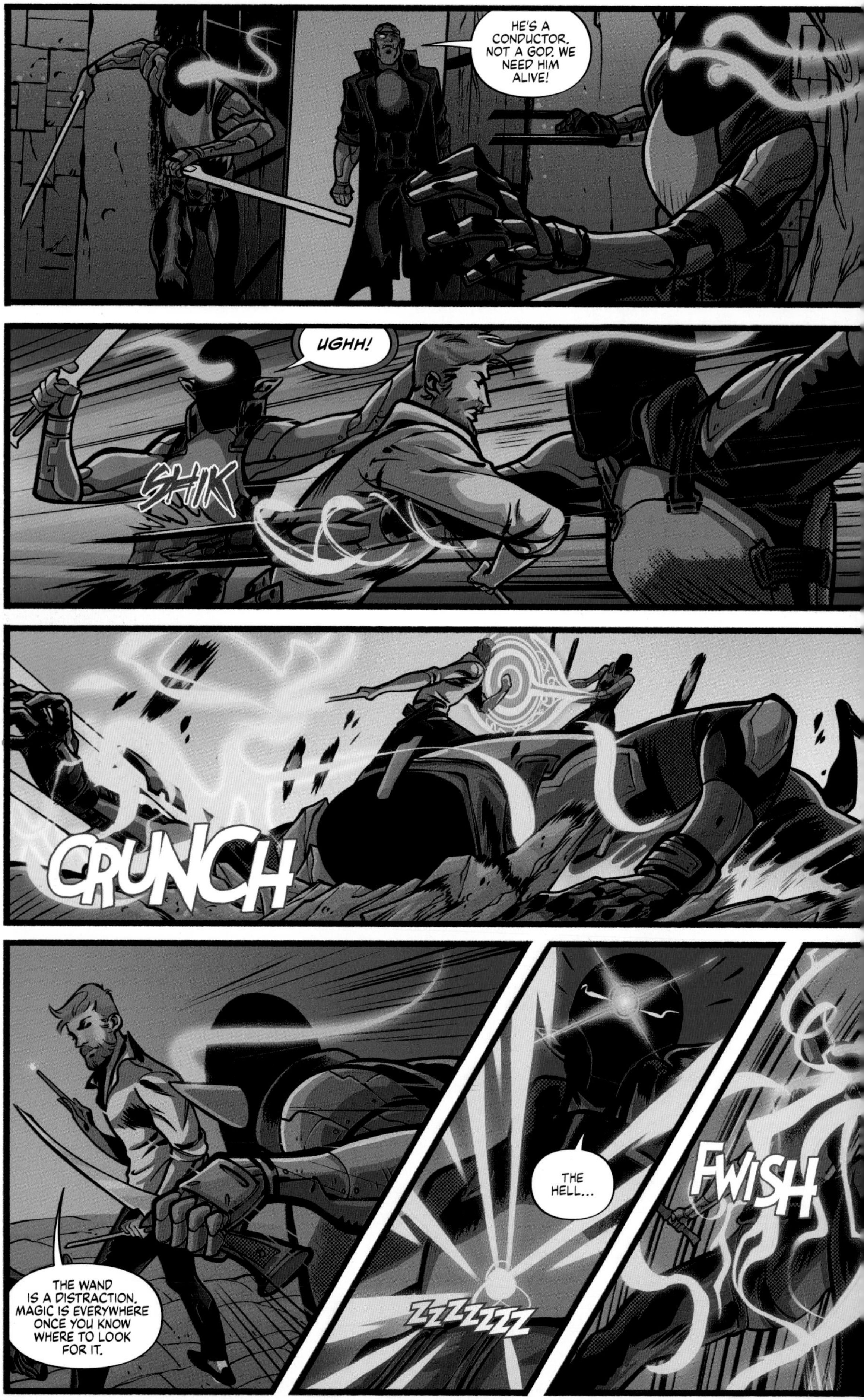
HE'S A CONDUCTOR. NOT A GOD. WE NEED HIM ALIVE!
UGHH!
SHIK
CRUNCH
THE WAND IS A DISTRACTION. MAGIC IS EVERYWHERE ONCE YOU KNOW WHERE TO LOOK FOR IT.
THE HELL...
ZZZZZZZ
FWISH

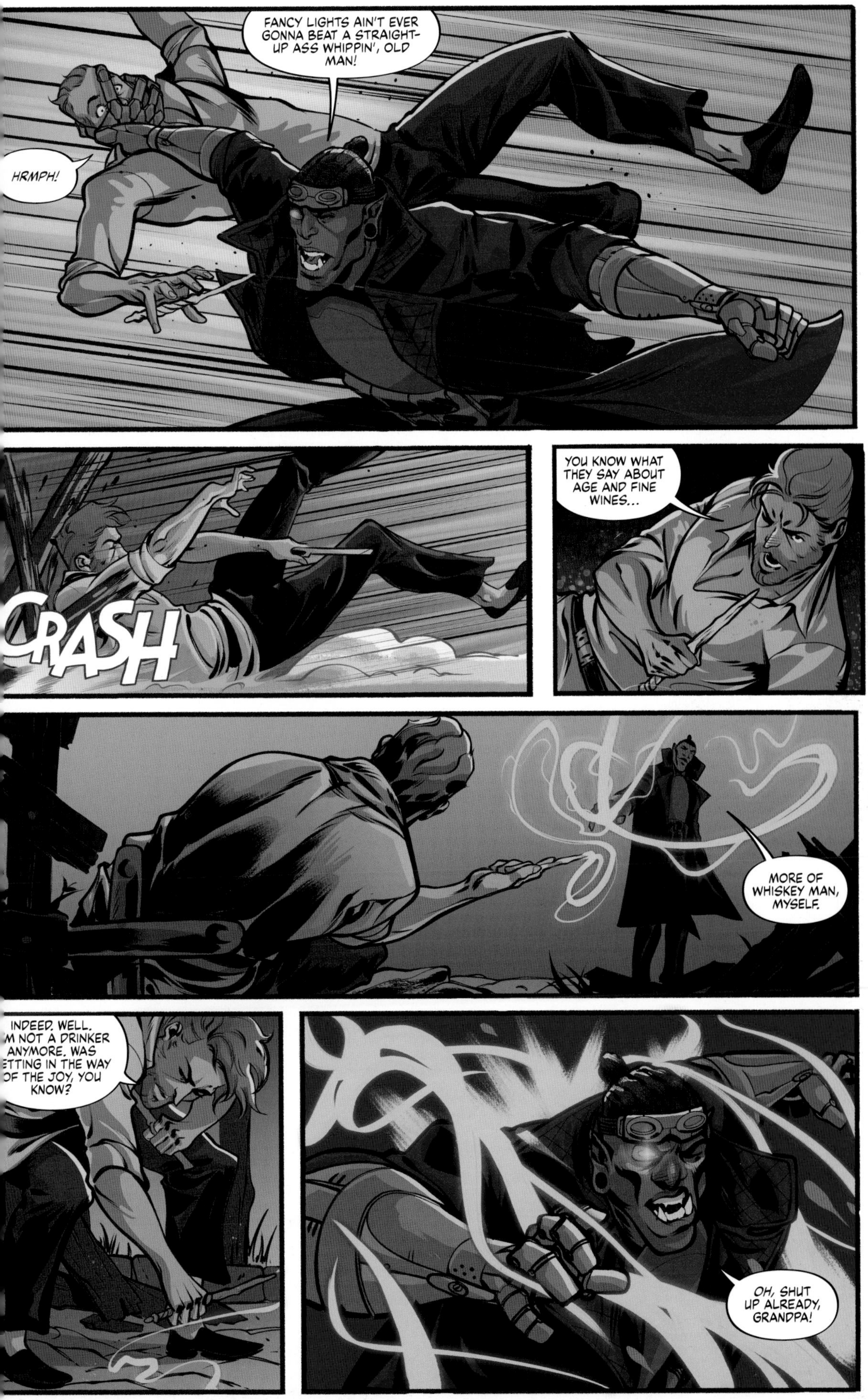
FANCY LIGHTS AIN'T EVER GONNA BEAT A STRAIGHT-UP ASS WHIPPIN', OLD MAN!
HRMPH!
CRASH
YOU KNOW WHAT THEY SAY ABOUT AGE AND FINE WINES...
MORE OF WHISKEY MAN, MYSELF.
INDEED. WELL. 'M NOT A DRINKER ANYMORE. WAS ETTING IN THE WAY OF THE JOY, YOU KNOW?
OH, SHUT UP ALREADY, GRANDPA!

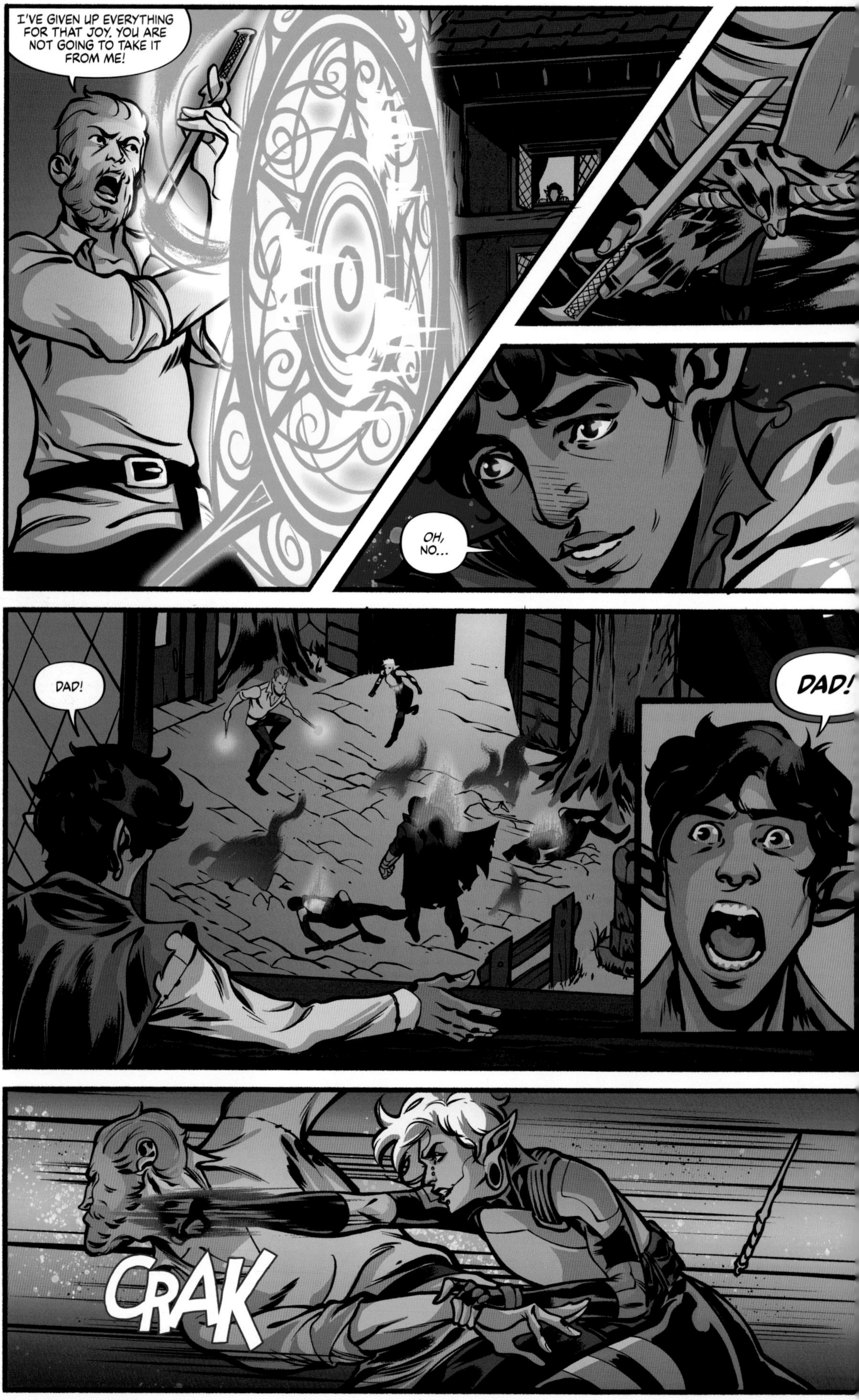
I'VE GIVEN UP EVERYTHING FOR THAT JOY. YOU ARE NOT GOING TO TAKE IT FROM ME!
OH, NO...
DAD!
DAD!
CRAK

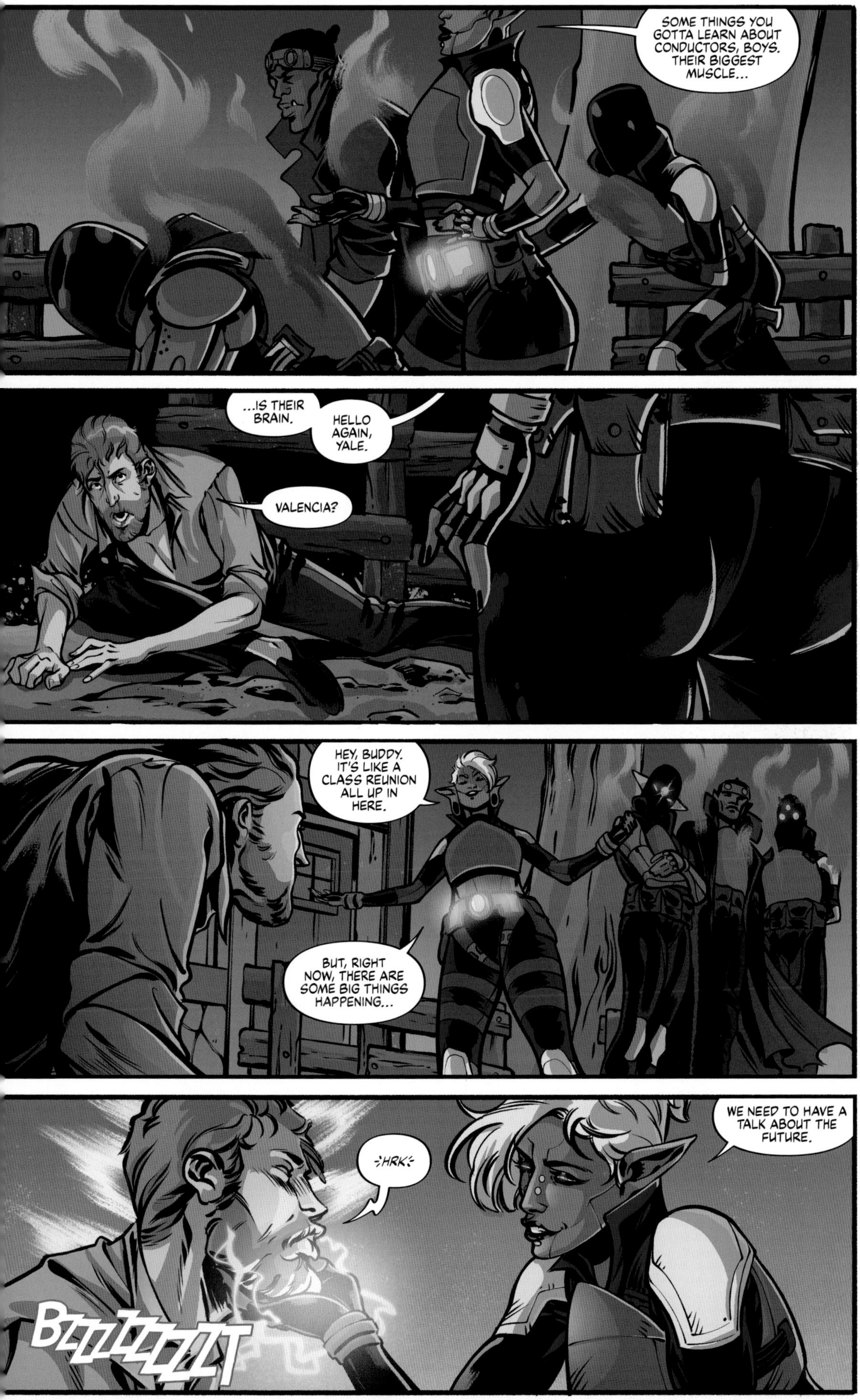
SOME THINGS YOU GOTTA LEARN ABOUT CONDUCTORS, BOYS. THEIR BIGGEST MUSCLE...
...IS THEIR BRAIN.
HELLO AGAIN, YALE.
VALENCIA?
HEY, BUDDY. IT'S LIKE A CLASS REUNION ALL UP IN HERE.
BUT, RIGHT NOW, THERE ARE SOME BIG THINGS HAPPENING...
HRK
WE NEED TO HAVE A TALK ABOUT THE FUTURE.
BZZZZZZZT

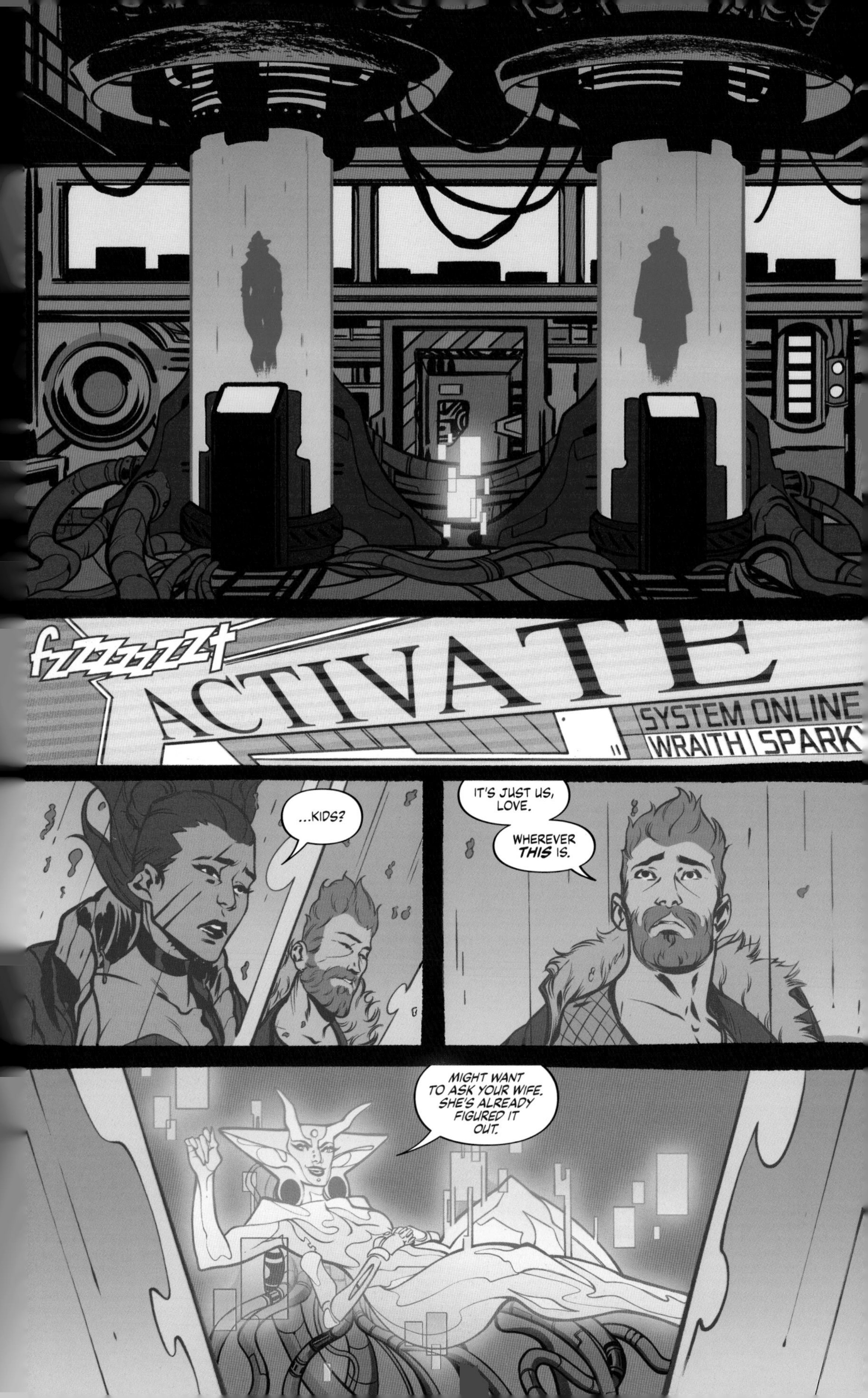

fzzzzzzzzt
ACTIVATE
SYSTEM ONLINE
WRAITH | SPARK
...KIDS?
IT'S JUST US, LOVE.
WHEREVER THIS IS.
MIGHT WANT TO ASK YOUR WIFE. SHE'S ALREADY FIGURED IT OUT.

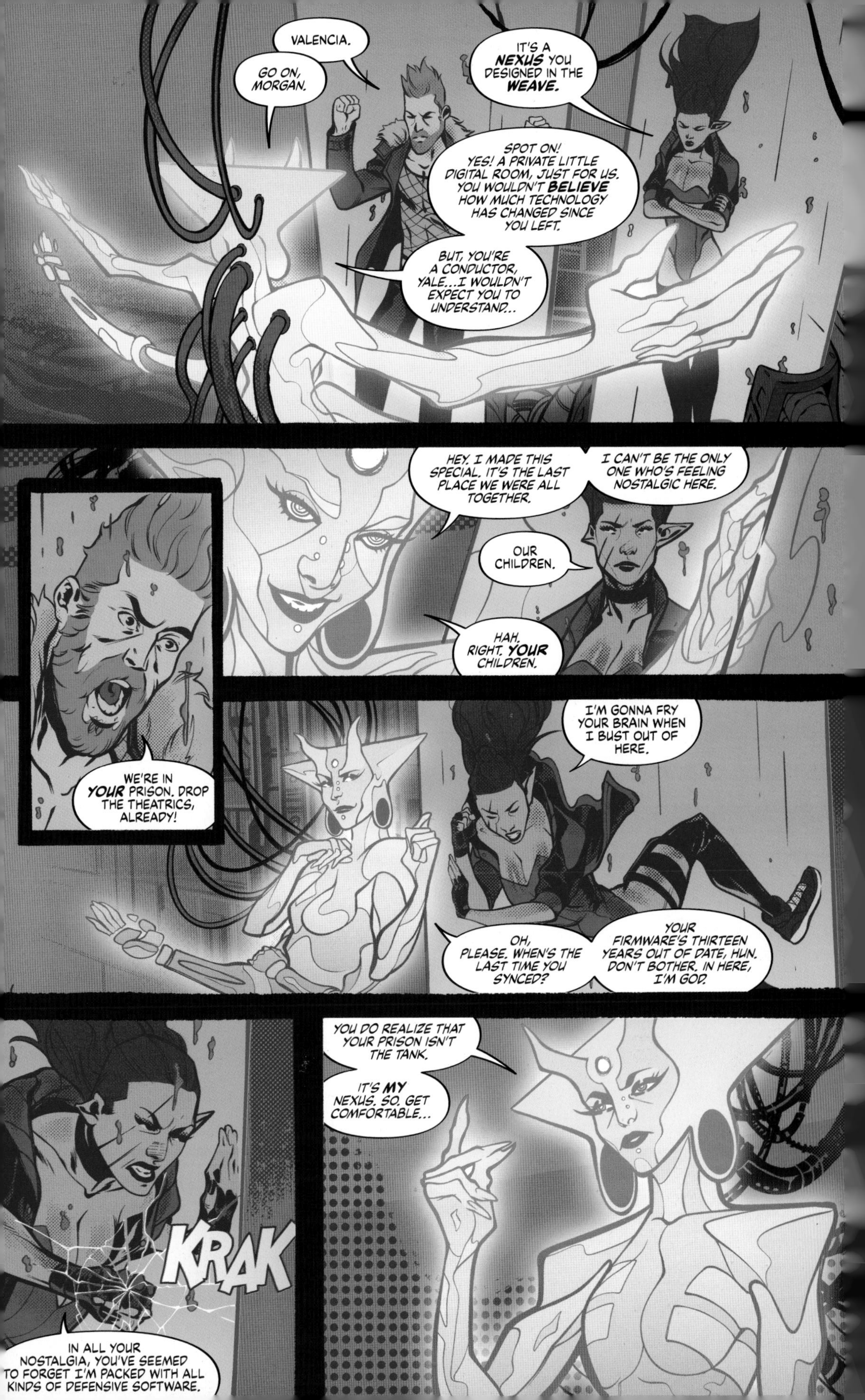
VALENCIA.
GO ON, MORGAN.
IT'S A NEXUS YOU DESIGNED IN THE WEAVE.
SPOT ON! YES! A PRIVATE LITTLE DIGITAL ROOM, JUST FOR US. YOU WOULDN'T BELIEVE HOW MUCH TECHNOLOGY HAS CHANGED SINCE YOU LEFT.
BUT, YOU'RE A CONDUCTOR, YALE...I WOULDN'T EXPECT YOU TO UNDERSTAND...
HEY. I MADE THIS SPECIAL. IT'S THE LAST PLACE WE WERE ALL TOGETHER.
I CAN'T BE THE ONLY ONE WHO'S FEELING NOSTALGIC HERE.
OUR CHILDREN.
HAH. RIGHT. YOUR CHILDREN.
WE'RE IN YOUR PRISON. DROP THE THEATRICS, ALREADY!
I'M GONNA FRY YOUR BRAIN WHEN I BUST OUT OF HERE.
OH, PLEASE. WHEN'S THE LAST TIME YOU SYNCED?
YOUR FIRMWARE'S THIRTEEN YEARS OUT OF DATE, HUN. DON'T BOTHER. IN HERE, I'M GOD.
KRAK
IN ALL YOUR NOSTALGIA, YOU'VE SEEMED TO FORGET I'M PACKED WITH ALL KINDS OF DEFENSIVE SOFTWARE.
YOU DO REALIZE THAT YOUR PRISON ISN'T THE TANK.
IT'S MY NEXUS. SO, GET COMFORTABLE...

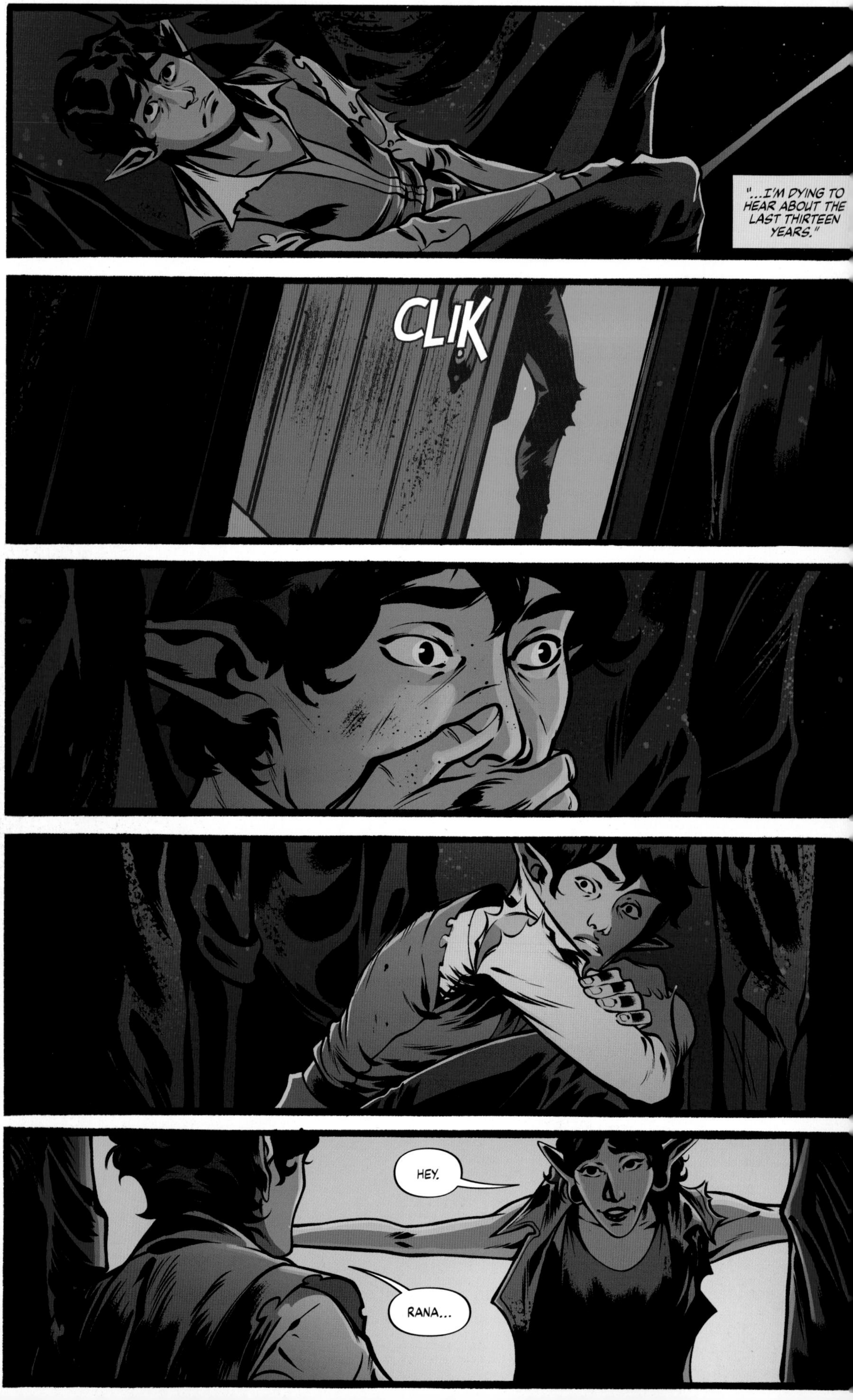
"...I'M DYING TO HEAR ABOUT THE LAST THIRTEEN YEARS."
CLIK
HEY.
RANA...

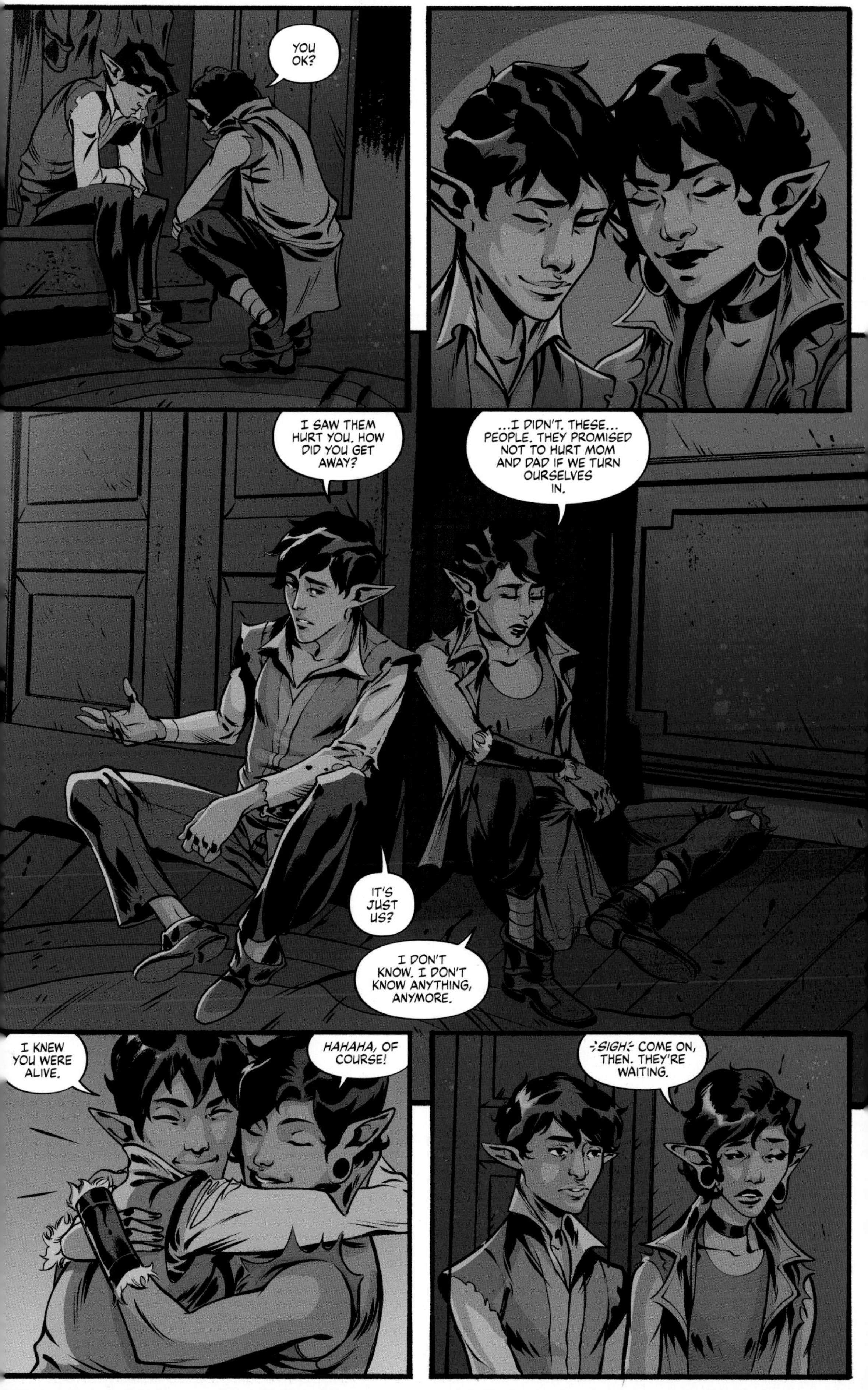
YOU OK?
I SAW THEM HURT YOU. HOW DID YOU GET AWAY?
...I DIDN'T. THESE... PEOPLE. THEY PROMISED NOT TO HURT MOM AND DAD IF WE TURN OURSELVES IN.
IT'S JUST US?
I DON'T KNOW. I DON'T KNOW ANYTHING, ANYMORE.
I KNEW YOU WERE ALIVE.
HAHAHA, OF COURSE!
-*SIGH*- COME ON, THEN. THEY'RE WAITING.

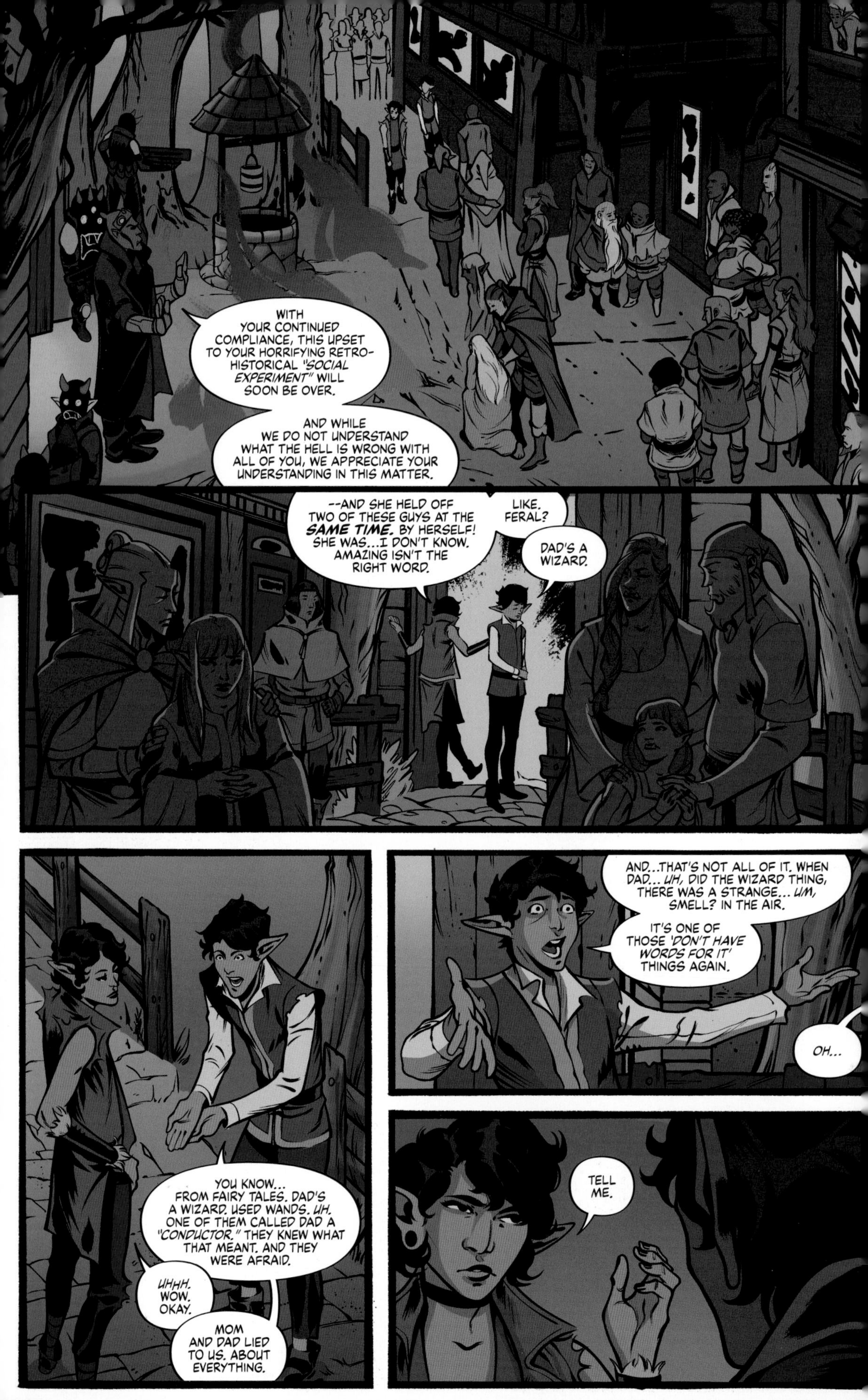
WITH YOUR CONTINUED COMPLIANCE, THIS UPSET TO YOUR HORRIFYING RETRO-HISTORICAL *"SOCIAL EXPERIMENT"* WILL SOON BE OVER.
AND WHILE WE DO NOT UNDERSTAND WHAT THE HELL IS WRONG WITH ALL OF YOU, WE APPRECIATE YOUR UNDERSTANDING IN THIS MATTER.
--AND SHE HELD OFF TWO OF THESE GUYS AT THE ***SAME TIME.*** BY HERSELF! SHE WAS...I DON'T KNOW. AMAZING ISN'T THE RIGHT WORD.
LIKE. FERAL?
DAD'S A WIZARD.
YOU KNOW... FROM FAIRY TALES. DAD'S A WIZARD. USED WANDS. *UH.* ONE OF THEM CALLED DAD A *"CONDUCTOR."* THEY KNEW WHAT THAT MEANT. AND THEY WERE AFRAID.
UHHH. WOW. OKAY.
MOM AND DAD LIED TO US. ABOUT EVERYTHING.
AND...THAT'S NOT ALL OF IT. WHEN DAD... *UH,* DID THE WIZARD THING, THERE WAS A STRANGE... *UM,* SMELL? IN THE AIR.
IT'S ONE OF THOSE *'DON'T HAVE WORDS FOR IT'* THINGS AGAIN.
OH...
TELL ME.

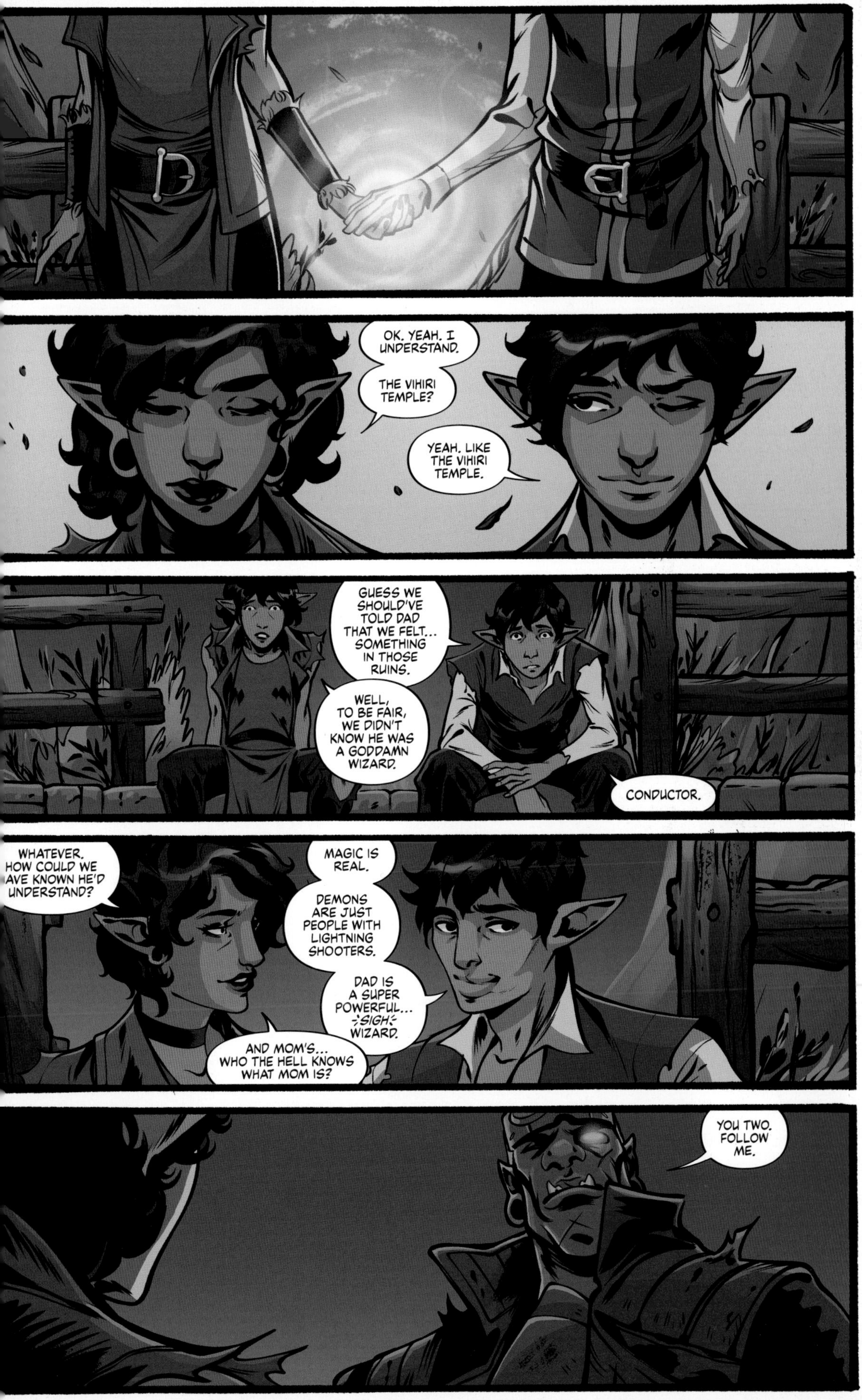
OK. YEAH. I UNDERSTAND.
THE VIHIRI TEMPLE?
YEAH. LIKE THE VIHIRI TEMPLE.
GUESS WE SHOULD'VE TOLD DAD THAT WE FELT... SOMETHING IN THOSE RUINS.
WELL, TO BE FAIR, WE DIDN'T KNOW HE WAS A GODDAMN WIZARD.
CONDUCTOR.
WHATEVER. HOW COULD WE AVE KNOWN HE'D UNDERSTAND?
MAGIC IS REAL.
DEMONS ARE JUST PEOPLE WITH LIGHTNING SHOOTERS.
DAD IS A SUPER POWERFUL... SIGH WIZARD.
AND MOM'S... WHO THE HELL KNOWS WHAT MOM IS?
YOU TWO. FOLLOW ME.

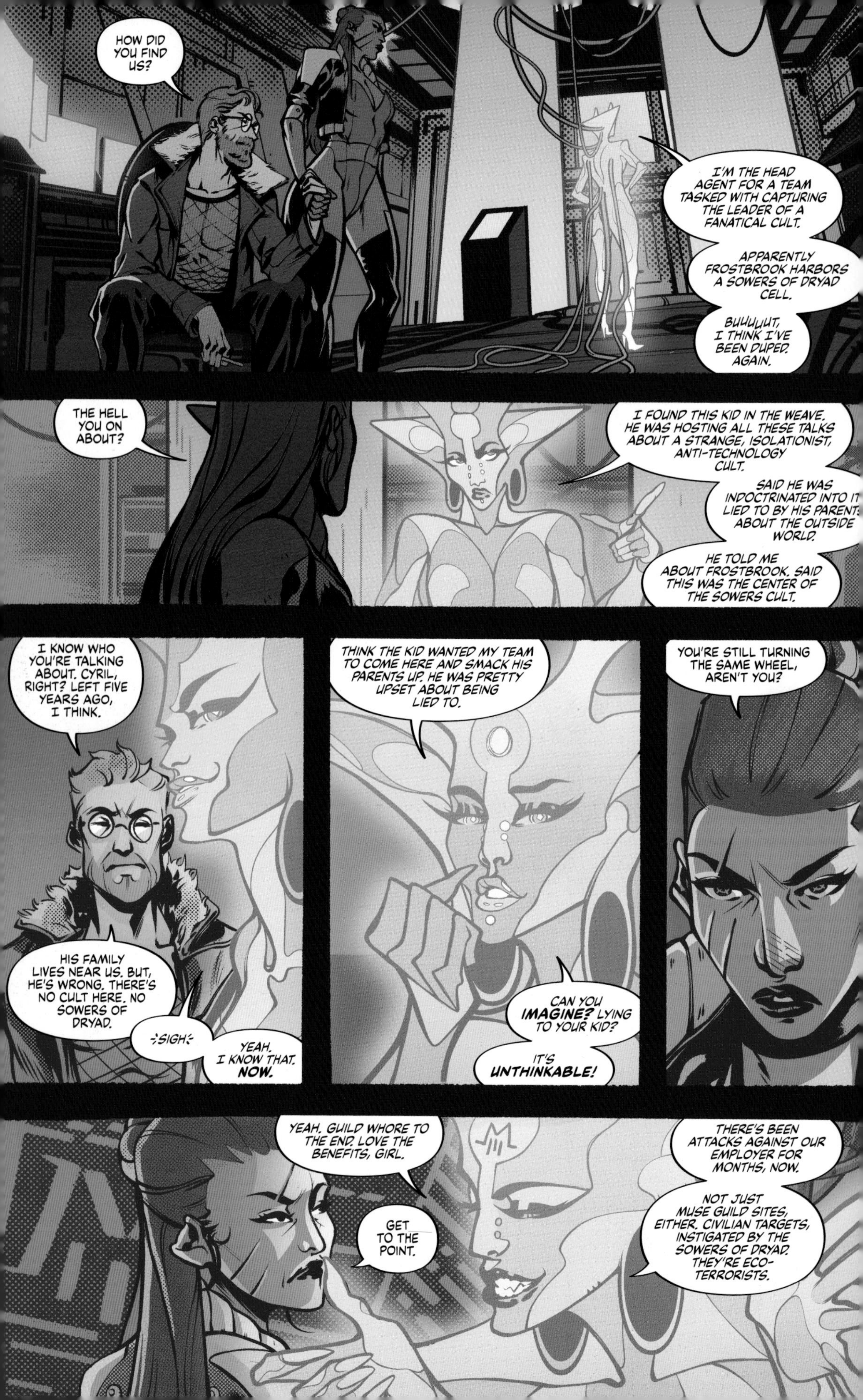
HOW DID YOU FIND US?
I'M THE HEAD AGENT FOR A TEAM TASKED WITH CAPTURING THE LEADER OF A FANATICAL CULT.
APPARENTLY FROSTBROOK HARBORS A SOWERS OF DRYAD CELL.
BUUUUUT, I THINK I'VE BEEN DUPED. AGAIN.
THE HELL YOU ON ABOUT?
I FOUND THIS KID IN THE WEAVE. HE WAS HOSTING ALL THESE TALKS ABOUT A STRANGE, ISOLATIONIST, ANTI-TECHNOLOGY CULT.
SAID HE WAS INDOCTRINATED INTO IT, LIED TO BY HIS PARENTS ABOUT THE OUTSIDE WORLD.
HE TOLD ME ABOUT FROSTBROOK. SAID THIS WAS THE CENTER OF THE SOWERS CULT.
I KNOW WHO YOU'RE TALKING ABOUT. CYRIL, RIGHT? LEFT FIVE YEARS AGO, I THINK.
HIS FAMILY LIVES NEAR US. BUT, HE'S WRONG. THERE'S NO CULT HERE. NO SOWERS OF DRYAD.
SIGH
YEAH. I KNOW THAT. **NOW.**
THINK THE KID WANTED MY TEAM TO COME HERE AND SMACK HIS PARENTS UP. HE WAS PRETTY UPSET ABOUT BEING LIED TO.
CAN YOU **IMAGINE?** LYING TO YOUR KID?
IT'S **UNTHINKABLE!**
YOU'RE STILL TURNING THE SAME WHEEL, AREN'T YOU?
YEAH. GUILD WHORE TO THE END. LOVE THE BENEFITS, GIRL.
GET TO THE POINT.
THERE'S BEEN ATTACKS AGAINST OUR EMPLOYER FOR MONTHS, NOW.
NOT JUST MUSE GUILD SITES, EITHER. CIVILIAN TARGETS, INSTIGATED BY THE SOWERS OF DRYAD. THEY'RE ECO-TERRORISTS.

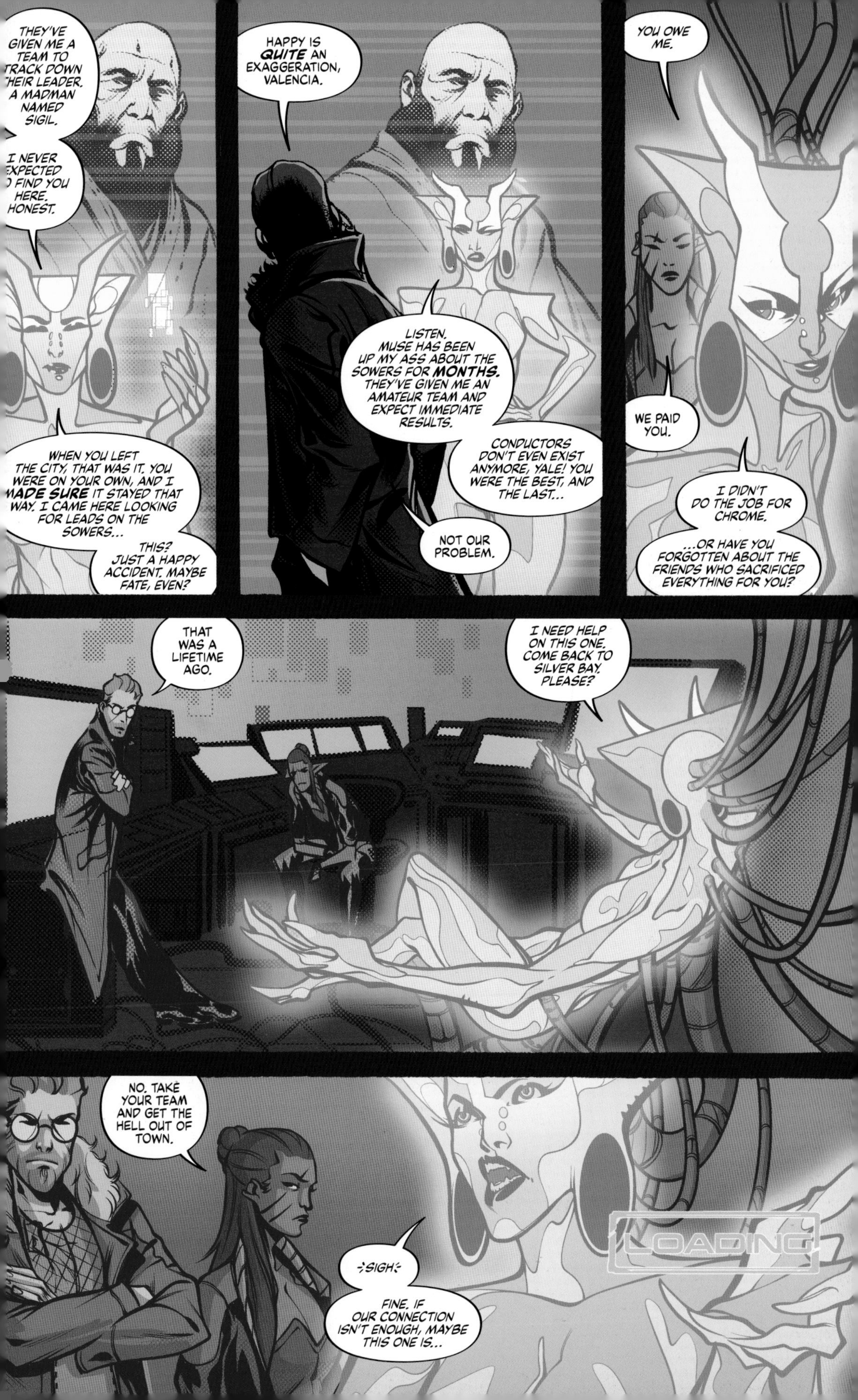
THEY'VE GIVEN ME A TEAM TO TRACK DOWN THEIR LEADER. A MADMAN NAMED SIGIL.
I NEVER EXPECTED TO FIND YOU HERE. HONEST.
WHEN YOU LEFT THE CITY, THAT WAS IT. YOU WERE ON YOUR OWN, AND I MADE SURE IT STAYED THAT WAY. I CAME HERE LOOKING FOR LEADS ON THE SOWERS...
THIS? JUST A HAPPY ACCIDENT. MAYBE FATE, EVEN?
HAPPY IS QUITE AN EXAGGERATION, VALENCIA.
LISTEN. MUSE HAS BEEN UP MY ASS ABOUT THE SOWERS FOR MONTHS. THEY'VE GIVEN ME AN AMATEUR TEAM AND EXPECT IMMEDIATE RESULTS.
CONDUCTORS DON'T EVEN EXIST ANYMORE, YALE! YOU WERE THE BEST, AND THE LAST...
NOT OUR PROBLEM.
YOU OWE ME.
WE PAID YOU.
I DIDN'T DO THE JOB FOR CHROME.
...OR HAVE YOU FORGOTTEN ABOUT THE FRIENDS WHO SACRIFICED EVERYTHING FOR YOU?
THAT WAS A LIFETIME AGO.
I NEED HELP ON THIS ONE. COME BACK TO SILVER BAY. PLEASE?
NO. TAKE YOUR TEAM AND GET THE HELL OUT OF TOWN.
SIGH
FINE. IF OUR CONNECTION ISN'T ENOUGH, MAYBE THIS ONE IS...
LOADING

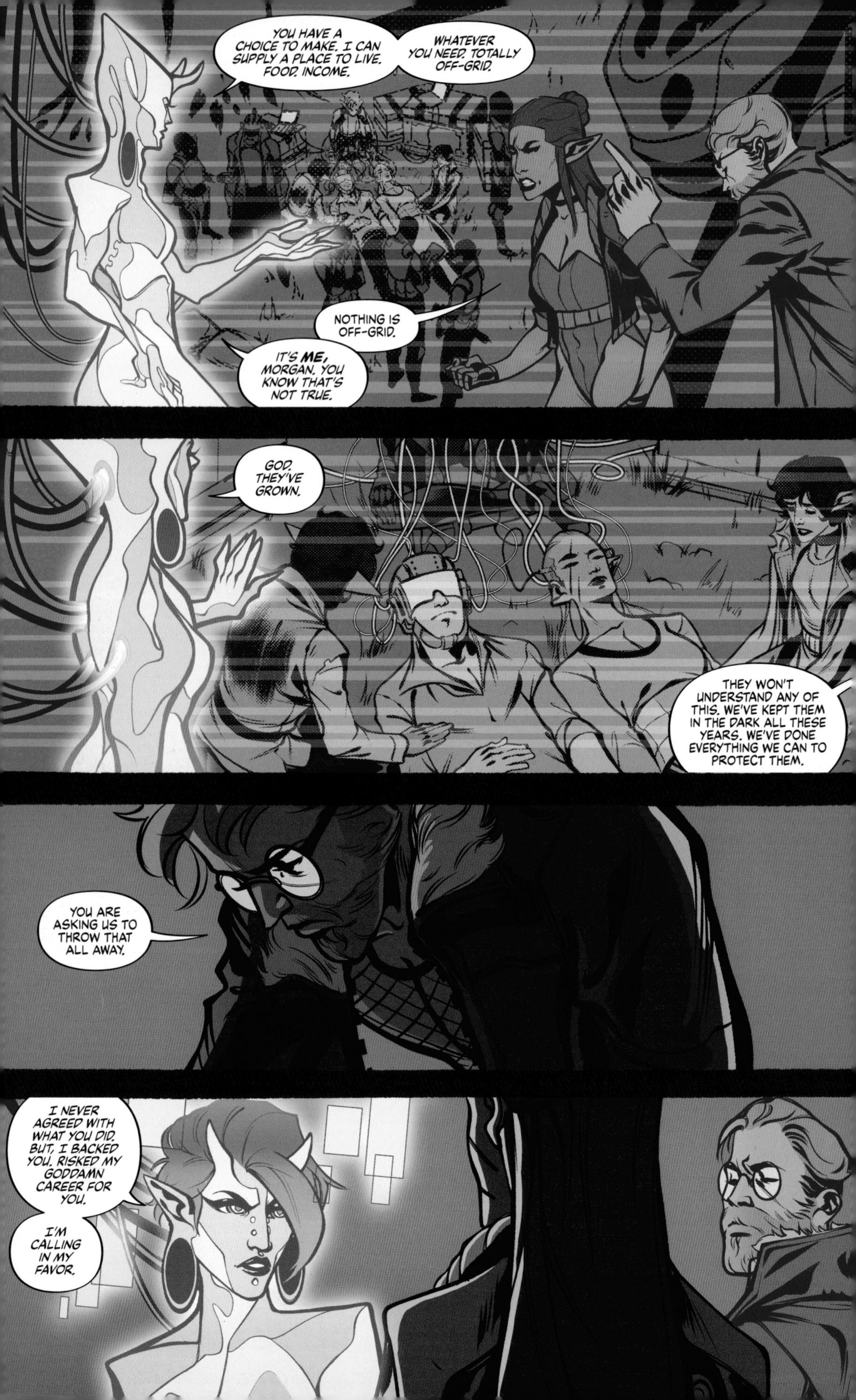
YOU HAVE A CHOICE TO MAKE. I CAN SUPPLY A PLACE TO LIVE. FOOD. INCOME.
WHATEVER YOU NEED. TOTALLY OFF-GRID.
NOTHING IS OFF-GRID.
IT'S **ME,** MORGAN. YOU KNOW THAT'S NOT TRUE.
GOD. THEY'VE GROWN.
THEY WON'T UNDERSTAND ANY OF THIS. WE'VE KEPT THEM IN THE DARK ALL THESE YEARS. WE'VE DONE EVERYTHING WE CAN TO PROTECT THEM.
YOU ARE ASKING US TO THROW THAT ALL AWAY.
I NEVER AGREED WITH WHAT YOU DID. BUT, I BACKED YOU. RISKED MY GODDAMN CAREER FOR YOU.
I'M CALLING IN MY FAVOR.

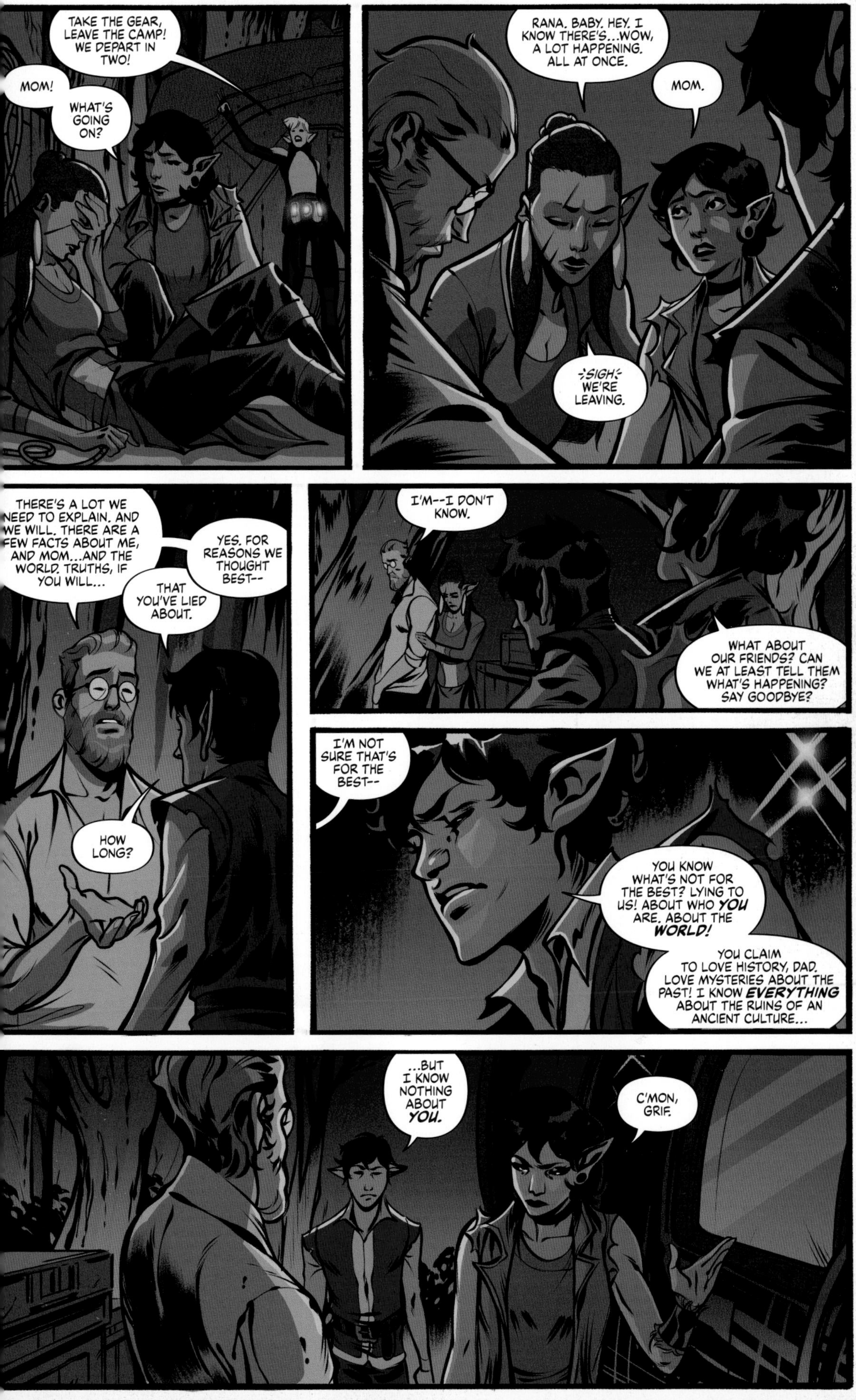
TAKE THE GEAR, LEAVE THE CAMP! WE DEPART IN TWO!
MOM!
WHAT'S GOING ON?
RANA. BABY. HEY. I KNOW THERE'S...WOW, A LOT HAPPENING. ALL AT ONCE.
MOM.
SIGH WE'RE LEAVING.
THERE'S A LOT WE NEED TO EXPLAIN. AND WE WILL. THERE ARE A FEW FACTS ABOUT ME, AND MOM...AND THE WORLD. TRUTHS, IF YOU WILL...
YES. FOR REASONS WE THOUGHT BEST--
THAT YOU'VE LIED ABOUT.
HOW LONG?
I'M--I DON'T KNOW.
WHAT ABOUT OUR FRIENDS? CAN WE AT LEAST TELL THEM WHAT'S HAPPENING? SAY GOODBYE?
I'M NOT SURE THAT'S FOR THE BEST--
YOU KNOW WHAT'S NOT FOR THE BEST? LYING TO US! ABOUT WHO YOU ARE. ABOUT THE WORLD!
YOU CLAIM TO LOVE HISTORY, DAD. LOVE MYSTERIES ABOUT THE PAST! I KNOW EVERYTHING ABOUT THE RUINS OF AN ANCIENT CULTURE...
...BUT I KNOW NOTHING ABOUT YOU.
C'MON, GRIF.

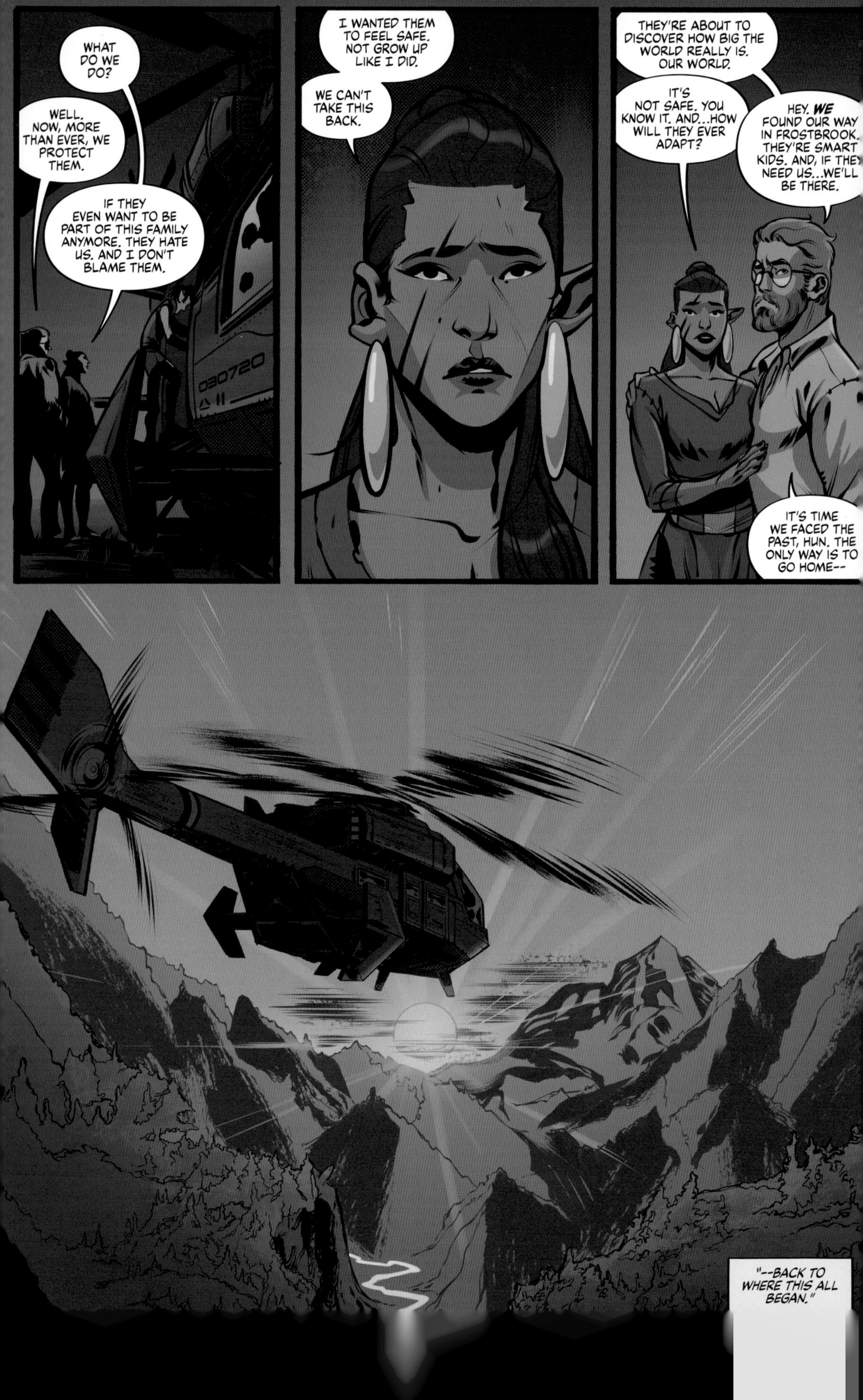
WHAT DO WE DO?
WELL. NOW, MORE THAN EVER, WE PROTECT THEM.
IF THEY EVEN WANT TO BE PART OF THIS FAMILY ANYMORE. THEY HATE US. AND I DON'T BLAME THEM.
030720
I WANTED THEM TO FEEL SAFE. NOT GROW UP LIKE I DID.
WE CAN'T TAKE THIS BACK.
THEY'RE ABOUT TO DISCOVER HOW BIG THE WORLD REALLY IS. OUR WORLD.
IT'S NOT SAFE. YOU KNOW IT. AND...HOW WILL THEY EVER ADAPT?
HEY. WE FOUND OUR WAY IN FROSTBROOK. THEY'RE SMART KIDS. AND, IF THEY NEED US...WE'LL BE THERE.
IT'S TIME WE FACED THE PAST, HUN. THE ONLY WAY IS TO GO HOME--
"--BACK TO WHERE THIS ALL BEGAN."

CHAPTER FOUR

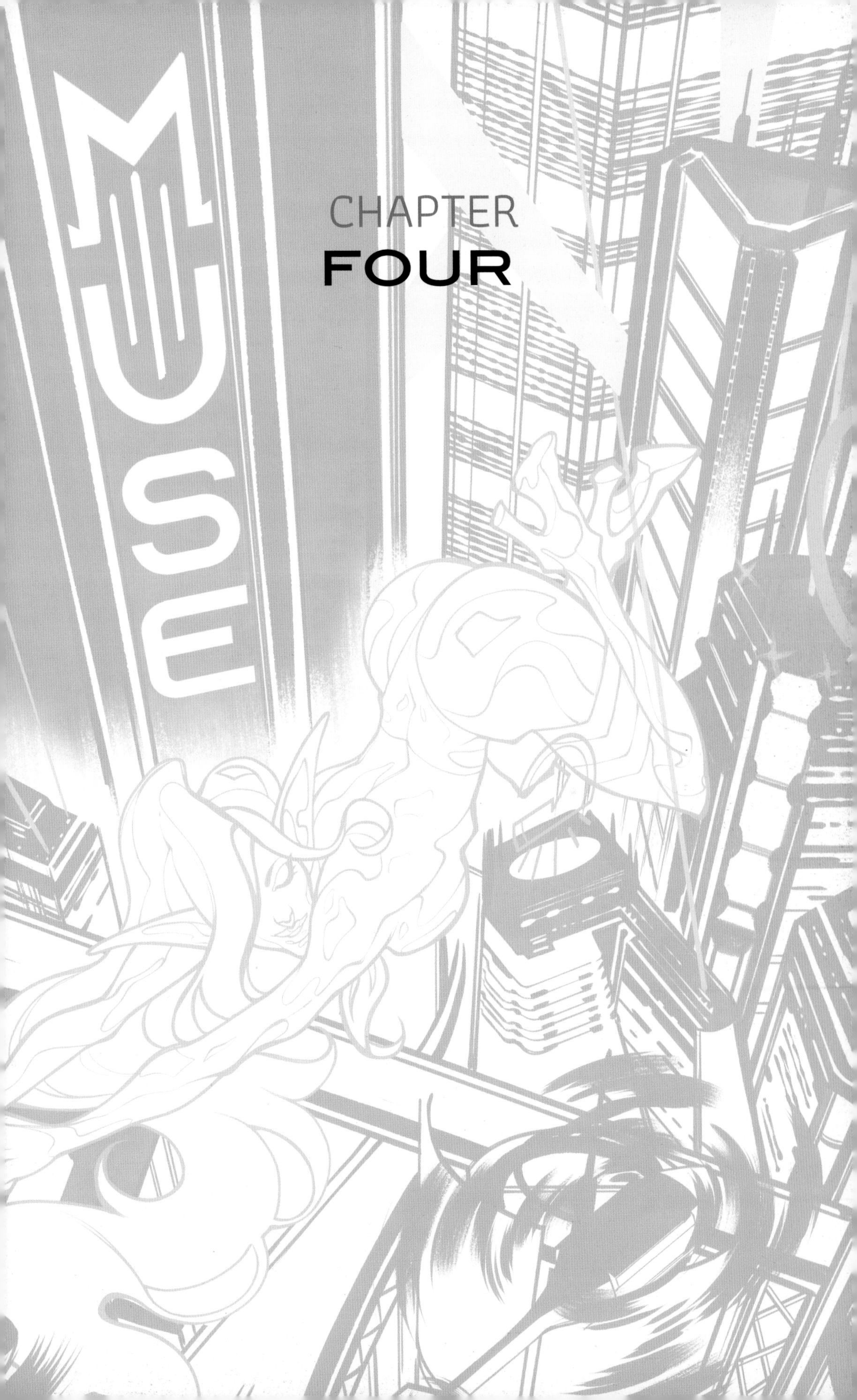
MUSE

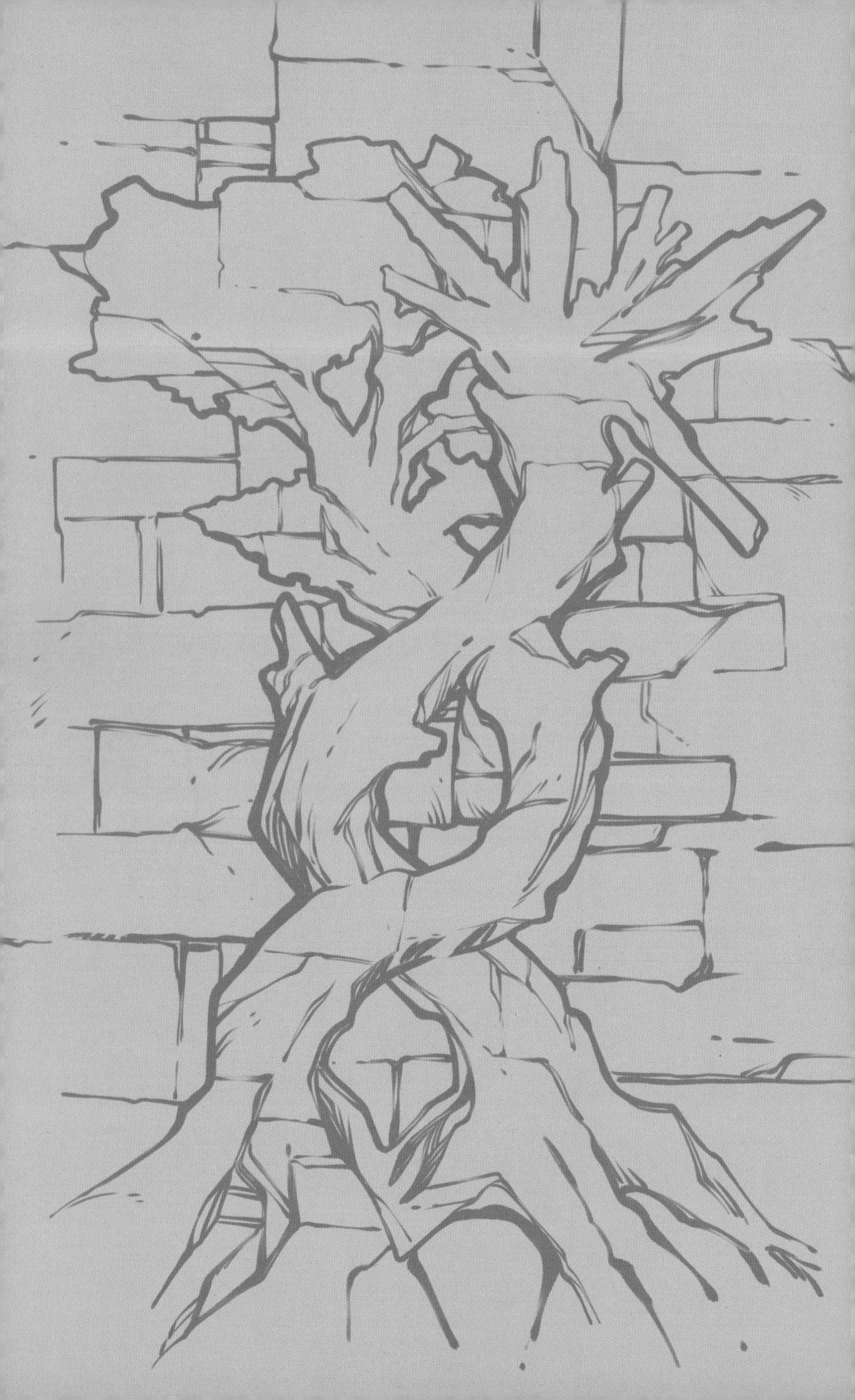

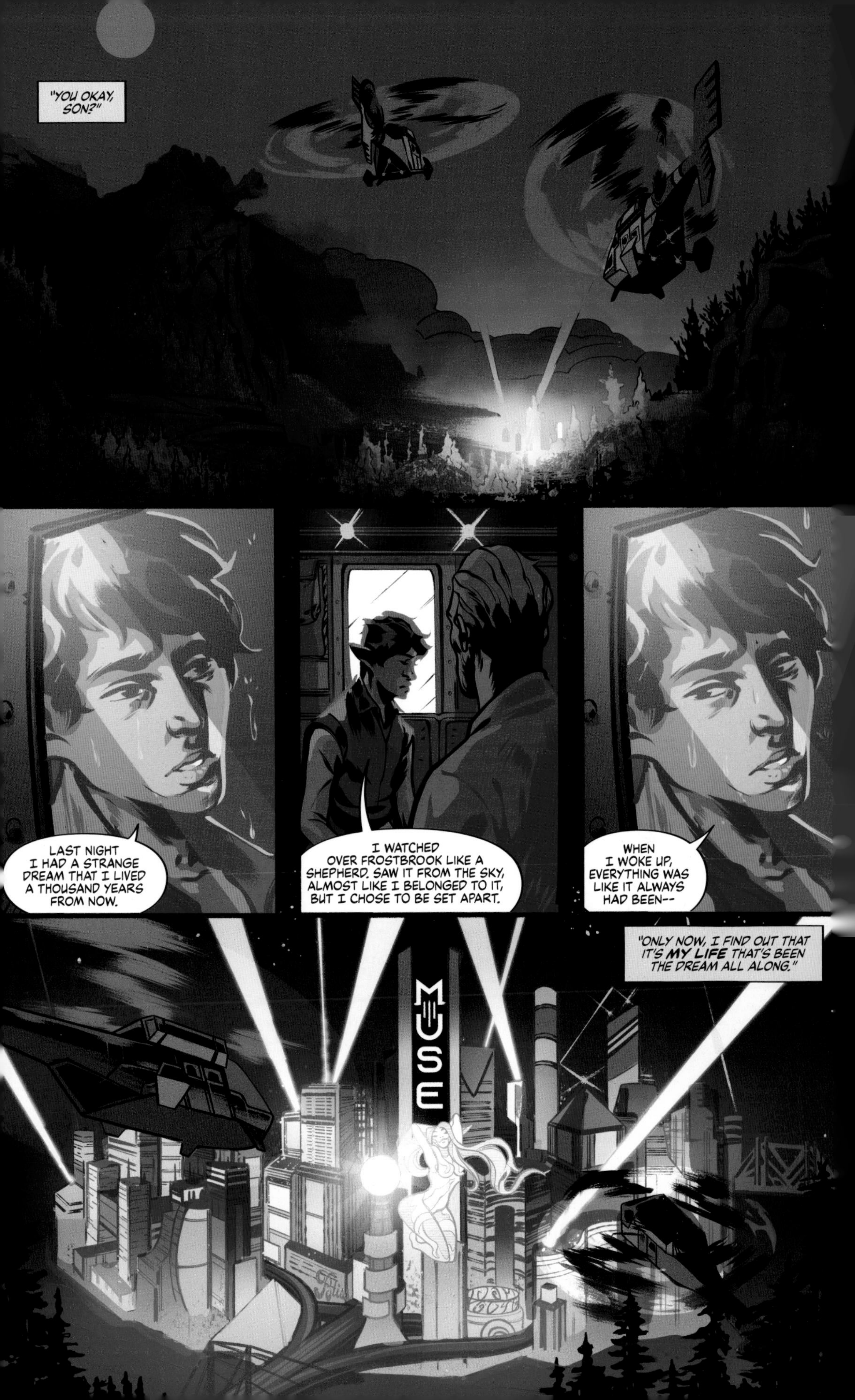
"YOU OKAY, SON?"
LAST NIGHT I HAD A STRANGE DREAM THAT I LIVED A THOUSAND YEARS FROM NOW.
I WATCHED OVER FROSTBROOK LIKE A SHEPHERD. SAW IT FROM THE SKY, ALMOST LIKE I BELONGED TO IT, BUT I CHOSE TO BE SET APART.
WHEN I WOKE UP, EVERYTHING WAS LIKE IT ALWAYS HAD BEEN--
"ONLY NOW, I FIND OUT THAT IT'S **MY LIFE** THAT'S BEEN THE DREAM ALL ALONG."
MUSE

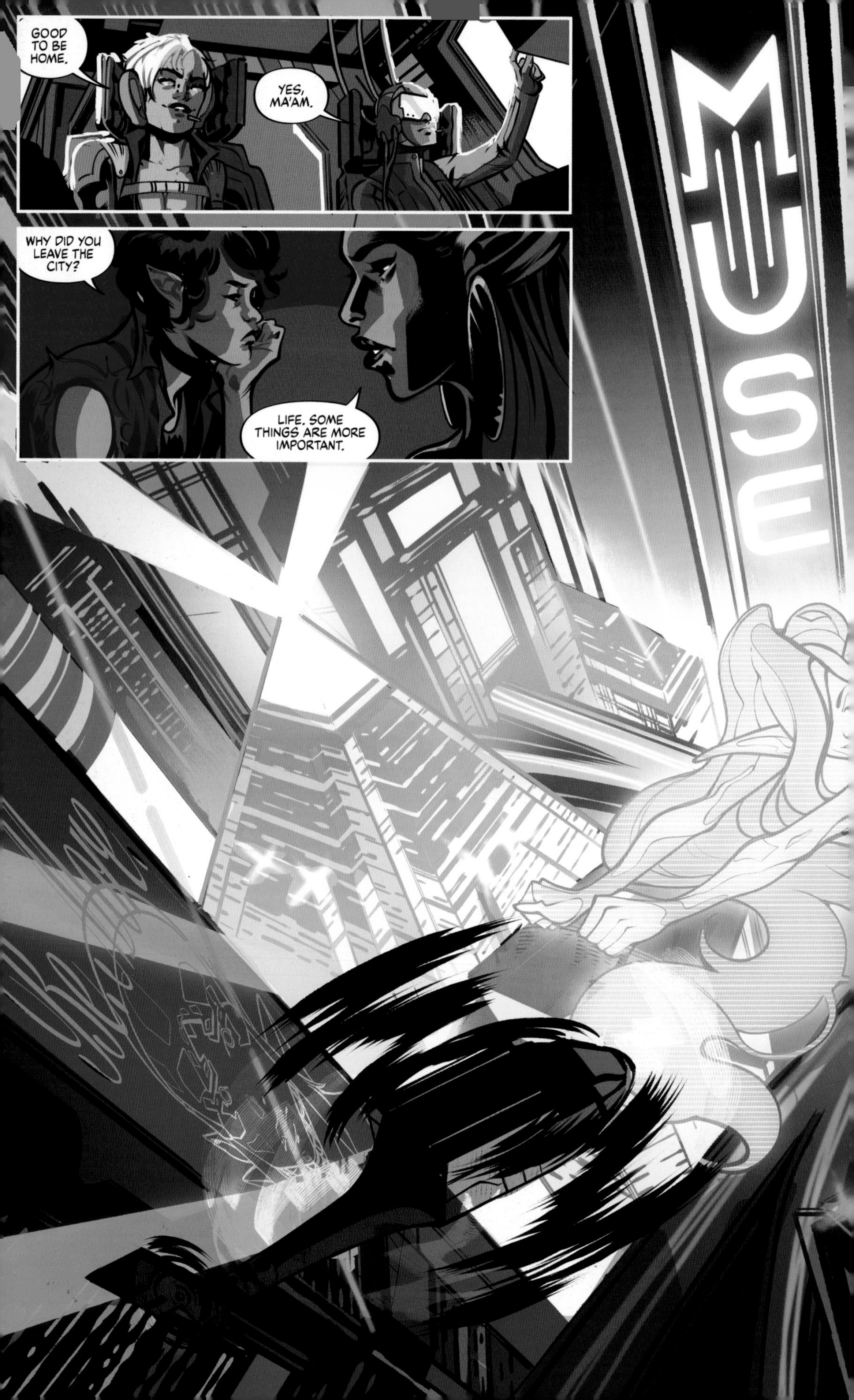
GOOD TO BE HOME.
YES, MA'AM.
WHY DID YOU LEAVE THE CITY?
LIFE. SOME THINGS ARE MORE IMPORTANT.
MUSE

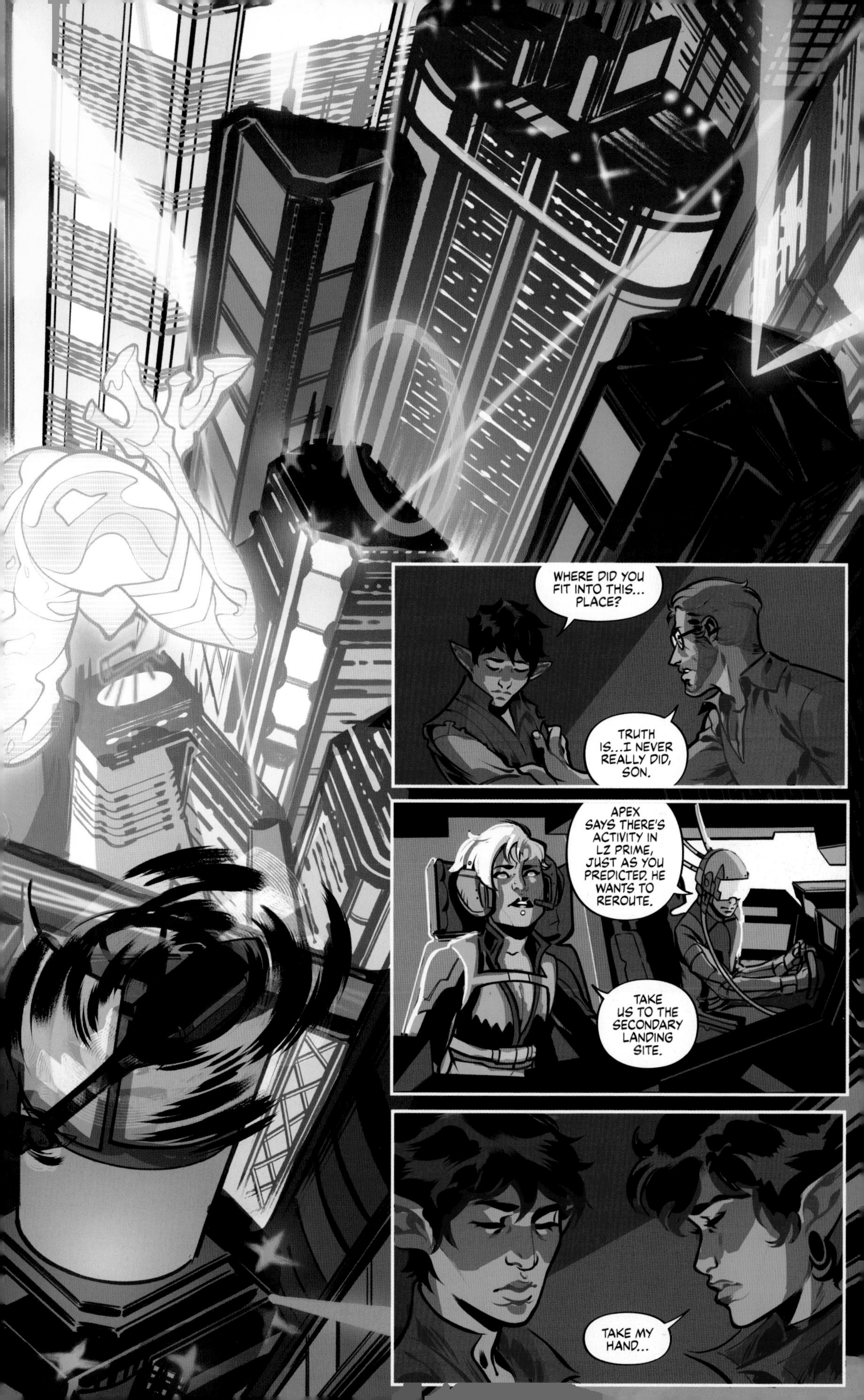
WHERE DID YOU FIT INTO THIS... PLACE?
TRUTH IS...I NEVER REALLY DID, SON.
APEX SAYS THERE'S ACTIVITY IN LZ PRIME, JUST AS YOU PREDICTED. HE WANTS TO REROUTE.
TAKE US TO THE SECONDARY LANDING SITE.
TAKE MY HAND...

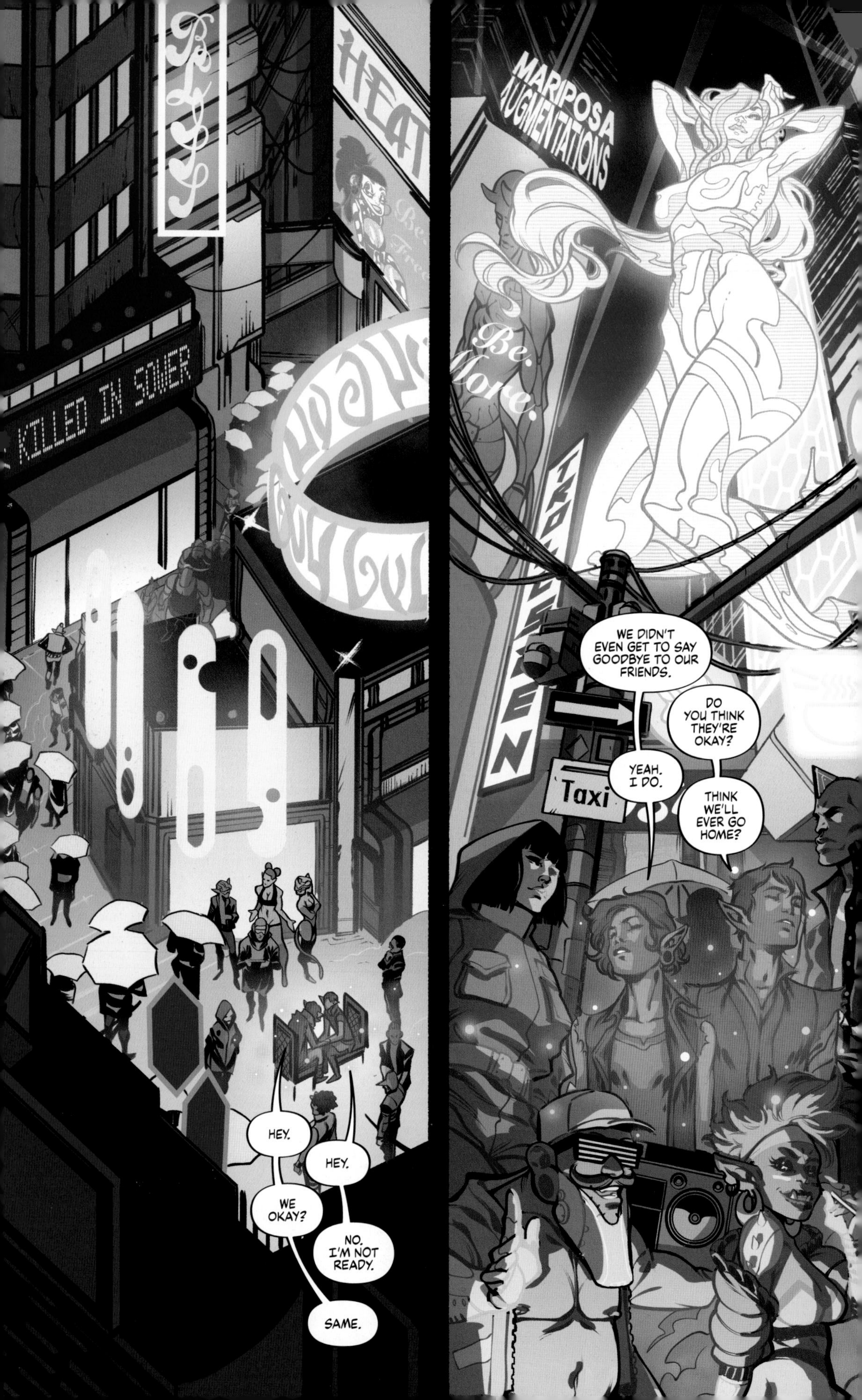
HEAT
KILLED IN SOWER
HEY.
HEY.
WE OKAY?
NO. I'M NOT READY.
SAME.
MARIPOSA AUGMENTATIONS
Be. More.
WE DIDN'T EVEN GET TO SAY GOODBYE TO OUR FRIENDS.
DO YOU THINK THEY'RE OKAY?
YEAH. I DO.
THINK WE'LL EVER GO HOME?
Taxi

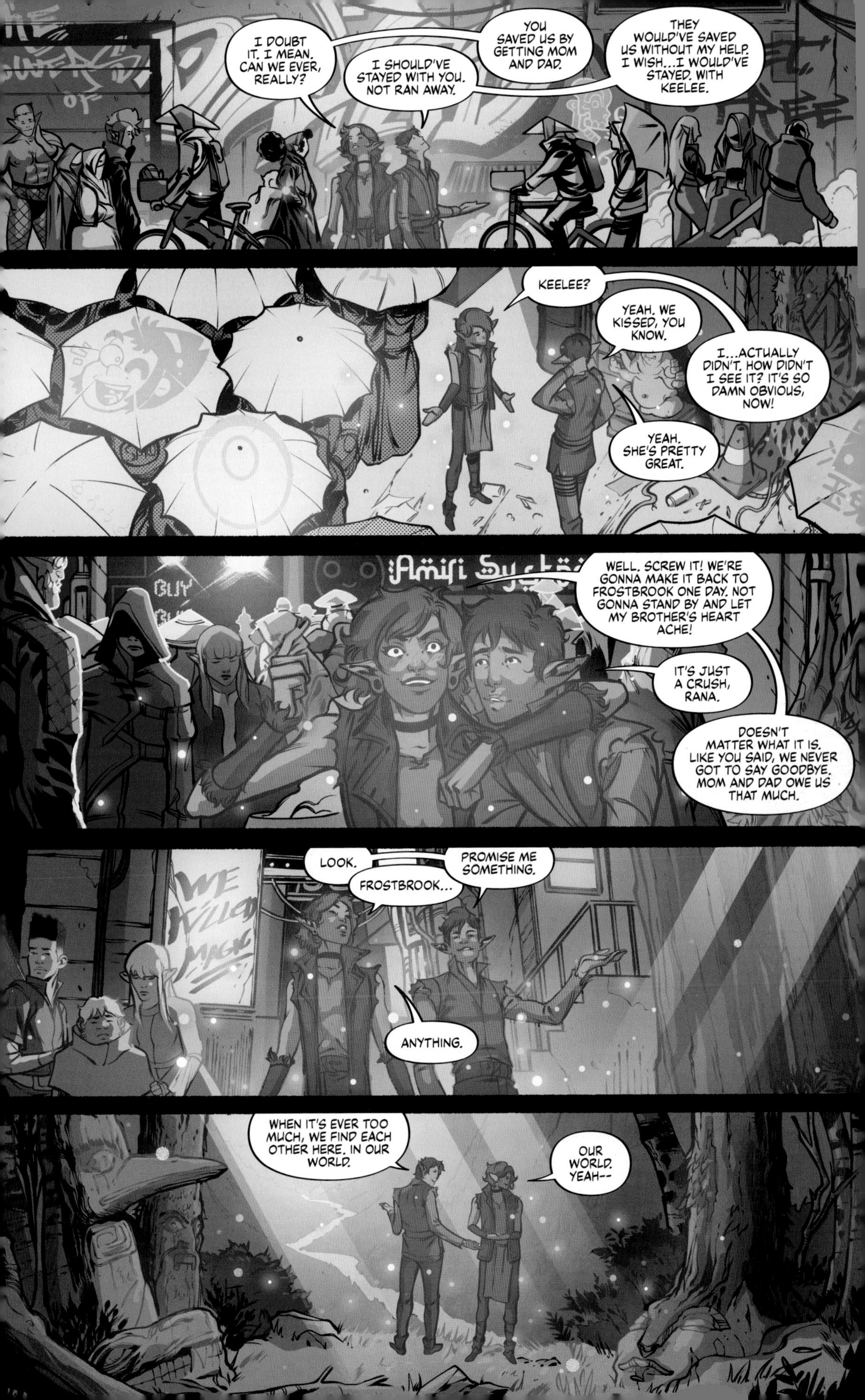
I DOUBT IT. I MEAN. CAN WE EVER, REALLY?
YOU SAVED US BY GETTING MOM AND DAD.
I SHOULD'VE STAYED WITH YOU. NOT RAN AWAY.
THEY WOULD'VE SAVED US WITHOUT MY HELP. I WISH...I WOULD'VE STAYED. WITH KEELEE.
KEELEE?
YEAH. WE KISSED, YOU KNOW.
I...ACTUALLY DIDN'T. HOW DIDN'T I SEE IT? IT'S SO DAMN OBVIOUS, NOW!
YEAH. SHE'S PRETTY GREAT.
BUY
WELL. SCREW IT! WE'RE GONNA MAKE IT BACK TO FROSTBROOK ONE DAY. NOT GONNA STAND BY AND LET MY BROTHER'S HEART ACHE!
IT'S JUST A CRUSH, RANA.
DOESN'T MATTER WHAT IT IS. LIKE YOU SAID, WE NEVER GOT TO SAY GOODBYE. MOM AND DAD OWE US THAT MUCH.
LOOK.
PROMISE ME SOMETHING.
FROSTBROOK...
ANYTHING.
WE KILLED MAGIC
WHEN IT'S EVER TOO MUCH, WE FIND EACH OTHER HERE. IN OUR WORLD.
OUR WORLD. YEAH--

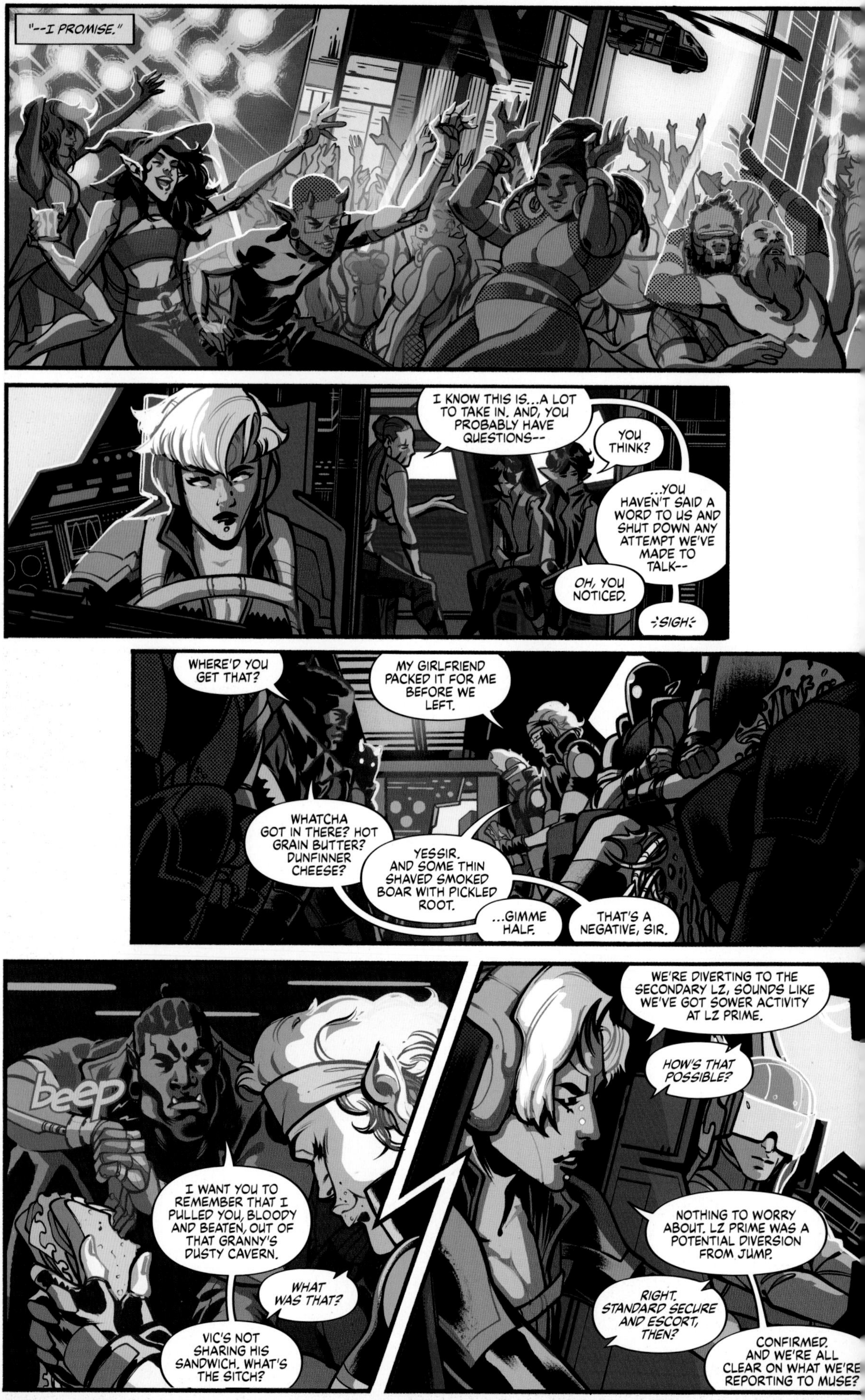
"--I PROMISE."
I KNOW THIS IS...A LOT TO TAKE IN. AND, YOU PROBABLY HAVE QUESTIONS--
YOU THINK?
...YOU HAVEN'T SAID A WORD TO US AND SHUT DOWN ANY ATTEMPT WE'VE MADE TO TALK--
OH, YOU NOTICED.
SIGH
WHERE'D YOU GET THAT?
MY GIRLFRIEND PACKED IT FOR ME BEFORE WE LEFT.
WHATCHA GOT IN THERE? HOT GRAIN BUTTER? DUNFINNER CHEESE?
YESSIR. AND SOME THIN SHAVED SMOKED BOAR WITH PICKLED ROOT.
...GIMME HALF.
THAT'S A NEGATIVE, SIR.
beep
I WANT YOU TO REMEMBER THAT I PULLED YOU, BLOODY AND BEATEN, OUT OF THAT GRANNY'S DUSTY CAVERN.
WHAT WAS THAT?
VIC'S NOT SHARING HIS SANDWICH. WHAT'S THE SITCH?
WE'RE DIVERTING TO THE SECONDARY LZ, SOUNDS LIKE WE'VE GOT SOWER ACTIVITY AT LZ PRIME.
HOW'S THAT POSSIBLE?
NOTHING TO WORRY ABOUT. LZ PRIME WAS A POTENTIAL DIVERSION FROM JUMP.
RIGHT. STANDARD SECURE AND ESCORT, THEN?
CONFIRMED. AND WE'RE ALL CLEAR ON WHAT WE'RE REPORTING TO MUSE?

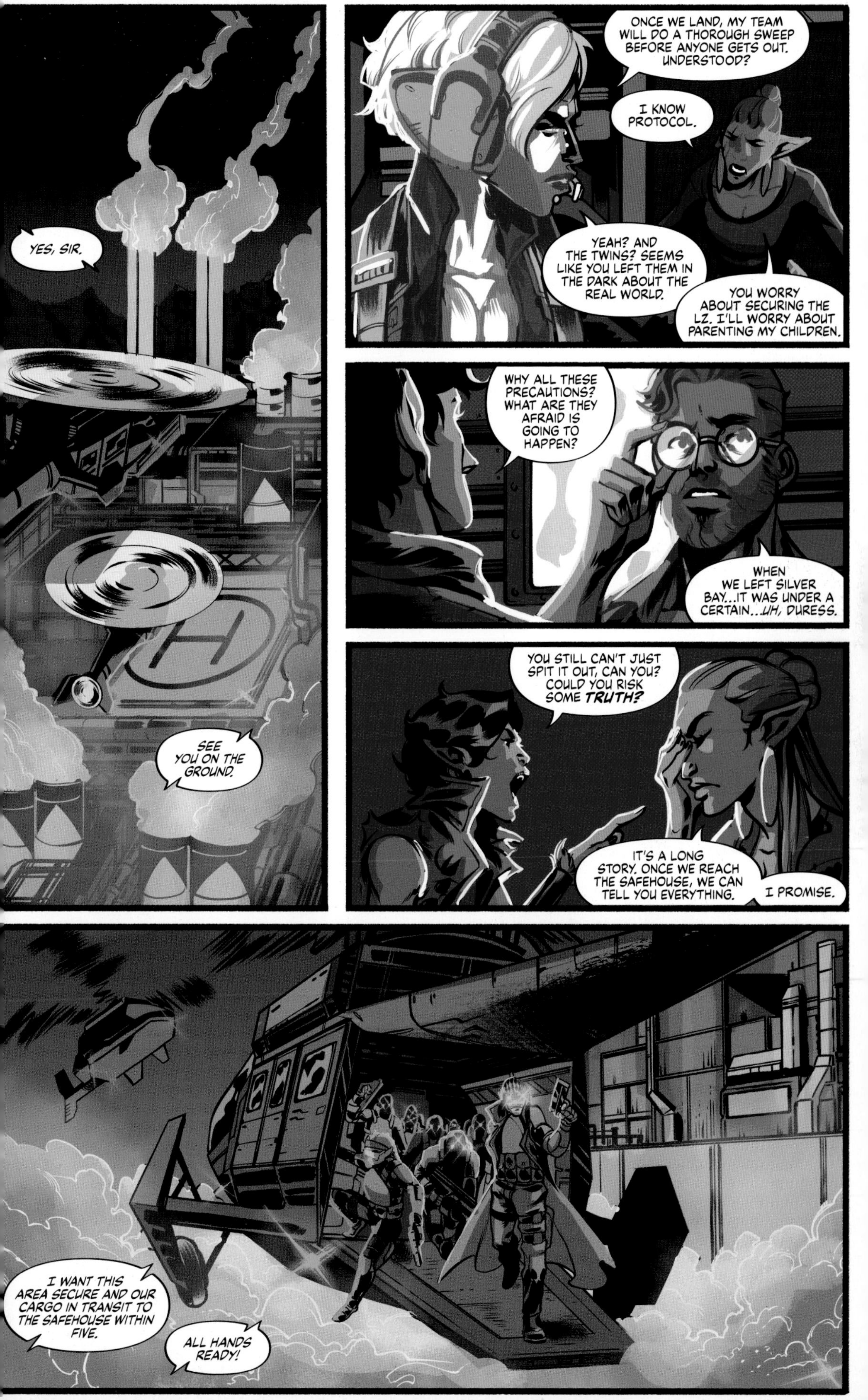
YES, SIR.
SEE YOU ON THE GROUND.
ONCE WE LAND, MY TEAM WILL DO A THOROUGH SWEEP BEFORE ANYONE GETS OUT. UNDERSTOOD?
I KNOW PROTOCOL.
YEAH? AND THE TWINS? SEEMS LIKE YOU LEFT THEM IN THE DARK ABOUT THE REAL WORLD.
YOU WORRY ABOUT SECURING THE LZ. I'LL WORRY ABOUT PARENTING MY CHILDREN.
WHY ALL THESE PRECAUTIONS? WHAT ARE THEY AFRAID IS GOING TO HAPPEN?
WHEN WE LEFT SILVER BAY...IT WAS UNDER A CERTAIN...*UH,* DURESS.
YOU STILL CAN'T JUST SPIT IT OUT, CAN YOU? COULD YOU RISK SOME ***TRUTH?***
IT'S A LONG STORY. ONCE WE REACH THE SAFEHOUSE, WE CAN TELL YOU EVERYTHING.
I PROMISE.
I WANT THIS AREA SECURE AND OUR CARGO IN TRANSIT TO THE SAFEHOUSE WITHIN FIVE.
ALL HANDS READY!

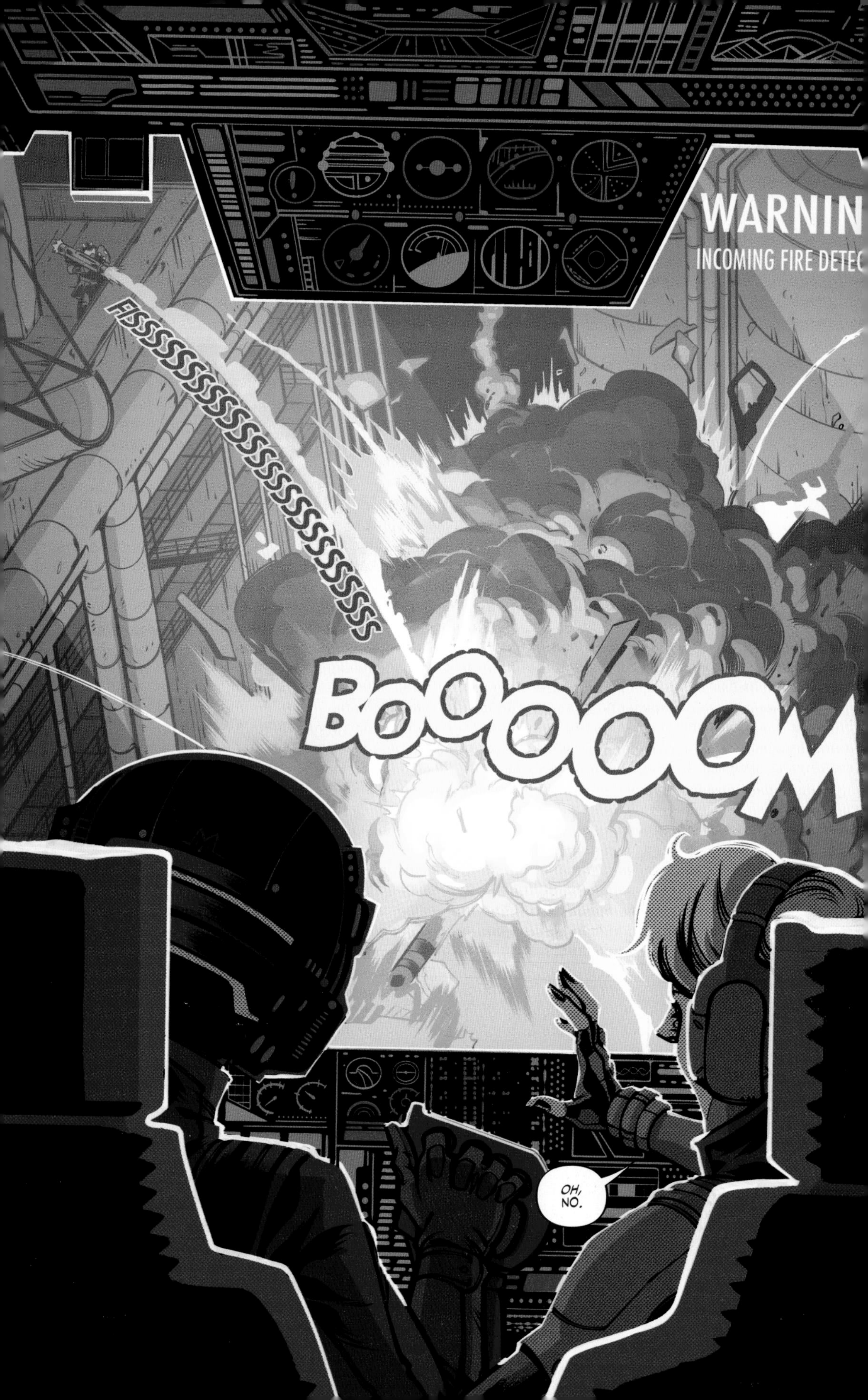
WARNIN
INCOMING FIRE DETEC
FSSSSSSSSSSSSSSSSSSSSSSSSSS
BOOOOOOM
OH, NO.

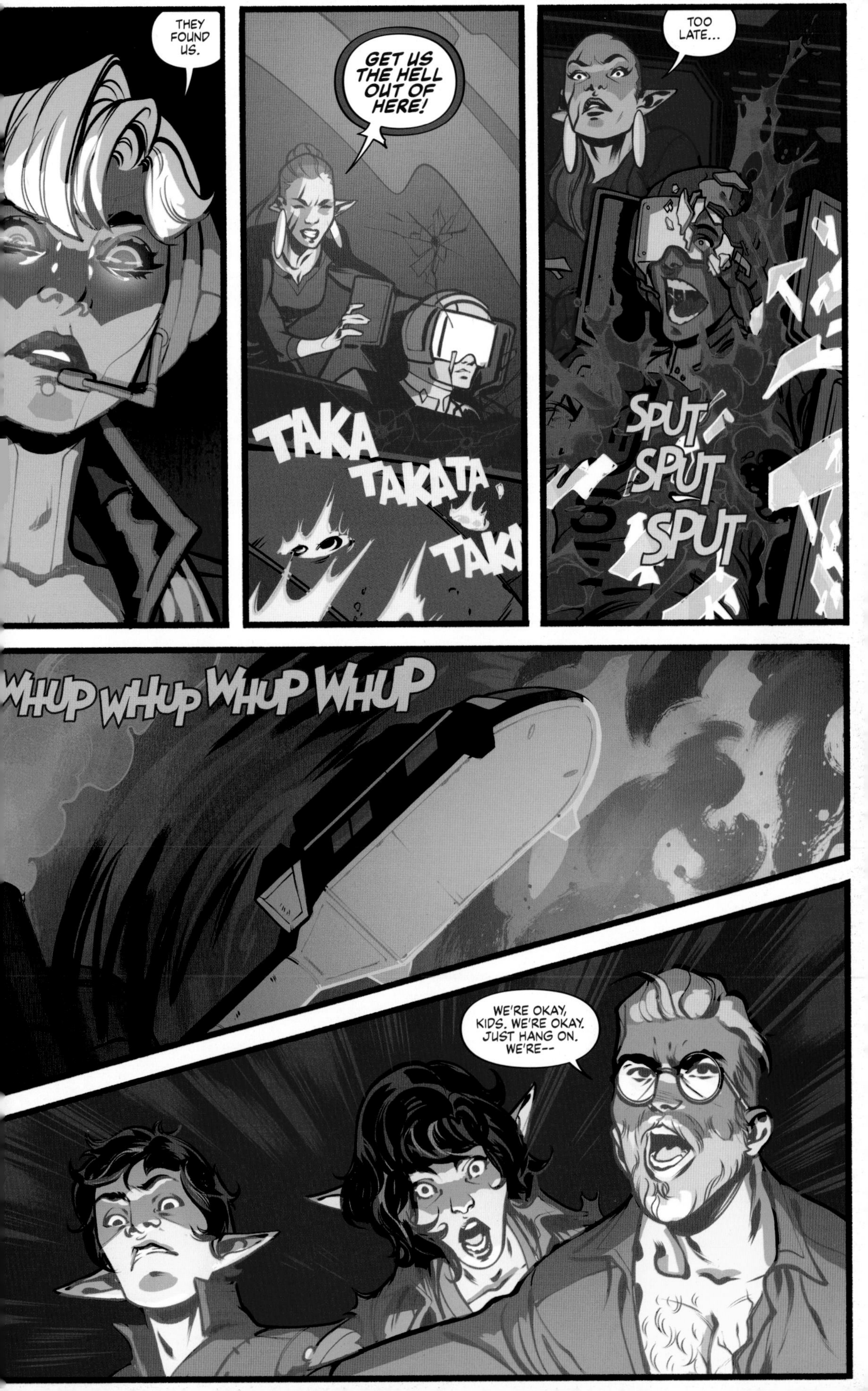
THEY FOUND US.
GET US THE HELL OUT OF HERE!
TAKA TAKATA TAK
TOO LATE...
SPUT SPUT SPUT
WHUP WHUP WHUP WHUP
WE'RE OKAY, KIDS. WE'RE OKAY. JUST HANG ON. WE'RE--

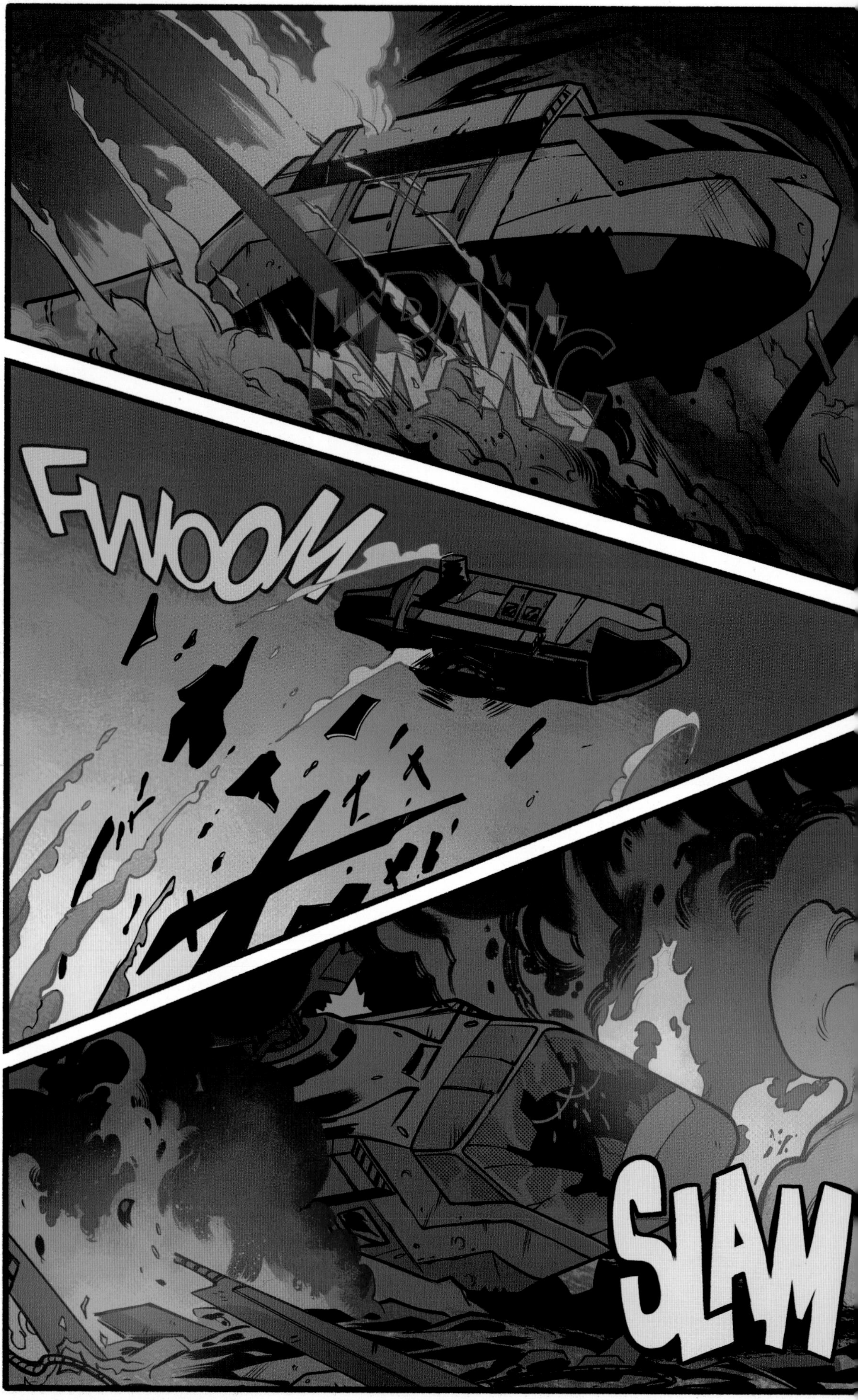
FWOOM
SLAM

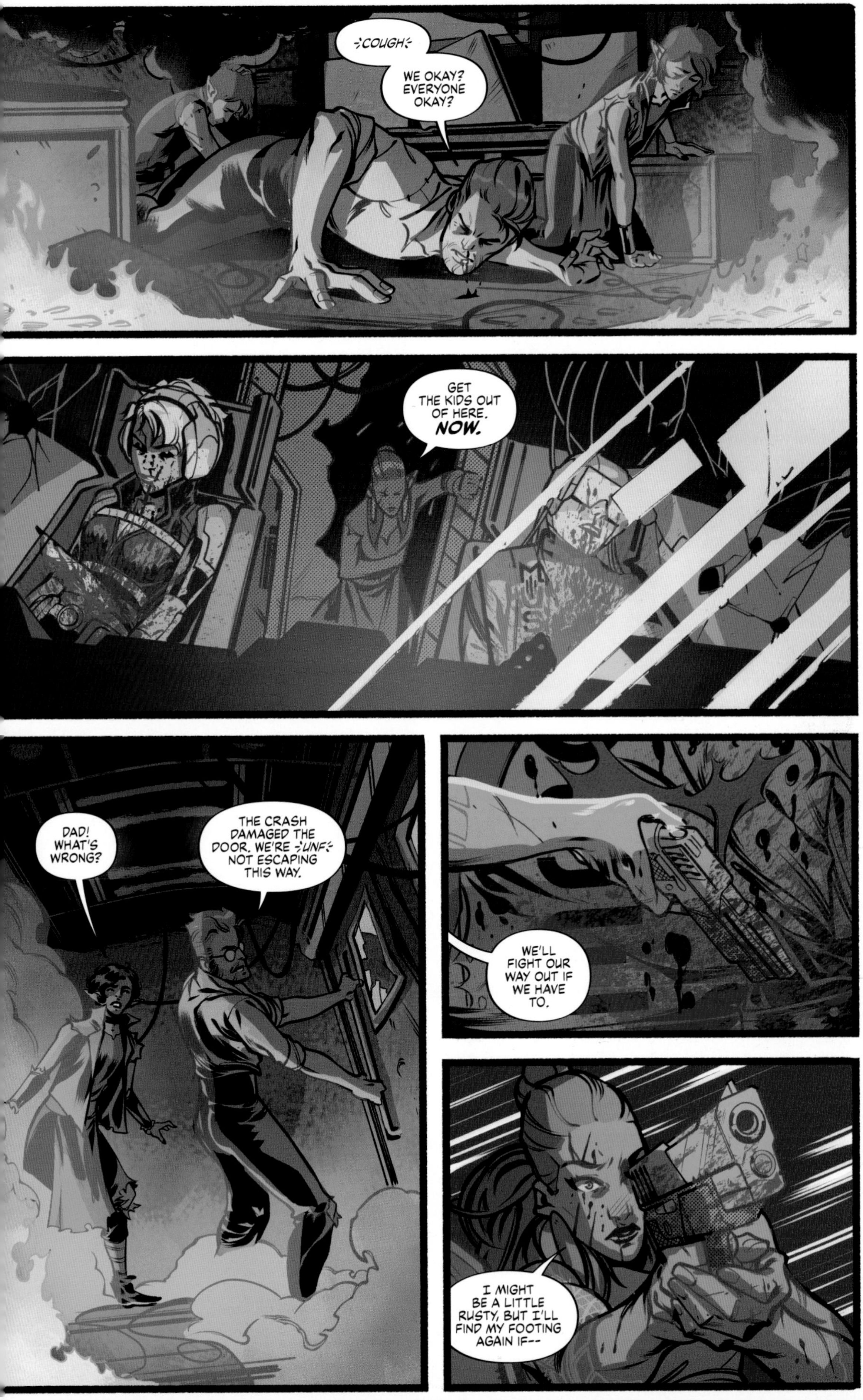

-COUGH-
WE OKAY? EVERYONE OKAY?
GET THE KIDS OUT OF HERE. NOW.
DAD! WHAT'S WRONG?
THE CRASH DAMAGED THE DOOR. WE'RE -UNF- NOT ESCAPING THIS WAY.
WE'LL FIGHT OUR WAY OUT IF WE HAVE TO.
I MIGHT BE A LITTLE RUSTY, BUT I'LL FIND MY FOOTING AGAIN IF--

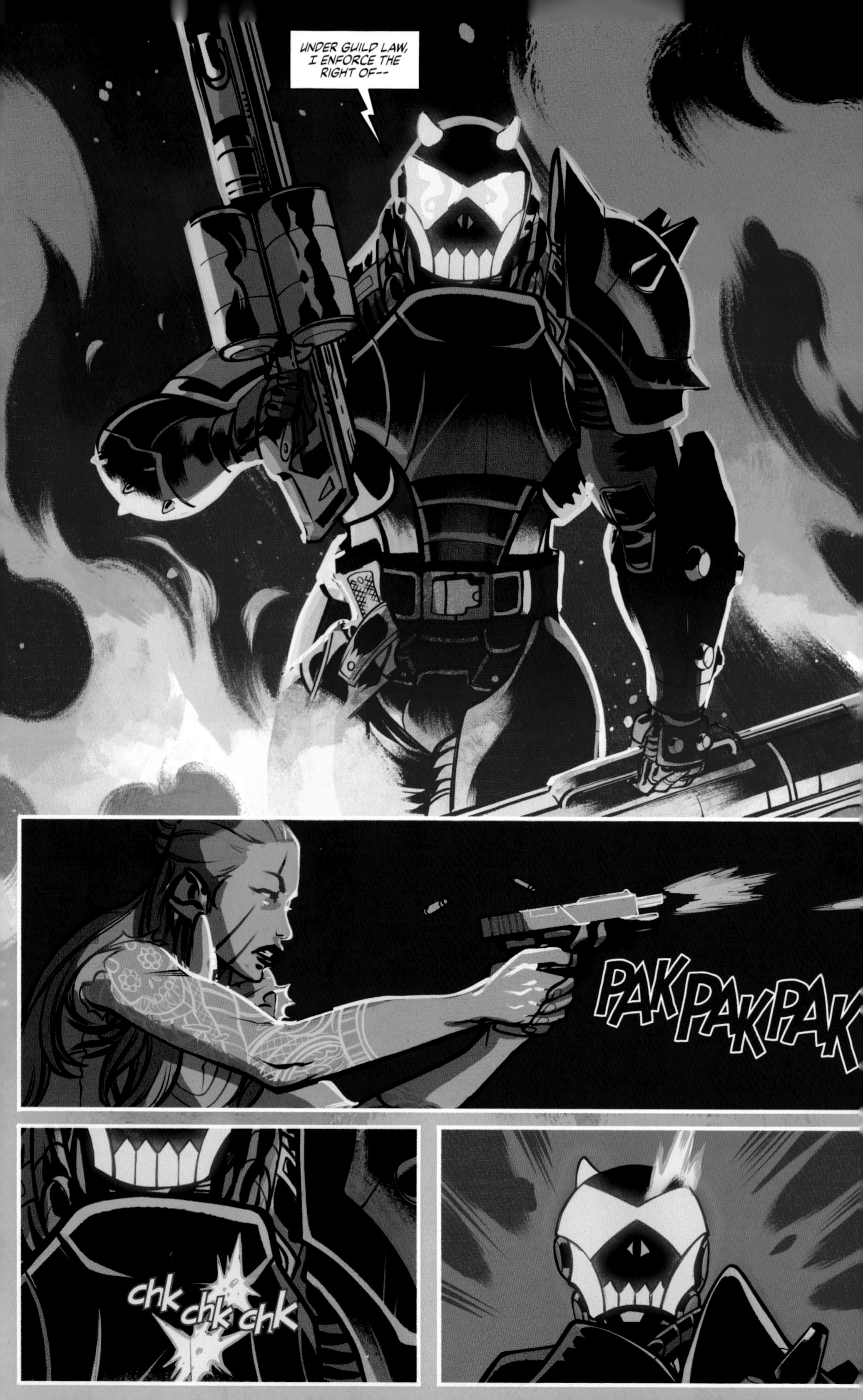
UNDER GUILD LAW, I ENFORCE THE RIGHT OF--
PAK PAK PAK
chk chk chk

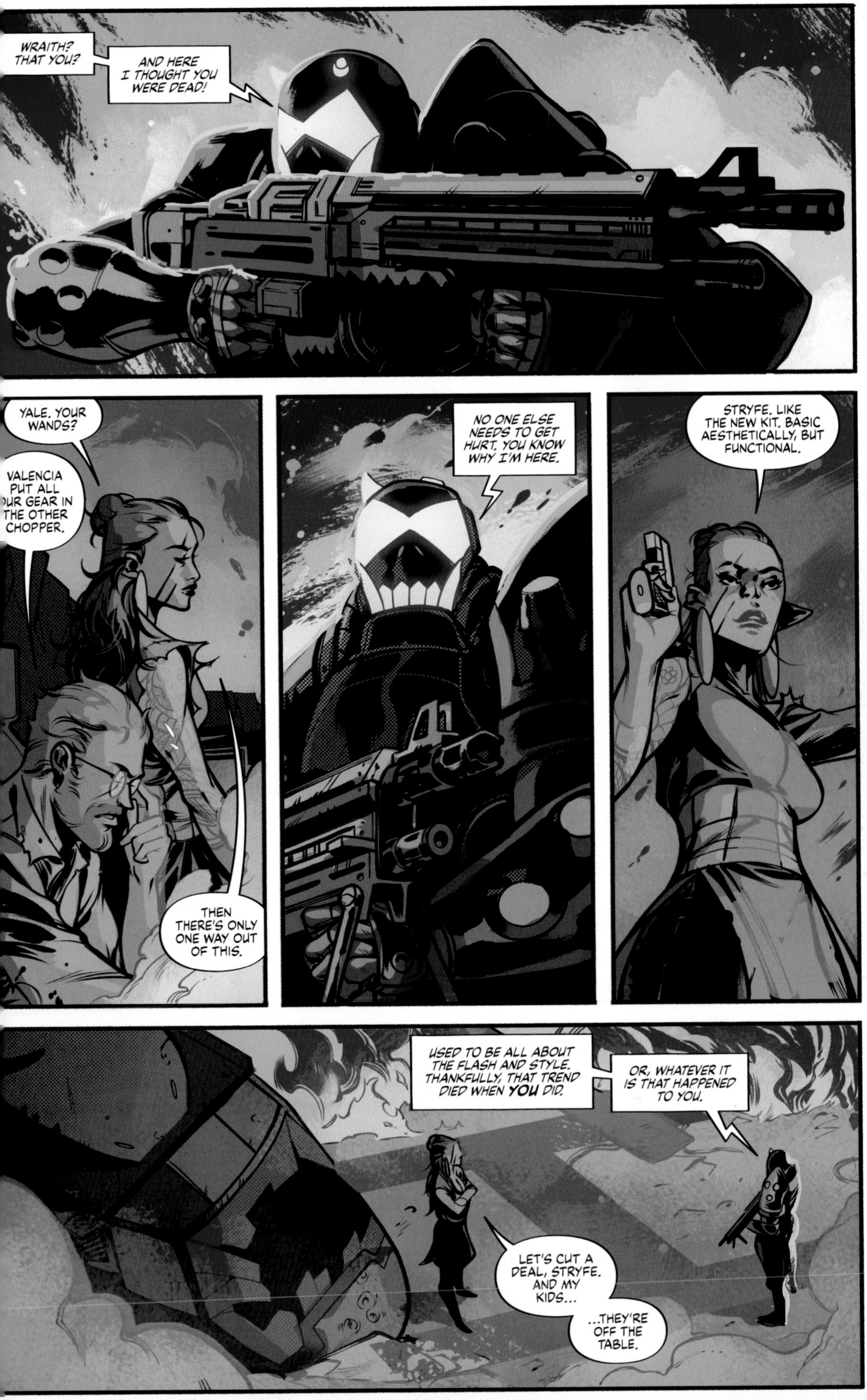

WRAITH? THAT YOU?
AND HERE I THOUGHT YOU WERE DEAD!
YALE. YOUR WANDS?
VALENCIA PUT ALL OUR GEAR IN THE OTHER CHOPPER.
THEN THERE'S ONLY ONE WAY OUT OF THIS.
NO ONE ELSE NEEDS TO GET HURT. YOU KNOW WHY I'M HERE.
STRYFE. LIKE THE NEW KIT. BASIC AESTHETICALLY, BUT FUNCTIONAL.
USED TO BE ALL ABOUT THE FLASH AND STYLE. THANKFULLY, THAT TREND DIED WHEN YOU DID.
OR, WHATEVER IT IS THAT HAPPENED TO YOU.
LET'S CUT A DEAL, STRYFE. AND MY KIDS...
...THEY'RE OFF THE TABLE.

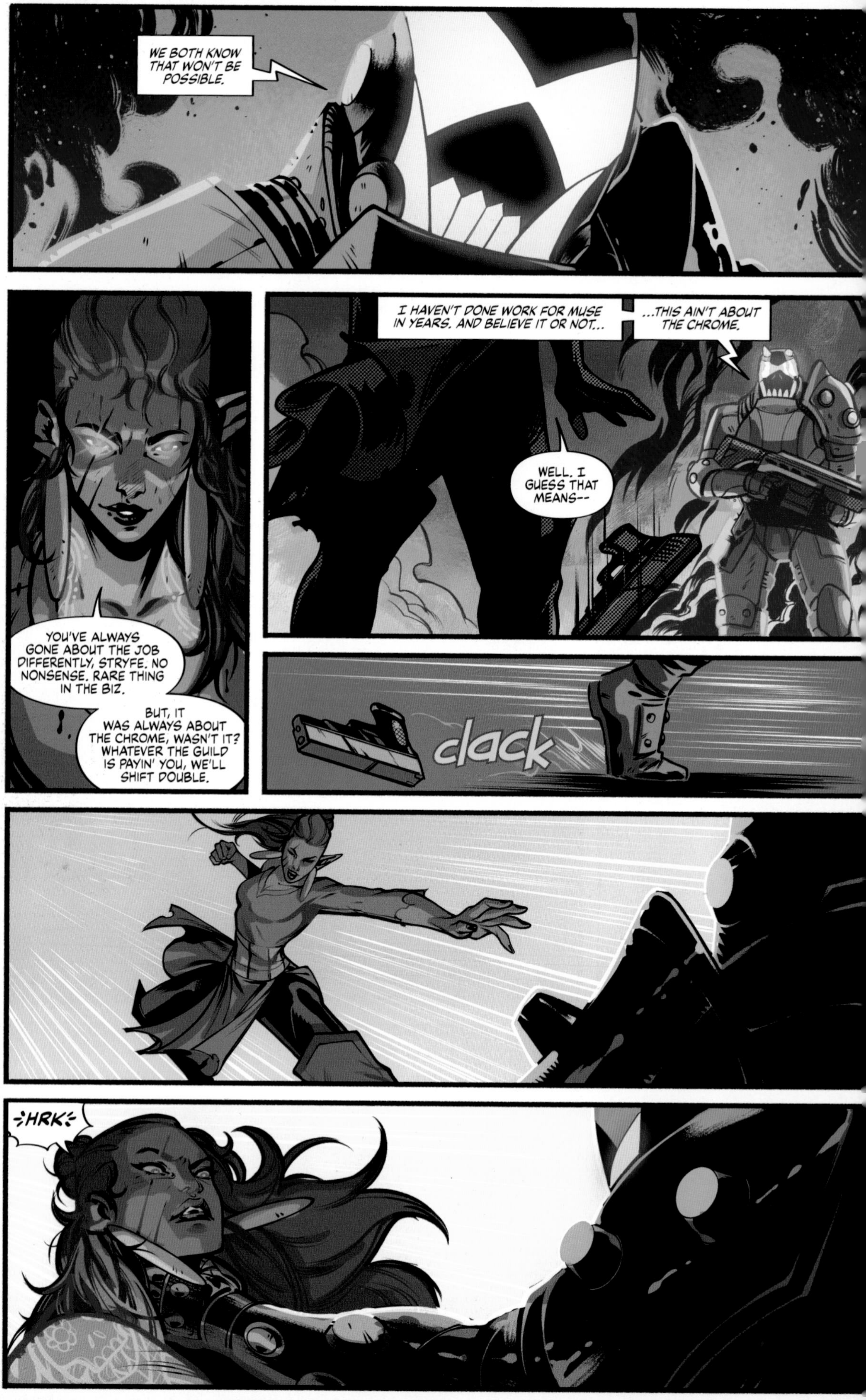
WE BOTH KNOW THAT WON'T BE POSSIBLE.
YOU'VE ALWAYS GONE ABOUT THE JOB DIFFERENTLY, STRYFE. NO NONSENSE. RARE THING IN THE BIZ.
BUT, IT WAS ALWAYS ABOUT THE CHROME, WASN'T IT? WHATEVER THE GUILD IS PAYIN' YOU, WE'LL SHIFT DOUBLE.
I HAVEN'T DONE WORK FOR MUSE IN YEARS. AND BELIEVE IT OR NOT...
...THIS AIN'T ABOUT THE CHROME.
WELL. I GUESS THAT MEANS--
clack
HRK

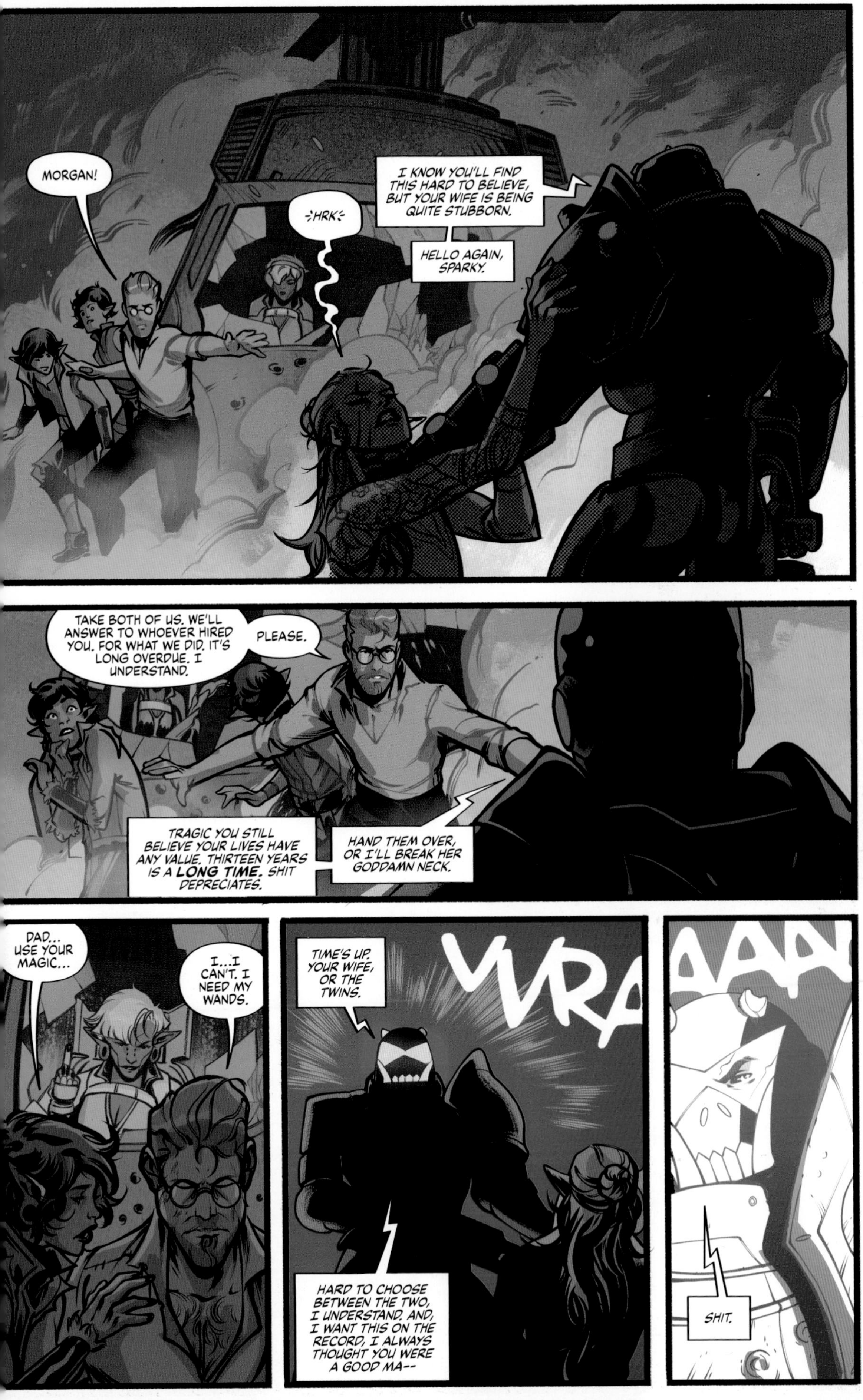

MORGAN!
-HRK-
I KNOW YOU'LL FIND THIS HARD TO BELIEVE, BUT YOUR WIFE IS BEING QUITE STUBBORN.
HELLO AGAIN, SPARKY.
TAKE BOTH OF US. WE'LL ANSWER TO WHOEVER HIRED YOU. FOR WHAT WE DID. IT'S LONG OVERDUE. I UNDERSTAND.
PLEASE.
TRAGIC YOU STILL BELIEVE YOUR LIVES HAVE ANY VALUE. THIRTEEN YEARS IS A **LONG TIME.** SHIT DEPRECIATES.
HAND THEM OVER, OR I'LL BREAK HER GODDAMN NECK.
DAD... USE YOUR MAGIC...
I...I CAN'T. I NEED MY WANDS.
TIME'S UP. YOUR WIFE, OR THE TWINS.
VVRAAAA
HARD TO CHOOSE BETWEEN THE TWO, I UNDERSTAND. AND, I WANT THIS ON THE RECORD, I ALWAYS THOUGHT YOU WERE A GOOD MA--
SHIT.

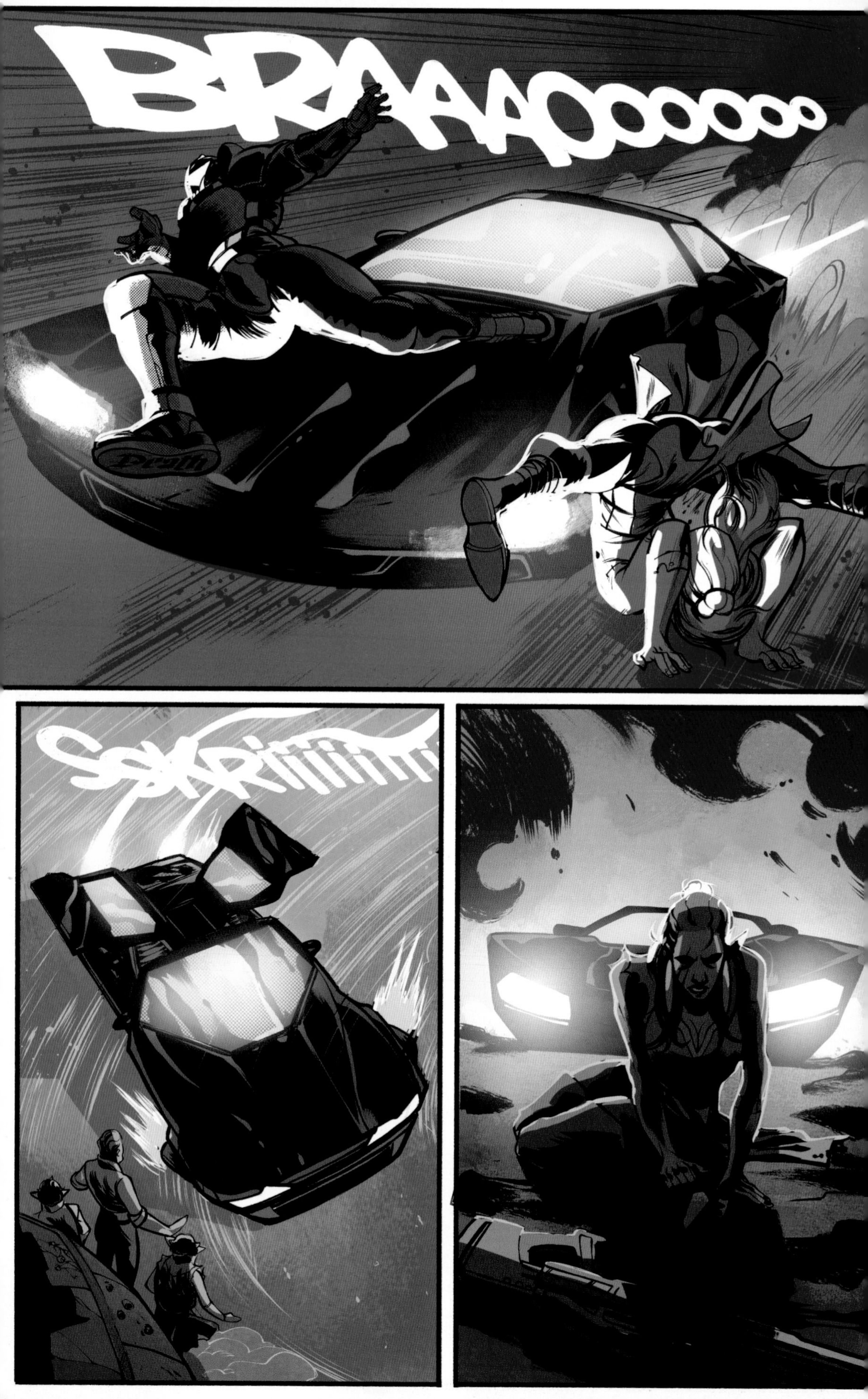
BRAAAOOOOOO
SSKRIIIIIII

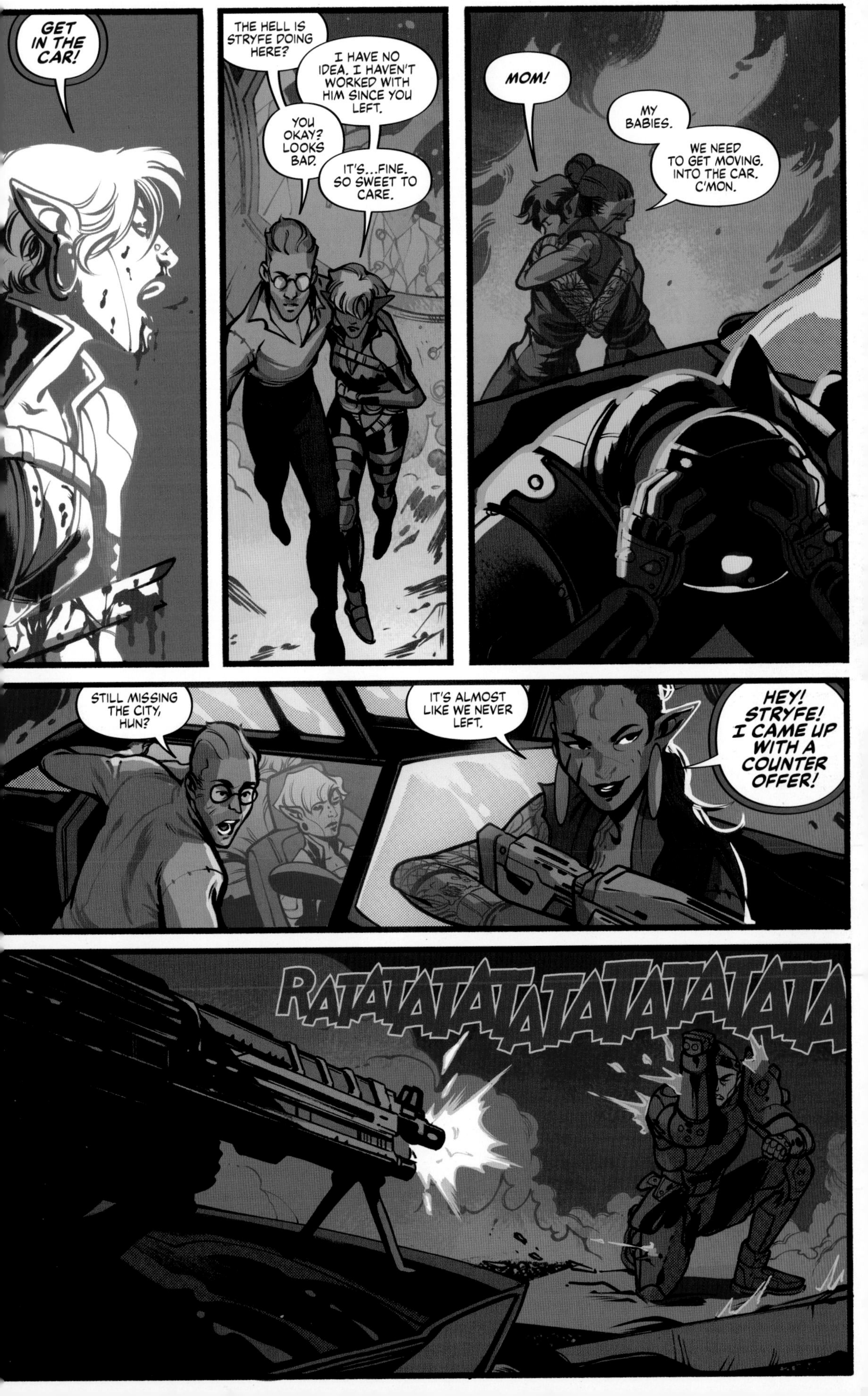
GET IN THE CAR!
THE HELL IS STRYFE DOING HERE?
I HAVE NO IDEA. I HAVEN'T WORKED WITH HIM SINCE YOU LEFT.
YOU OKAY? LOOKS BAD.
IT'S...FINE. SO SWEET TO CARE.
MOM!
MY BABIES.
WE NEED TO GET MOVING. INTO THE CAR. C'MON.
STILL MISSING THE CITY, HUN?
IT'S ALMOST LIKE WE NEVER LEFT.
HEY! STRYFE! I CAME UP WITH A COUNTER OFFER!
RATATATATATATATATATATA

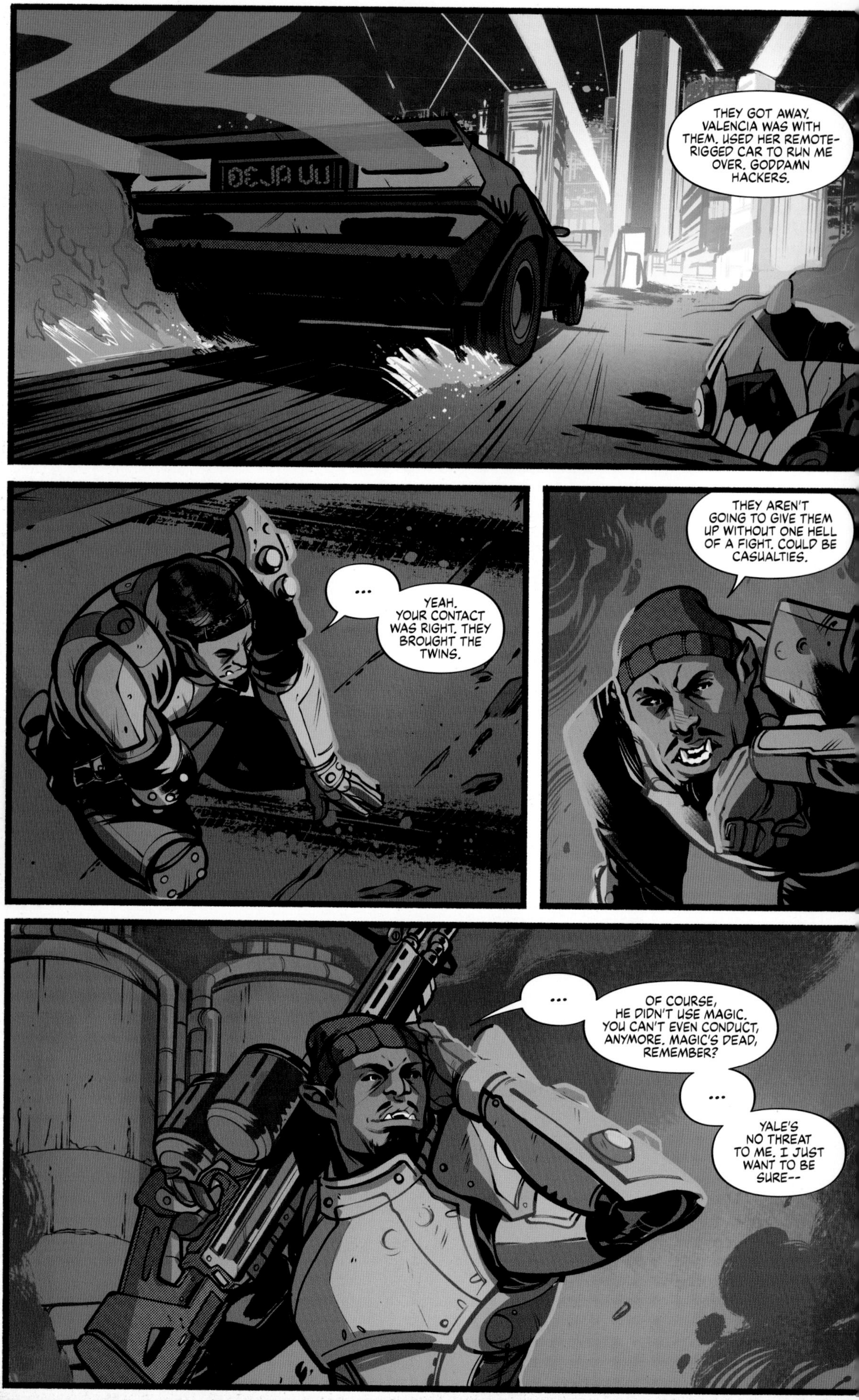
DEJA VU
THEY GOT AWAY. VALENCIA WAS WITH THEM. USED HER REMOTE-RIGGED CAR TO RUN ME OVER. GODDAMN HACKERS.
...
YEAH. YOUR CONTACT WAS RIGHT. THEY BROUGHT THE TWINS.
THEY AREN'T GOING TO GIVE THEM UP WITHOUT ONE HELL OF A FIGHT. COULD BE CASUALTIES.
...
OF COURSE, HE DIDN'T USE MAGIC. YOU CAN'T EVEN CONDUCT, ANYMORE. MAGIC'S DEAD, REMEMBER?
...
YALE'S NO THREAT TO ME. I JUST WANT TO BE SURE--

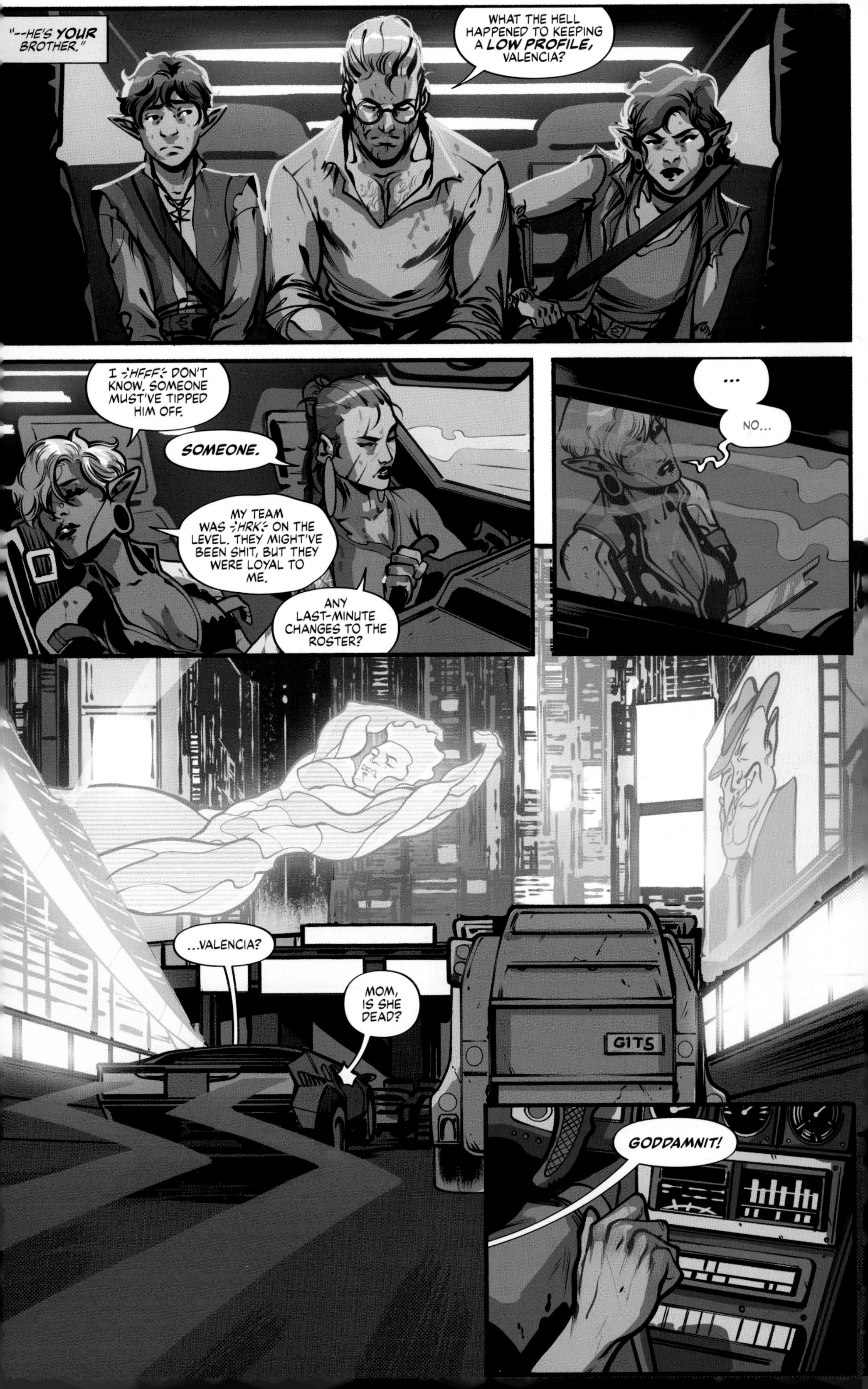
"--HE'S YOUR BROTHER."
WHAT THE HELL HAPPENED TO KEEPING A LOW PROFILE, VALENCIA?
I -HFFF- DON'T KNOW. SOMEONE MUST'VE TIPPED HIM OFF.
SOMEONE.
MY TEAM WAS -HRK- ON THE LEVEL. THEY MIGHT'VE BEEN SHIT, BUT THEY WERE LOYAL TO ME.
ANY LAST-MINUTE CHANGES TO THE ROSTER?
...
NO...
...VALENCIA?
MOM, IS SHE DEAD?
G1TS
GODDAMNIT!

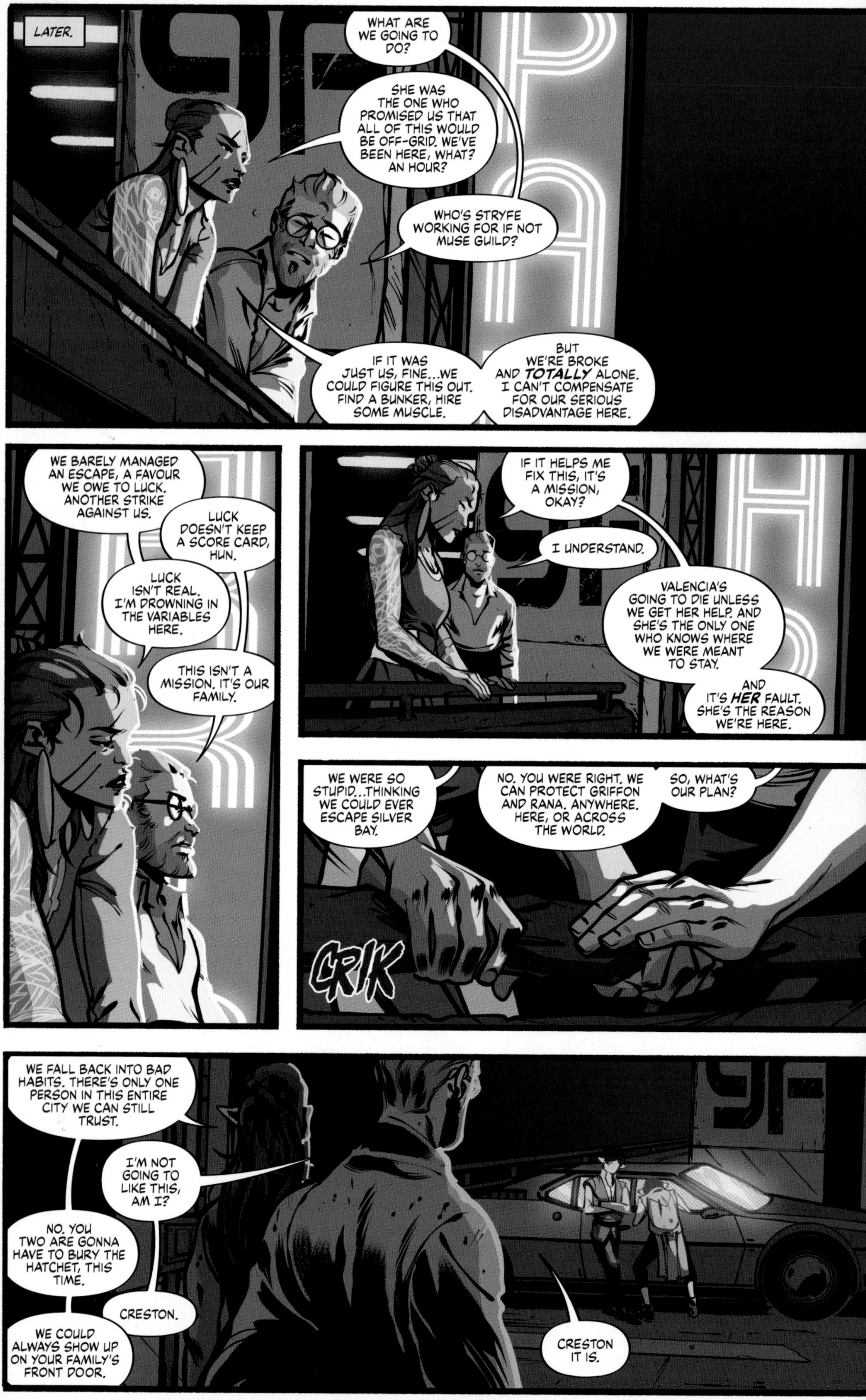
LATER.
WHAT ARE WE GOING TO DO?
SHE WAS THE ONE WHO PROMISED US THAT ALL OF THIS WOULD BE OFF-GRID. WE'VE BEEN HERE, WHAT? AN HOUR?
WHO'S STRYFE WORKING FOR IF NOT MUSE GUILD?
IF IT WAS JUST US, FINE...WE COULD FIGURE THIS OUT. FIND A BUNKER, HIRE SOME MUSCLE.
BUT WE'RE BROKE AND ***TOTALLY*** ALONE. I CAN'T COMPENSATE FOR OUR SERIOUS DISADVANTAGE HERE.
WE BARELY MANAGED AN ESCAPE, A FAVOUR WE OWE TO LUCK. ANOTHER STRIKE AGAINST US.
LUCK DOESN'T KEEP A SCORE CARD, HUN.
LUCK ISN'T REAL. I'M DROWNING IN THE VARIABLES HERE.
THIS ISN'T A MISSION. IT'S OUR FAMILY.
IF IT HELPS ME FIX THIS, IT'S A MISSION, OKAY?
I UNDERSTAND.
VALENCIA'S GOING TO DIE UNLESS WE GET HER HELP. AND SHE'S THE ONLY ONE WHO KNOWS WHERE WE WERE MEANT TO STAY.
AND IT'S ***HER*** FAULT. SHE'S THE REASON WE'RE HERE.
WE WERE SO STUPID...THINKING WE COULD EVER ESCAPE SILVER BAY.
NO. YOU WERE RIGHT. WE CAN PROTECT GRIFFON AND RANA. ANYWHERE. HERE, OR ACROSS THE WORLD.
SO, WHAT'S OUR PLAN?
CRIK
WE FALL BACK INTO BAD HABITS. THERE'S ONLY ONE PERSON IN THIS ENTIRE CITY WE CAN STILL TRUST.
I'M NOT GOING TO LIKE THIS, AM I?
NO. YOU TWO ARE GONNA HAVE TO BURY THE HATCHET, THIS TIME.
CRESTON.
WE COULD ALWAYS SHOW UP ON YOUR FAMILY'S FRONT DOOR.
CRESTON IT IS.

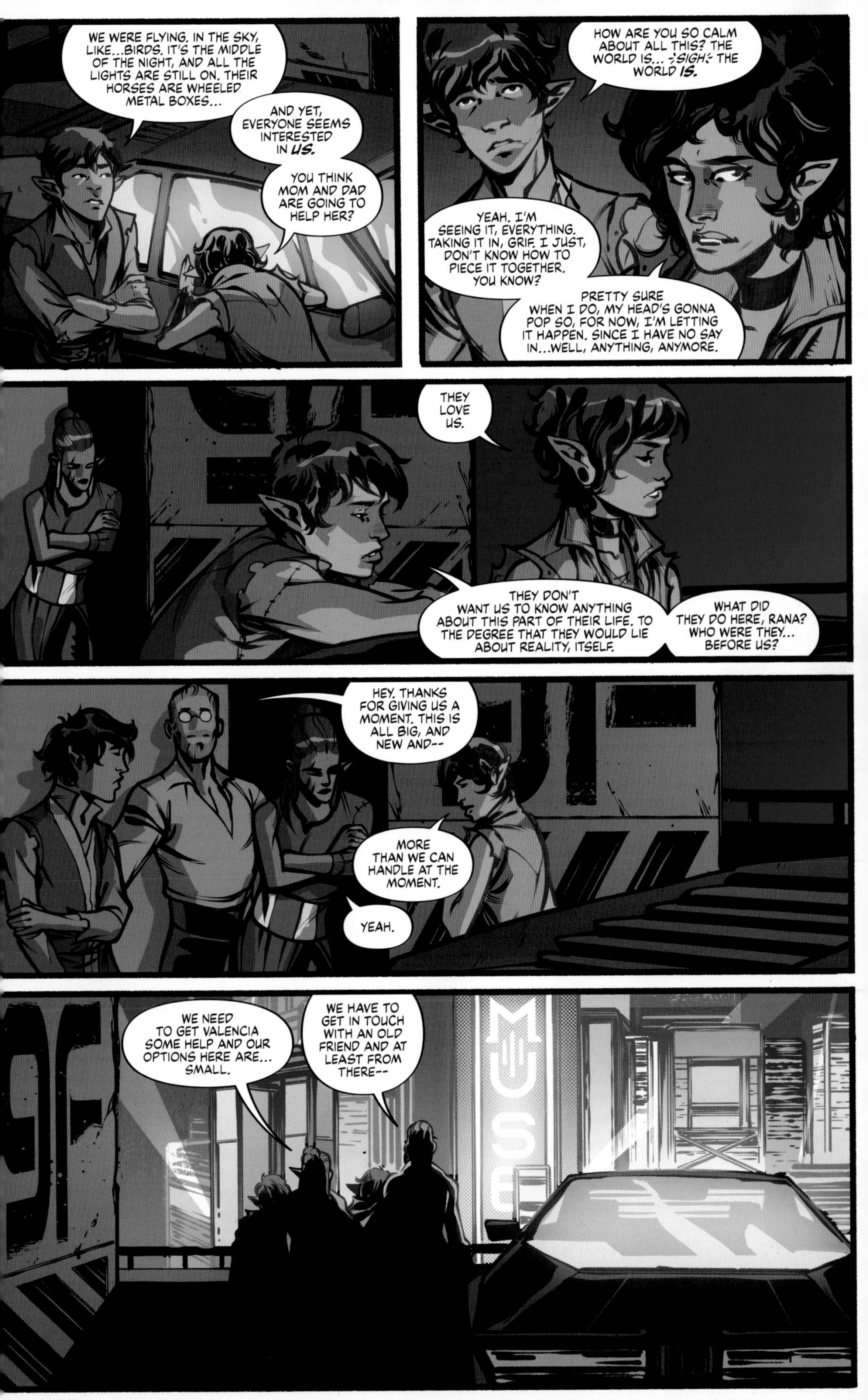
WE WERE FLYING. IN THE SKY, LIKE...BIRDS. IT'S THE MIDDLE OF THE NIGHT, AND ALL THE LIGHTS ARE STILL ON. THEIR HORSES ARE WHEELED METAL BOXES...
AND YET, EVERYONE SEEMS INTERESTED IN *US.*
YOU THINK MOM AND DAD ARE GOING TO HELP HER?
HOW ARE YOU SO CALM ABOUT ALL THIS? THE WORLD IS... -SIGH- THE WORLD *IS.*
YEAH. I'M SEEING IT, EVERYTHING. TAKING IT IN, GRIF. I JUST, DON'T KNOW HOW TO PIECE IT TOGETHER. YOU KNOW?
PRETTY SURE WHEN I DO, MY HEAD'S GONNA POP SO, FOR NOW, I'M LETTING IT HAPPEN. SINCE I HAVE NO SAY IN...WELL, ANYTHING, ANYMORE.
THEY LOVE US.
THEY DON'T WANT US TO KNOW ANYTHING ABOUT THIS PART OF THEIR LIFE. TO THE DEGREE THAT THEY WOULD LIE ABOUT REALITY, ITSELF.
WHAT DID THEY DO HERE, RANA? WHO WERE THEY... BEFORE US?
HEY. THANKS FOR GIVING US A MOMENT. THIS IS ALL BIG, AND NEW AND--
MORE THAN WE CAN HANDLE AT THE MOMENT.
YEAH.
WE NEED TO GET VALENCIA SOME HELP AND OUR OPTIONS HERE ARE... SMALL.
WE HAVE TO GET IN TOUCH WITH AN OLD FRIEND AND AT LEAST FROM THERE--
MUSE

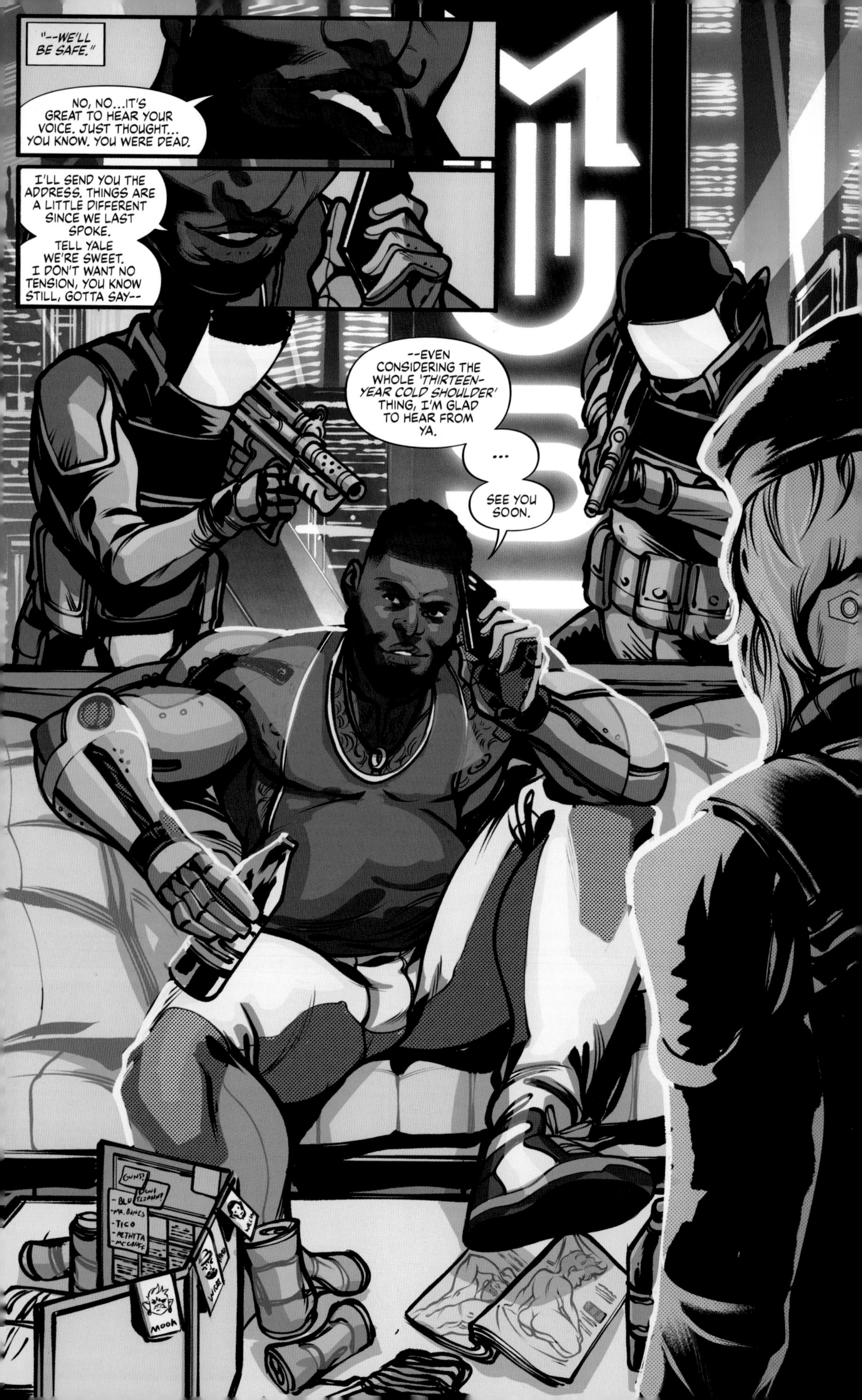
"--WE'LL BE SAFE."
NO, NO...IT'S GREAT TO HEAR YOUR VOICE. JUST THOUGHT... YOU KNOW. YOU WERE DEAD.
I'LL SEND YOU THE ADDRESS. THINGS ARE A LITTLE DIFFERENT SINCE WE LAST SPOKE.
TELL YALE WE'RE SWEET. I DON'T WANT NO TENSION, YOU KNOW STILL, GOTTA SAY--
--EVEN CONSIDERING THE WHOLE *'THIRTEEN-YEAR COLD SHOULDER'* THING, I'M GLAD TO HEAR FROM YA.
...
SEE YOU SOON.

CHAPTER FIVE

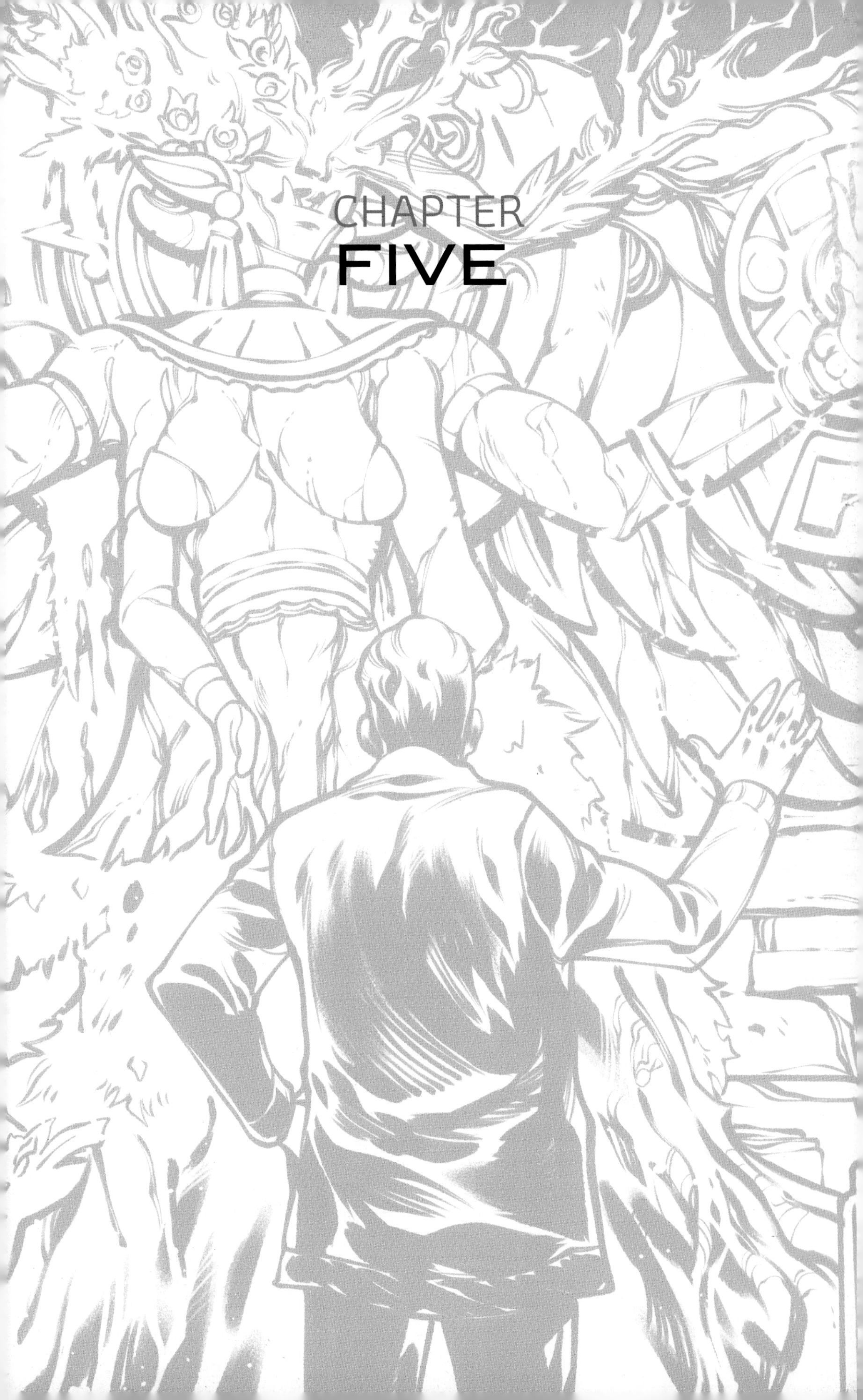

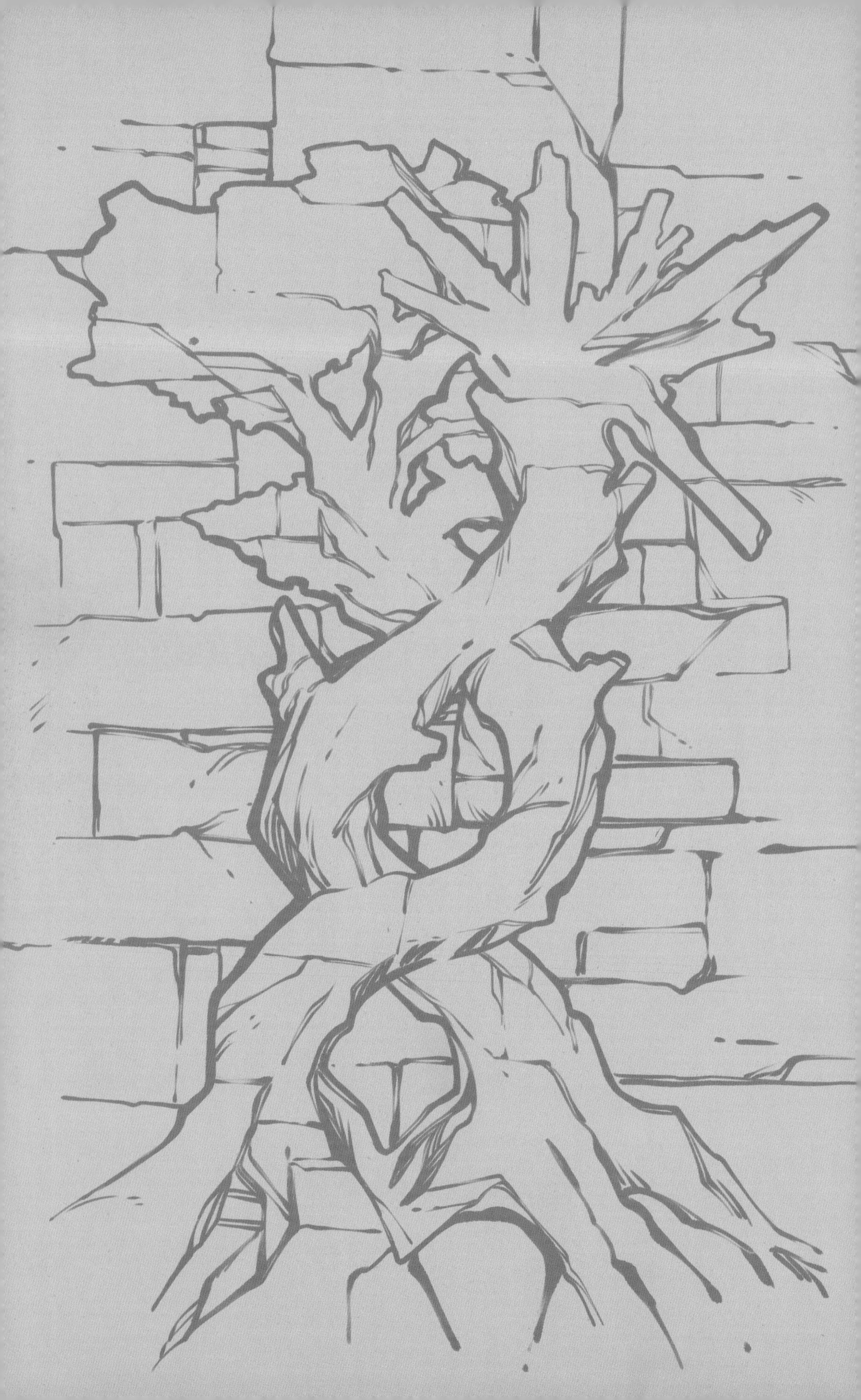

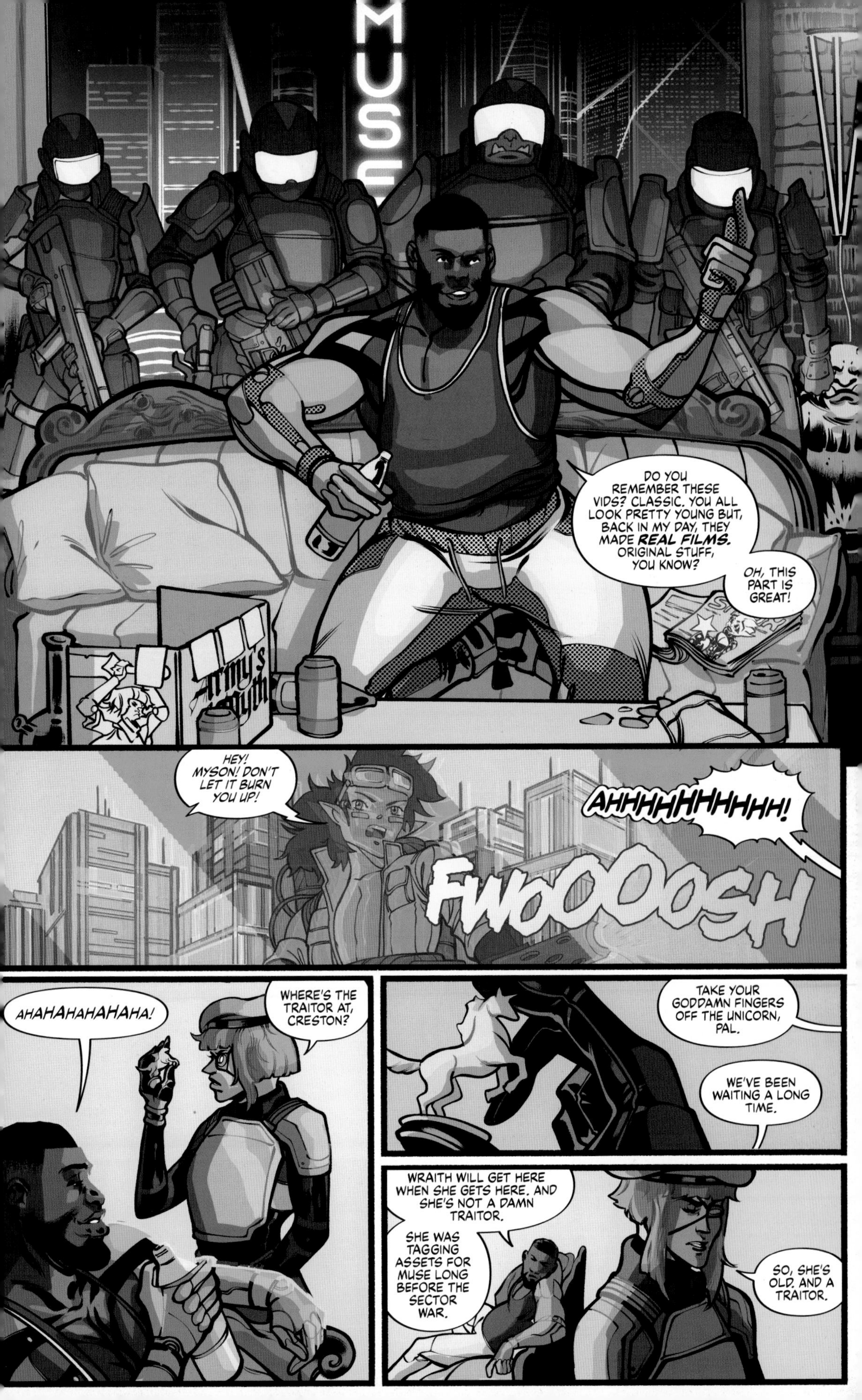
MUSE
DO YOU REMEMBER THESE VIDS? CLASSIC. YOU ALL LOOK PRETTY YOUNG BUT, BACK IN MY DAY, THEY MADE **REAL FILMS.** ORIGINAL STUFF, YOU KNOW?
OH, THIS PART IS GREAT!
HEY! MYSON! DON'T LET IT BURN YOU UP!
AHHHHHHHHHH!
FWOOOOOSH
AHAHAHAHAHAHA!
WHERE'S THE TRAITOR AT, CRESTON?
TAKE YOUR GODDAMN FINGERS OFF THE UNICORN, PAL.
WE'VE BEEN WAITING A LONG TIME.
WRAITH WILL GET HERE WHEN SHE GETS HERE. AND SHE'S NOT A DAMN TRAITOR.
SHE WAS TAGGING ASSETS FOR MUSE LONG BEFORE THE SECTOR WAR.
SO, SHE'S OLD, AND A TRAITOR.

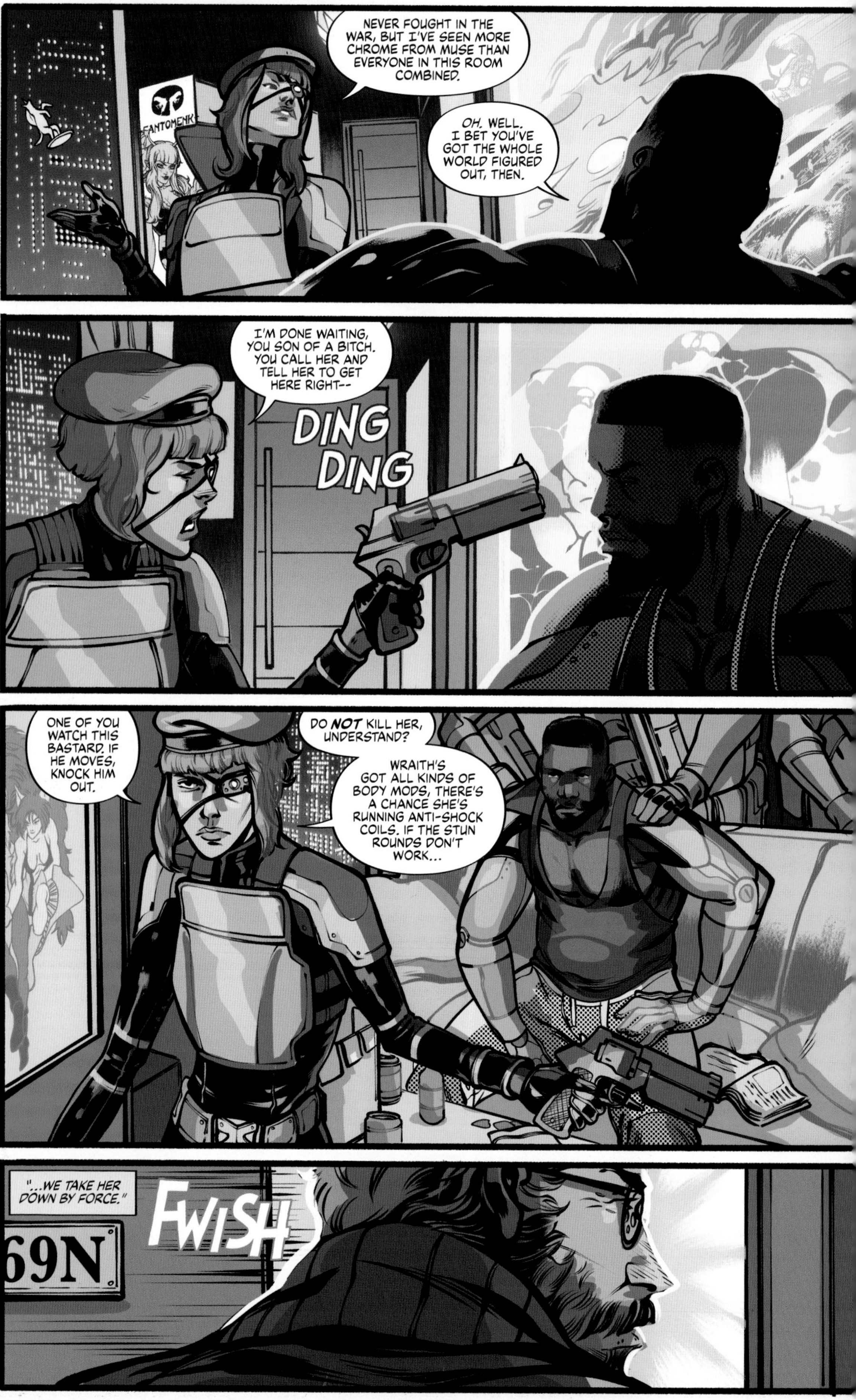
NEVER FOUGHT IN THE WAR, BUT I'VE SEEN MORE CHROME FROM MUSE THAN EVERYONE IN THIS ROOM COMBINED.
OH. WELL. I BET YOU'VE GOT THE WHOLE WORLD FIGURED OUT, THEN.
FANTOMENK
I'M DONE WAITING, YOU SON OF A BITCH. YOU CALL HER AND TELL HER TO GET HERE RIGHT--
DING DING
ONE OF YOU WATCH THIS BASTARD. IF HE MOVES, KNOCK HIM OUT.
DO NOT KILL HER, UNDERSTAND?
WRAITH'S GOT ALL KINDS OF BODY MODS, THERE'S A CHANCE SHE'S RUNNING ANTI-SHOCK COILS. IF THE STUN ROUNDS DON'T WORK...
"...WE TAKE HER DOWN BY FORCE."
FWISH
69N

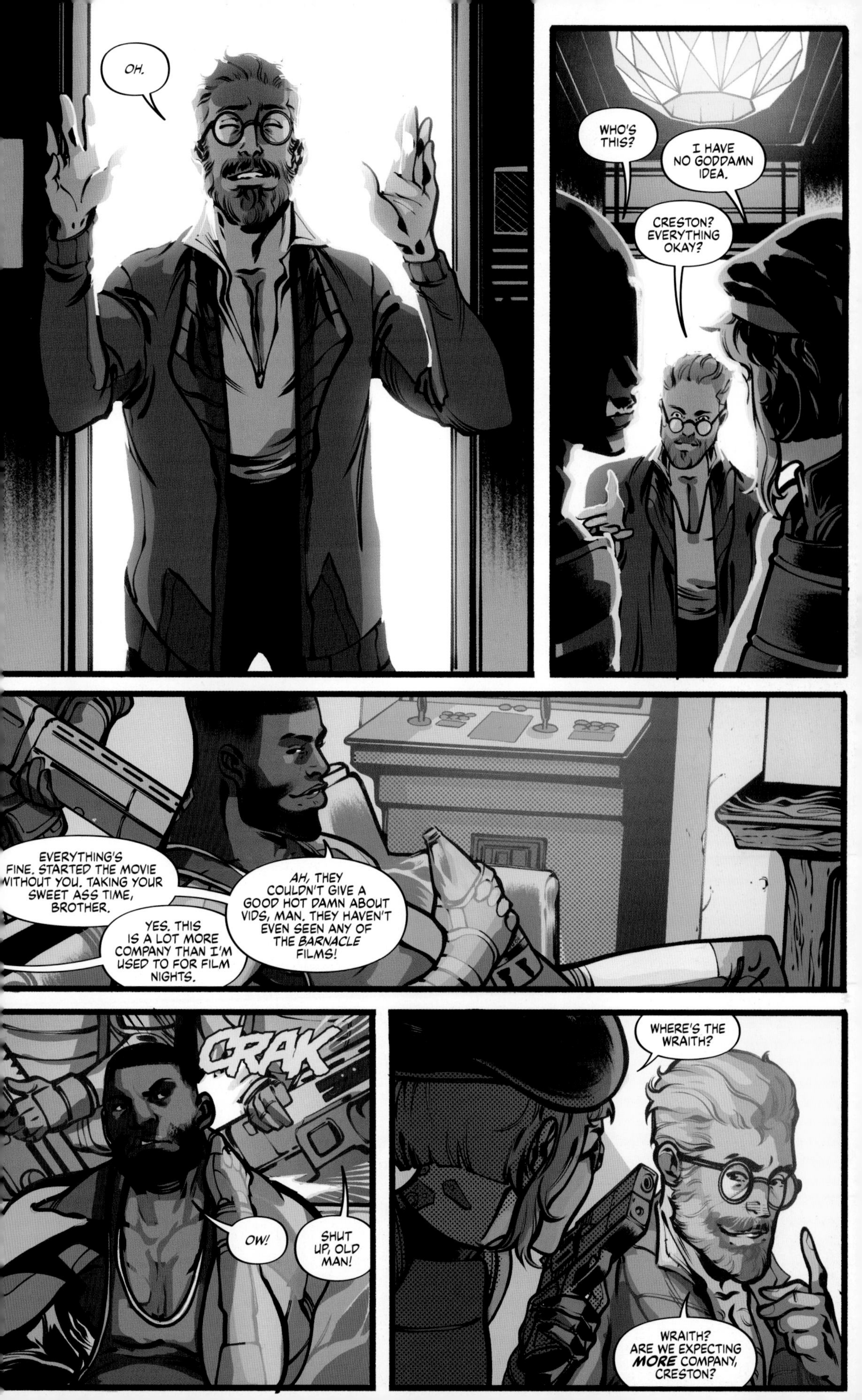
OH.
WHO'S THIS?
I HAVE NO GODDAMN IDEA.
CRESTON? EVERYTHING OKAY?
EVERYTHING'S FINE. STARTED THE MOVIE WITHOUT YOU. TAKING YOUR SWEET ASS TIME, BROTHER.
YES. THIS IS A LOT MORE COMPANY THAN I'M USED TO FOR FILM NIGHTS.
AH, THEY COULDN'T GIVE A GOOD HOT DAMN ABOUT VIDS, MAN. THEY HAVEN'T EVEN SEEN ANY OF THE BARNACLE FILMS!
CRAK
OW!
SHUT UP, OLD MAN!
WHERE'S THE WRAITH?
WRAITH? ARE WE EXPECTING MORE COMPANY, CRESTON?

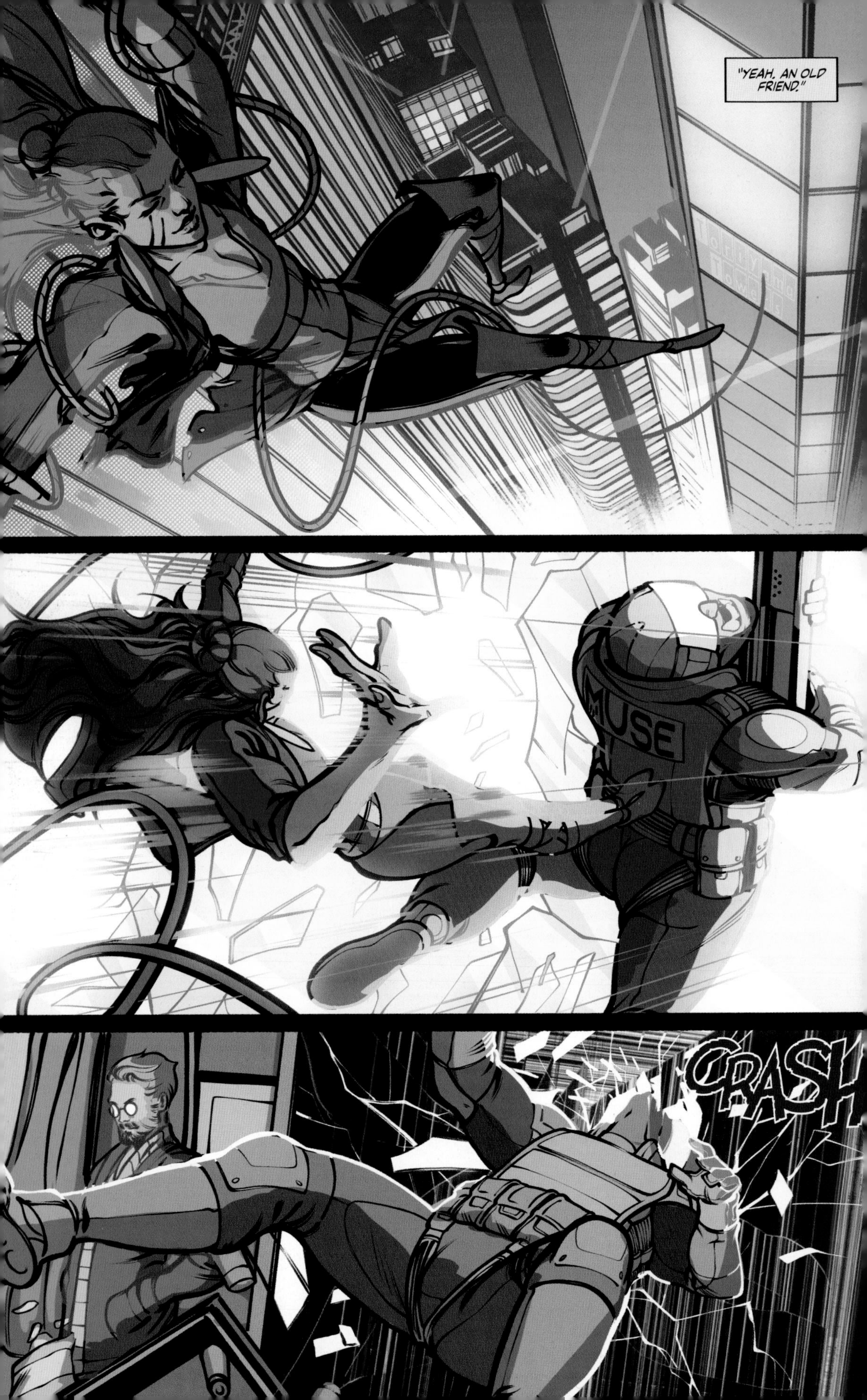
"YEAH. AN OLD FRIEND."
MUSE
CRASH

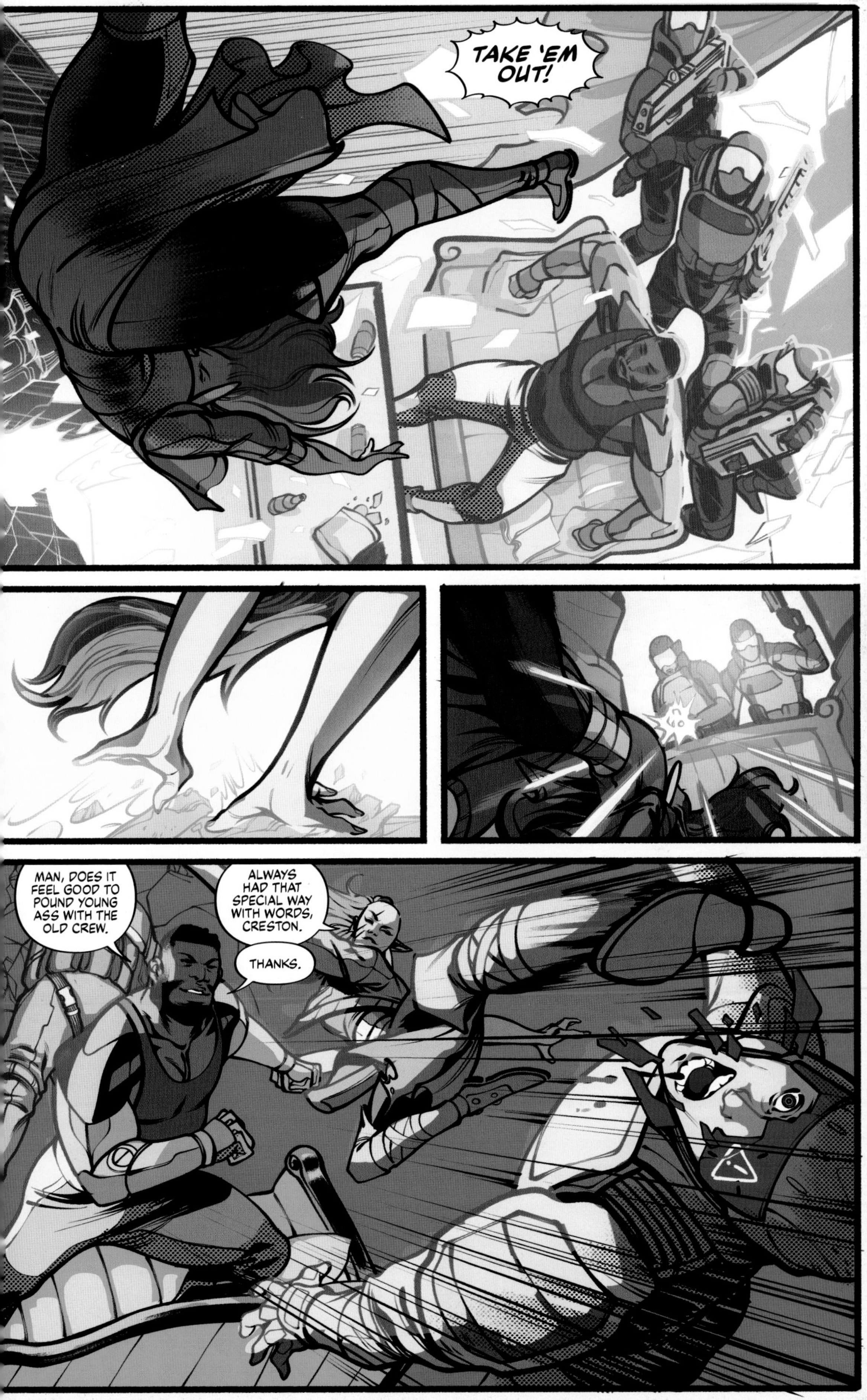
TAKE 'EM OUT!
MAN, DOES IT FEEL GOOD TO POUND YOUNG ASS WITH THE OLD CREW.
ALWAYS HAD THAT SPECIAL WAY WITH WORDS, CRESTON.
THANKS.

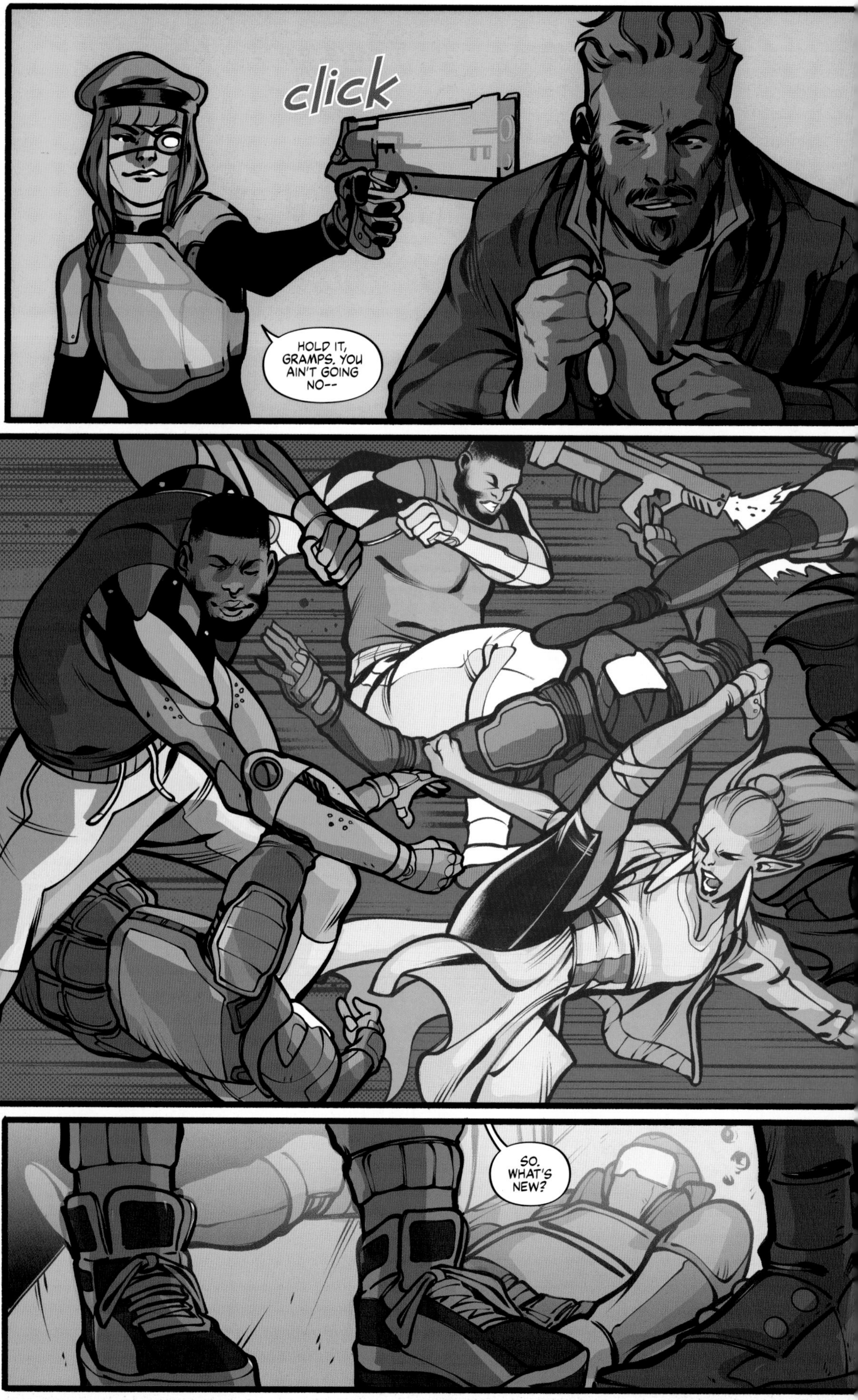
click
HOLD IT, GRAMPS. YOU AIN'T GOING NO--
SO, WHAT'S NEW?

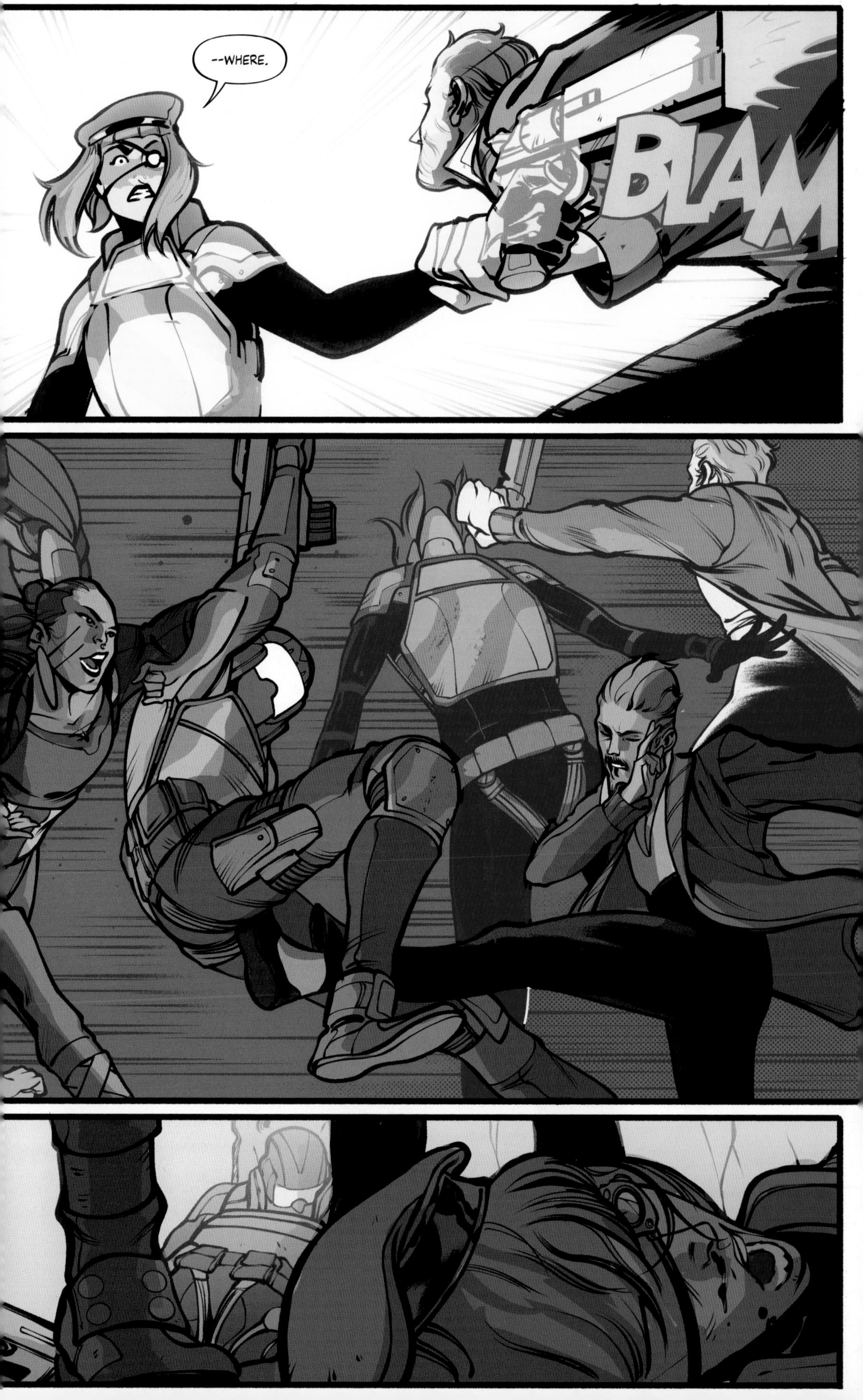
--WHERE.
BLAM

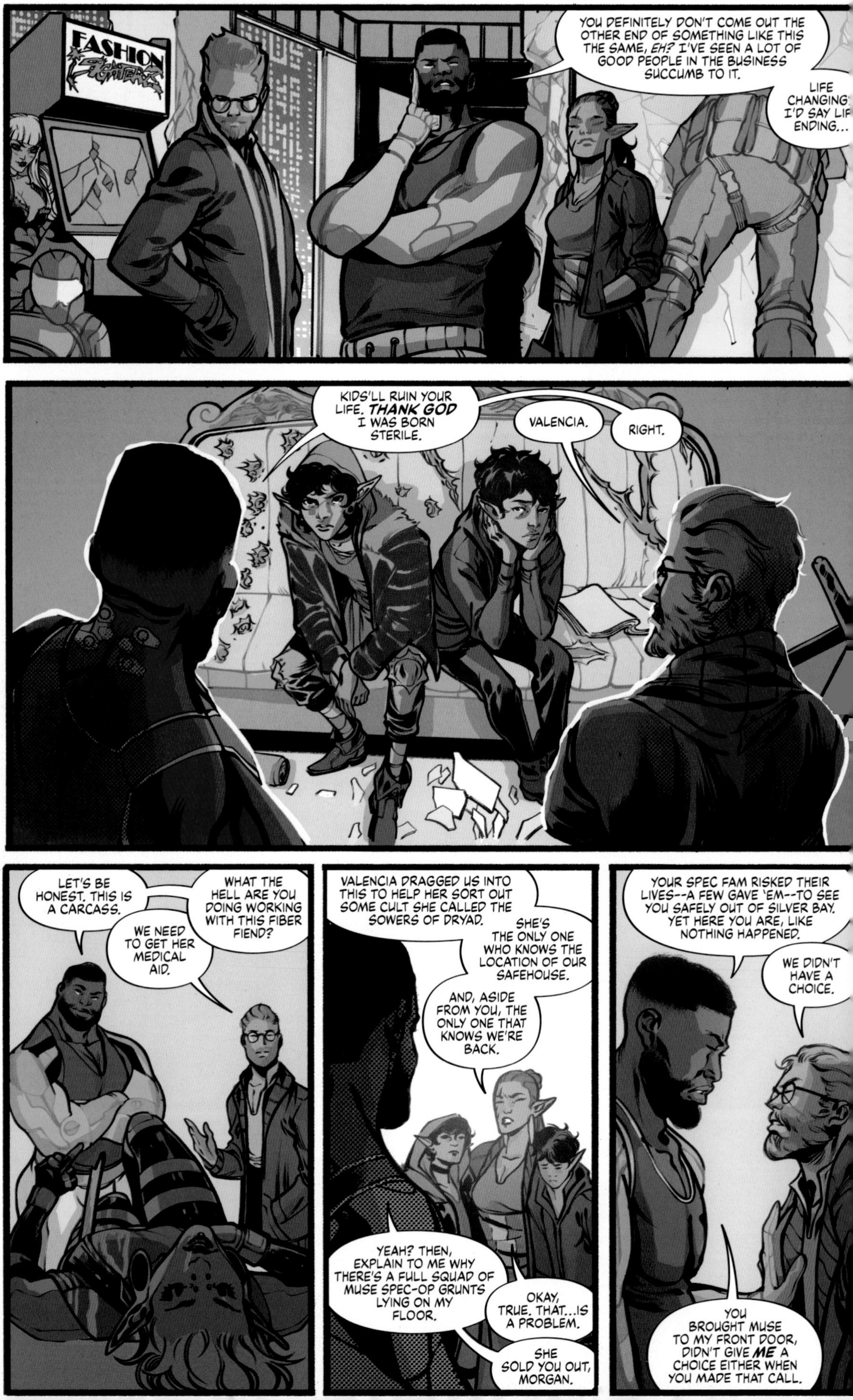
FASHION
YOU DEFINITELY DON'T COME OUT THE OTHER END OF SOMETHING LIKE THIS THE SAME, *EH?* I'VE SEEN A LOT OF GOOD PEOPLE IN THE BUSINESS SUCCUMB TO IT.
LIFE CHANGING? I'D SAY LIF ENDING...
KIDS'LL RUIN YOUR LIFE. ***THANK GOD*** I WAS BORN STERILE.
VALENCIA.
RIGHT.
LET'S BE HONEST. THIS IS A CARCASS.
WHAT THE HELL ARE YOU DOING WORKING WITH THIS FIBER FIEND?
WE NEED TO GET HER MEDICAL AID.
VALENCIA DRAGGED US INTO THIS TO HELP HER SORT OUT SOME CULT SHE CALLED THE SOWERS OF DRYAD.
SHE'S THE ONLY ONE WHO KNOWS THE LOCATION OF OUR SAFEHOUSE.
AND, ASIDE FROM YOU, THE ONLY ONE THAT KNOWS WE'RE BACK.
YEAH? THEN, EXPLAIN TO ME WHY THERE'S A FULL SQUAD OF MUSE SPEC-OP GRUNTS LYING ON MY FLOOR.
OKAY, TRUE. THAT...IS A PROBLEM.
SHE SOLD YOU OUT, MORGAN.
YOUR SPEC FAM RISKED THEIR LIVES--A FEW GAVE 'EM--TO SEE YOU SAFELY OUT OF SILVER BAY. YET HERE YOU ARE, LIKE NOTHING HAPPENED.
WE DIDN'T HAVE A CHOICE.
YOU BROUGHT MUSE TO MY FRONT DOOR, DIDN'T GIVE ***ME*** A CHOICE EITHER WHEN YOU MADE THAT CALL.

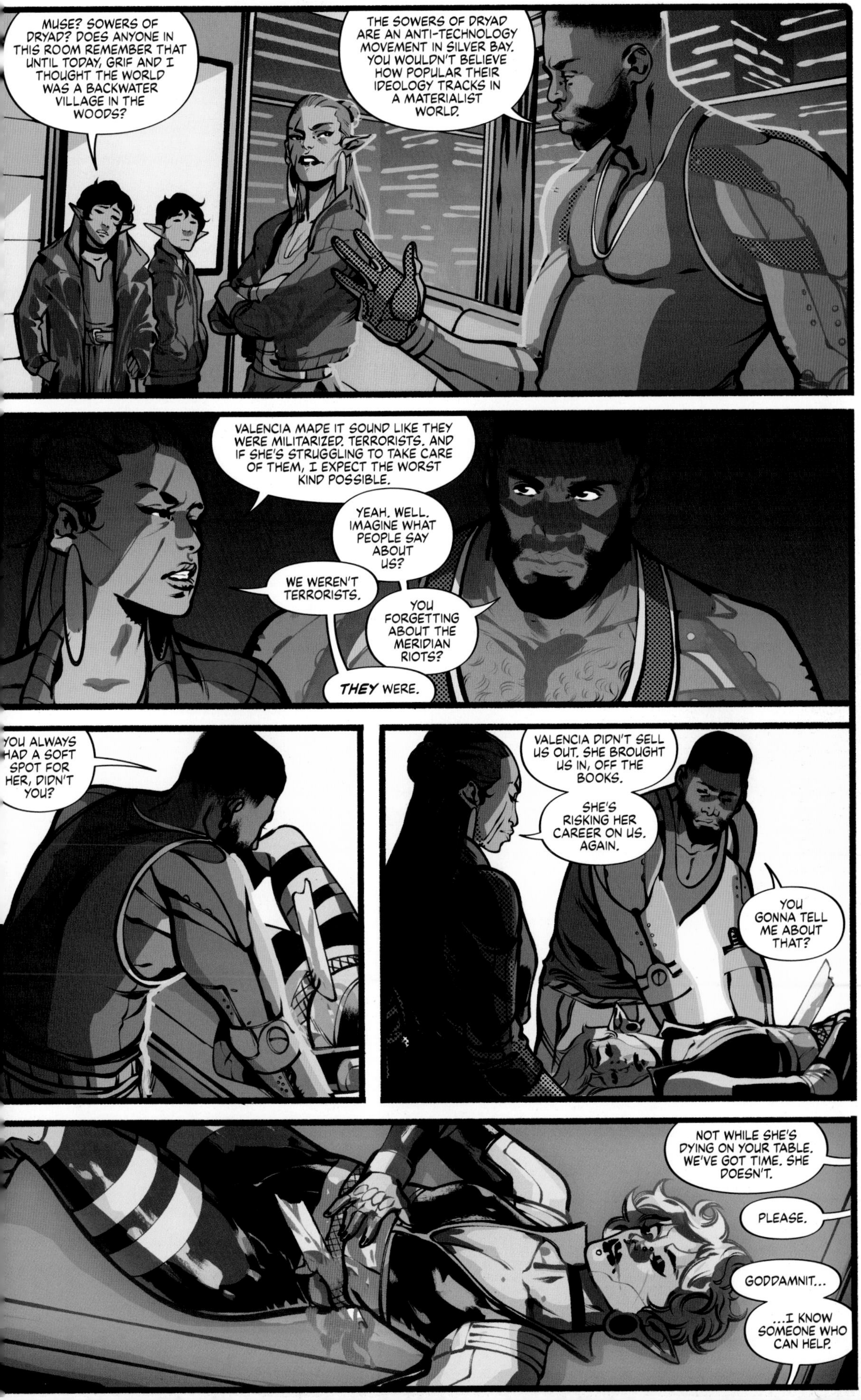
MUSE? SOWERS OF DRYAD? DOES ANYONE IN THIS ROOM REMEMBER THAT UNTIL TODAY, GRIF AND I THOUGHT THE WORLD WAS A BACKWATER VILLAGE IN THE WOODS?
THE SOWERS OF DRYAD ARE AN ANTI-TECHNOLOGY MOVEMENT IN SILVER BAY. YOU WOULDN'T BELIEVE HOW POPULAR THEIR IDEOLOGY TRACKS IN A MATERIALIST WORLD.
VALENCIA MADE IT SOUND LIKE THEY WERE MILITARIZED. TERRORISTS. AND IF SHE'S STRUGGLING TO TAKE CARE OF THEM, I EXPECT THE WORST KIND POSSIBLE.
YEAH. WELL. IMAGINE WHAT PEOPLE SAY ABOUT US?
WE WEREN'T TERRORISTS.
YOU FORGETTING ABOUT THE MERIDIAN RIOTS?
THEY WERE.
YOU ALWAYS HAD A SOFT SPOT FOR HER, DIDN'T YOU?
VALENCIA DIDN'T SELL US OUT. SHE BROUGHT US IN, OFF THE BOOKS.
SHE'S RISKING HER CAREER ON US. AGAIN.
YOU GONNA TELL ME ABOUT THAT?
NOT WHILE SHE'S DYING ON YOUR TABLE. WE'VE GOT TIME. SHE DOESN'T.
PLEASE.
GODDAMNIT...
...I KNOW SOMEONE WHO CAN HELP.

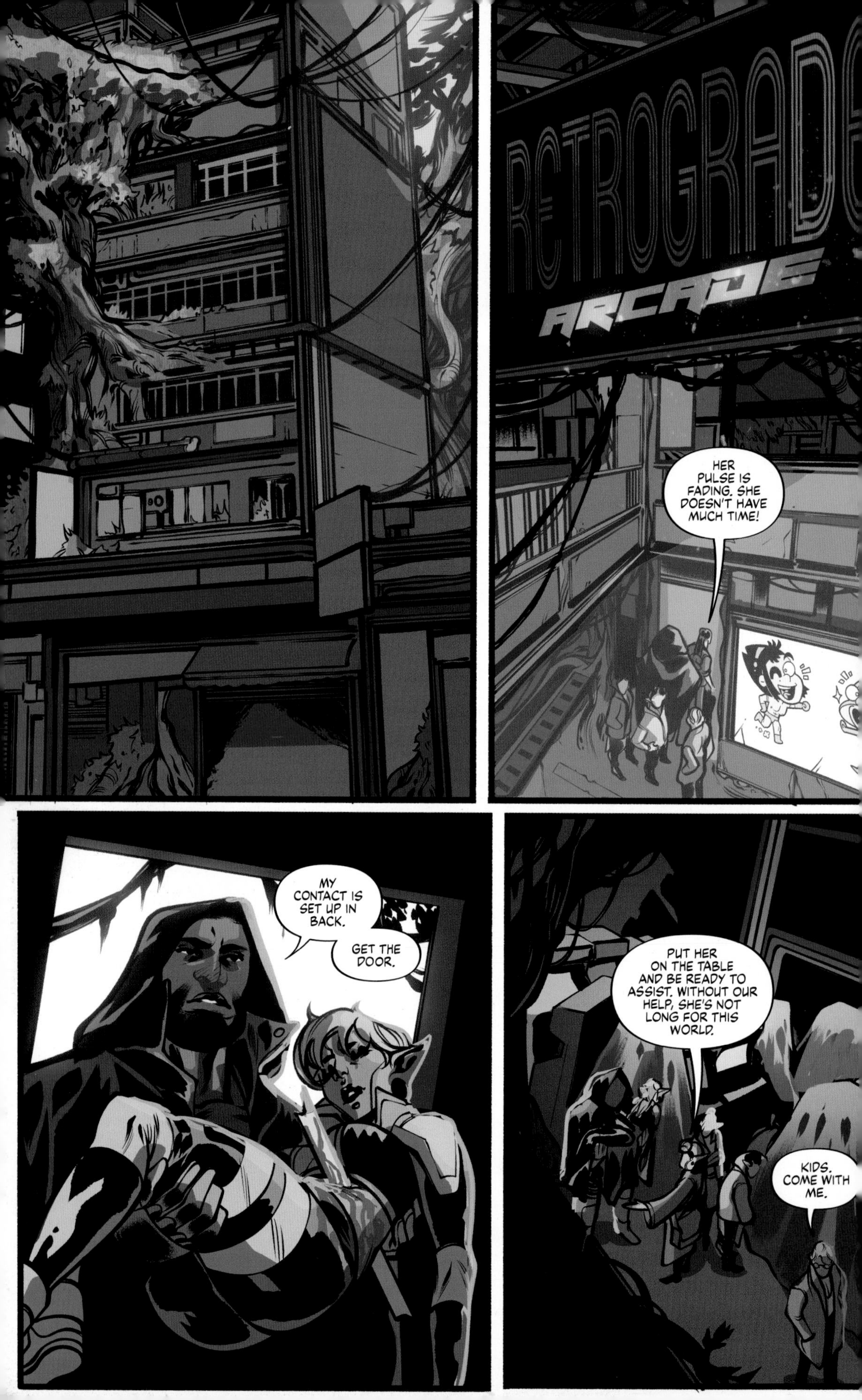
RETROGRADE
ARCADE
HER PULSE IS FADING. SHE DOESN'T HAVE MUCH TIME!
MY CONTACT IS SET UP IN BACK.
GET THE DOOR.
PUT HER ON THE TABLE AND BE READY TO ASSIST. WITHOUT OUR HELP, SHE'S NOT LONG FOR THIS WORLD.
KIDS. COME WITH ME.

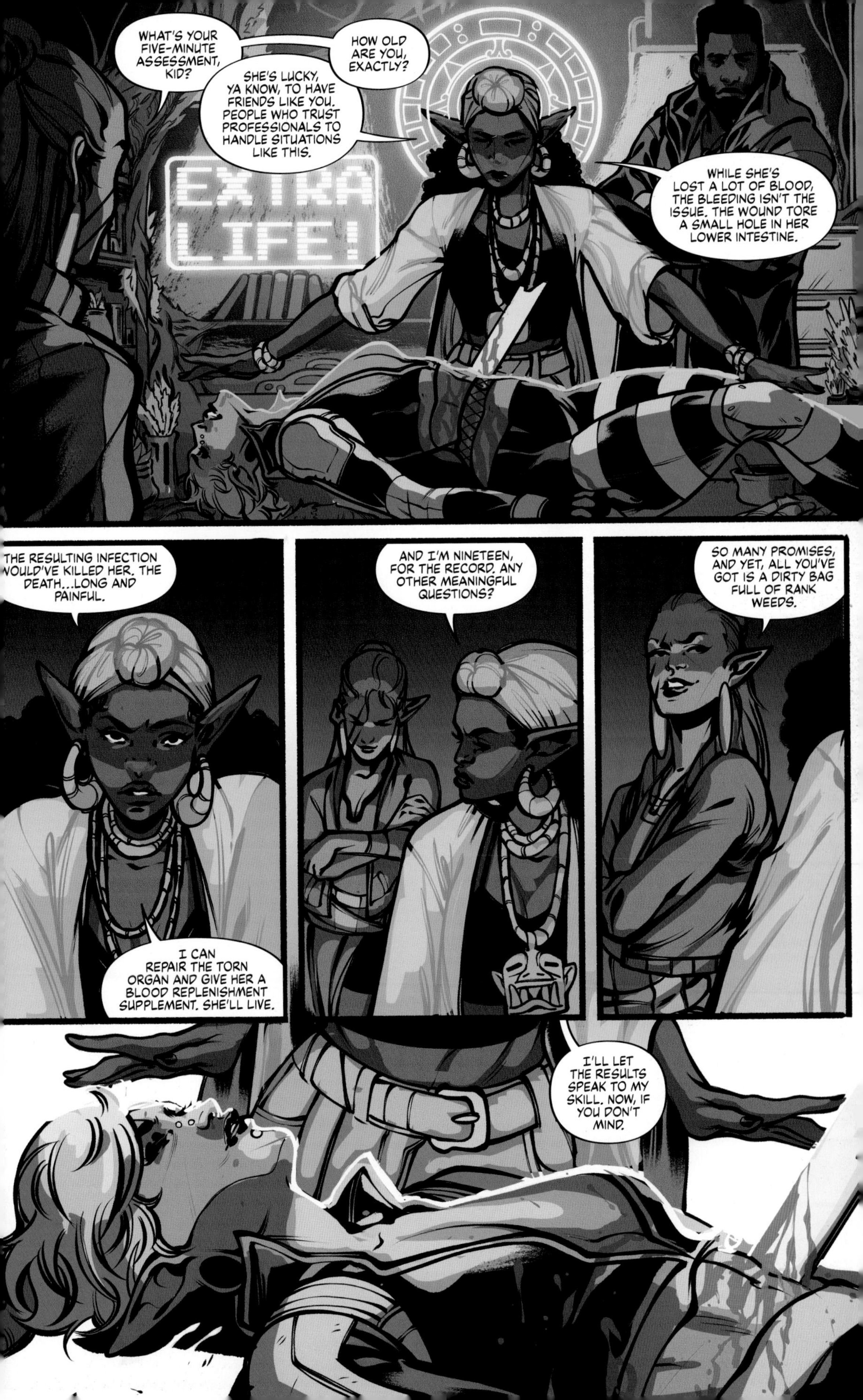
WHAT'S YOUR FIVE-MINUTE ASSESSMENT, KID?
HOW OLD ARE YOU, EXACTLY?
SHE'S LUCKY, YA KNOW, TO HAVE FRIENDS LIKE YOU. PEOPLE WHO TRUST PROFESSIONALS TO HANDLE SITUATIONS LIKE THIS.
EXTRA LIFE!
WHILE SHE'S LOST A LOT OF BLOOD, THE BLEEDING ISN'T THE ISSUE. THE WOUND TORE A SMALL HOLE IN HER LOWER INTESTINE.
THE RESULTING INFECTION WOULD'VE KILLED HER. THE DEATH...LONG AND PAINFUL.
I CAN REPAIR THE TORN ORGAN AND GIVE HER A BLOOD REPLENISHMENT SUPPLEMENT. SHE'LL LIVE.
AND I'M NINETEEN, FOR THE RECORD. ANY OTHER MEANINGFUL QUESTIONS?
SO MANY PROMISES, AND YET, ALL YOU'VE GOT IS A DIRTY BAG FULL OF RANK WEEDS.
I'LL LET THE RESULTS SPEAK TO MY SKILL. NOW, IF YOU DON'T MIND.

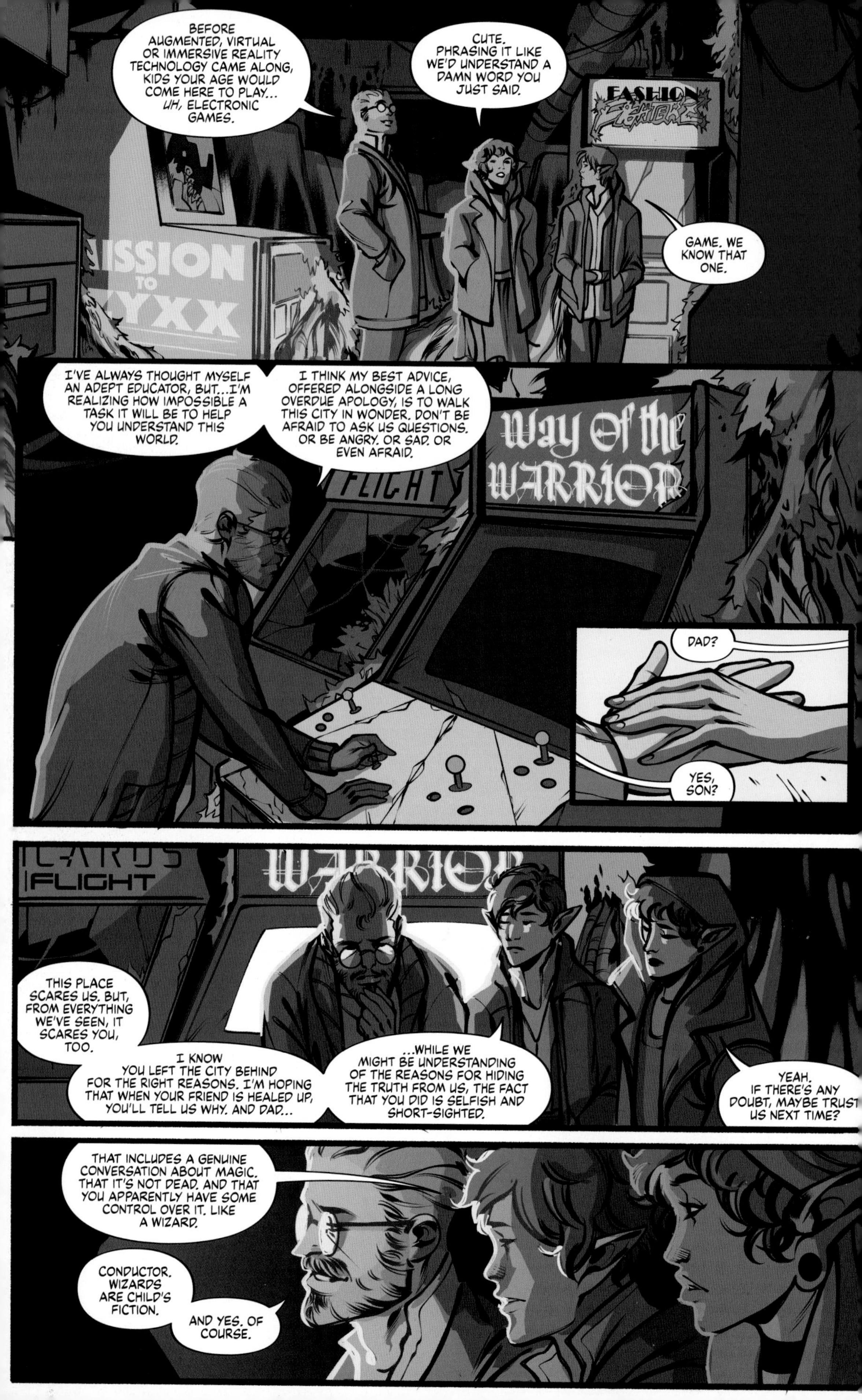
BEFORE AUGMENTED, VIRTUAL OR IMMERSIVE REALITY TECHNOLOGY CAME ALONG, KIDS YOUR AGE WOULD COME HERE TO PLAY... *UH,* ELECTRONIC GAMES.
CUTE. PHRASING IT LIKE WE'D UNDERSTAND A DAMN WORD YOU JUST SAID.
FASHION FIGHTERZ
ISSION TO YXX
GAME. WE KNOW THAT ONE.
I'VE ALWAYS THOUGHT MYSELF AN ADEPT EDUCATOR, BUT...I'M REALIZING HOW IMPOSSIBLE A TASK IT WILL BE TO HELP YOU UNDERSTAND THIS WORLD.
I THINK MY BEST ADVICE, OFFERED ALONGSIDE A LONG OVERDUE APOLOGY, IS TO WALK THIS CITY IN WONDER. DON'T BE AFRAID TO ASK US QUESTIONS. OR BE ANGRY. OR SAD. OR EVEN AFRAID.
FLIGHT
WAY OF THE WARRIOR
DAD?
YES, SON?
ICARUS FLIGHT
WARRIOR
THIS PLACE SCARES US. BUT, FROM EVERYTHING WE'VE SEEN, IT SCARES YOU, TOO.
I KNOW YOU LEFT THE CITY BEHIND FOR THE RIGHT REASONS. I'M HOPING THAT WHEN YOUR FRIEND IS HEALED UP, YOU'LL TELL US WHY. AND DAD...
...WHILE WE MIGHT BE UNDERSTANDING OF THE REASONS FOR HIDING THE TRUTH FROM US, THE FACT THAT YOU DID IS SELFISH AND SHORT-SIGHTED.
YEAH. IF THERE'S ANY DOUBT, MAYBE TRUST US NEXT TIME?
THAT INCLUDES A GENUINE CONVERSATION ABOUT MAGIC. THAT IT'S NOT DEAD. AND THAT YOU APPARENTLY HAVE SOME CONTROL OVER IT. LIKE A WIZARD.
CONDUCTOR. WIZARDS ARE CHILD'S FICTION.
AND YES. OF COURSE.

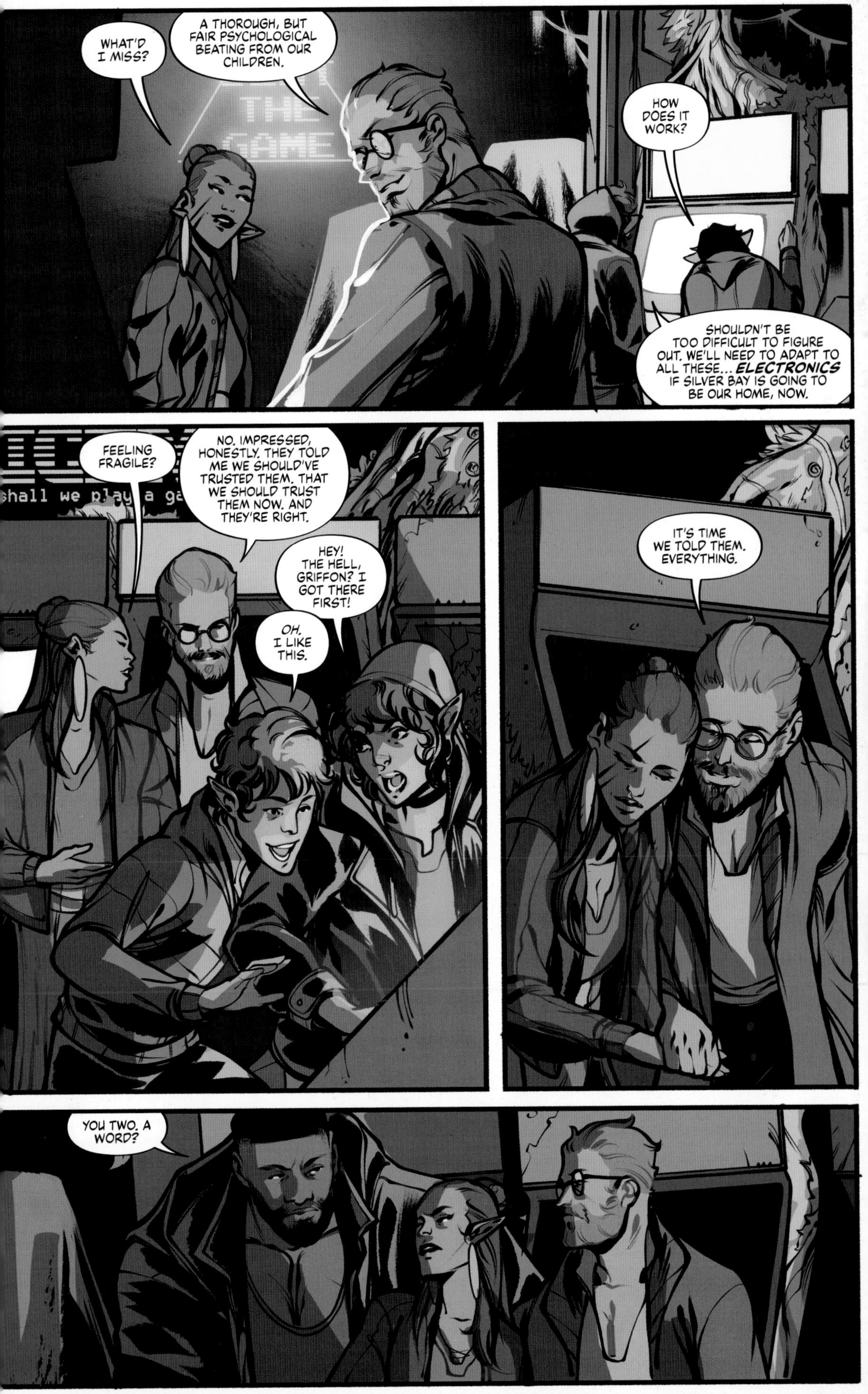
WHAT'D I MISS?
A THOROUGH, BUT FAIR PSYCHOLOGICAL BEATING FROM OUR CHILDREN.
THE GAME
HOW DOES IT WORK?
SHOULDN'T BE TOO DIFFICULT TO FIGURE OUT. WE'LL NEED TO ADAPT TO ALL THESE... ***ELECTRONICS*** IF SILVER BAY IS GOING TO BE OUR HOME, NOW.
shall we play a ga
FEELING FRAGILE?
NO. IMPRESSED, HONESTLY. THEY TOLD ME WE SHOULD'VE TRUSTED THEM. THAT WE SHOULD TRUST THEM NOW. AND THEY'RE RIGHT.
HEY! THE HELL, GRIFFON? I GOT THERE FIRST!
OH. I LIKE THIS.
IT'S TIME WE TOLD THEM. EVERYTHING.
YOU TWO. A WORD?

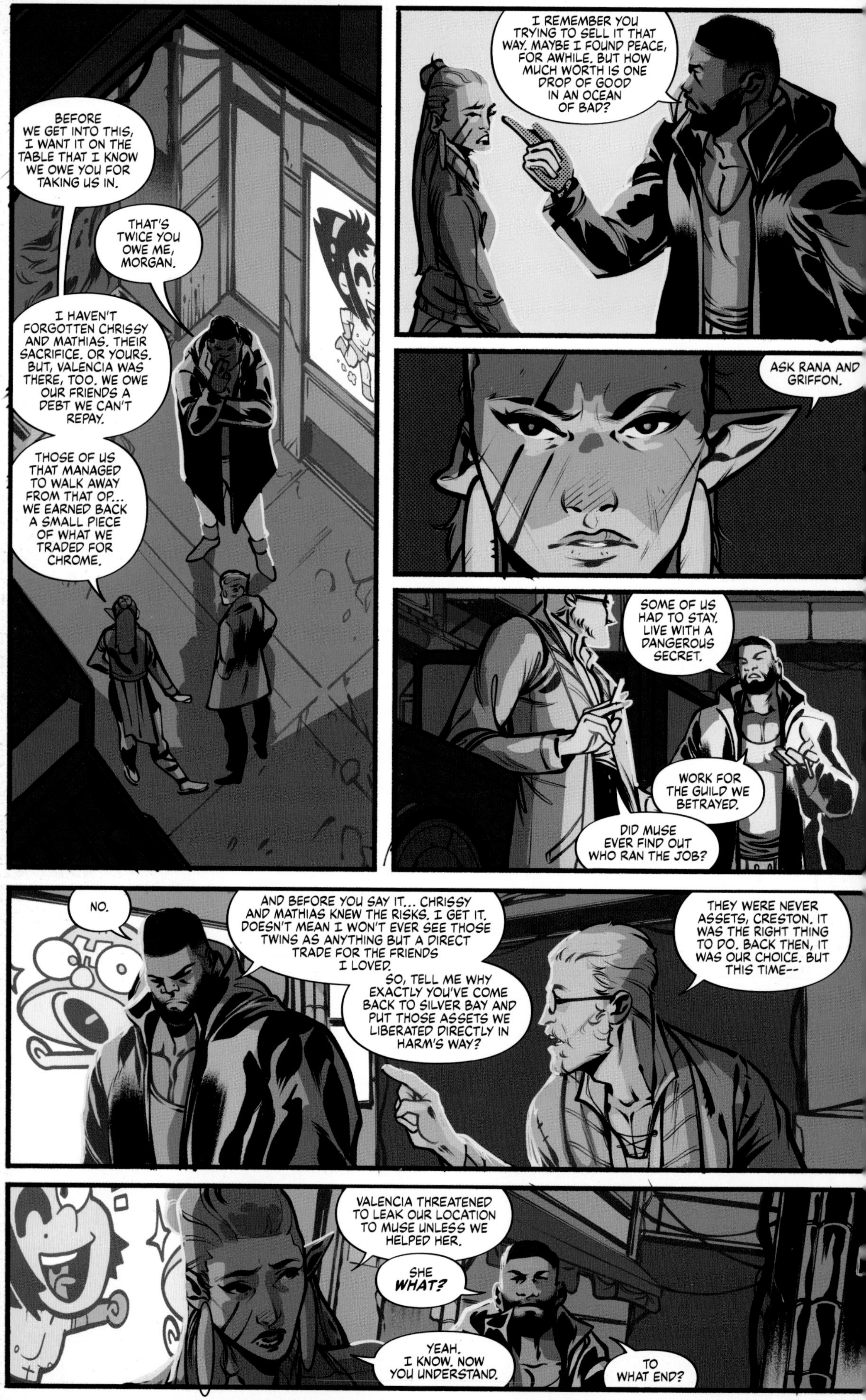
BEFORE WE GET INTO THIS, I WANT IT ON THE TABLE THAT I KNOW WE OWE YOU FOR TAKING US IN.
THAT'S TWICE YOU OWE ME, MORGAN.
I HAVEN'T FORGOTTEN CHRISSY AND MATHIAS. THEIR SACRIFICE. OR YOURS. BUT, VALENCIA WAS THERE, TOO. WE OWE OUR FRIENDS A DEBT WE CAN'T REPAY.
THOSE OF US THAT MANAGED TO WALK AWAY FROM THAT OP... WE EARNED BACK A SMALL PIECE OF WHAT WE TRADED FOR CHROME.
I REMEMBER YOU TRYING TO SELL IT THAT WAY. MAYBE I FOUND PEACE, FOR AWHILE. BUT HOW MUCH WORTH IS ONE DROP OF GOOD IN AN OCEAN OF BAD?
ASK RANA AND GRIFFON.
SOME OF US HAD TO STAY. LIVE WITH A DANGEROUS SECRET.
WORK FOR THE GUILD WE BETRAYED.
DID MUSE EVER FIND OUT WHO RAN THE JOB?
NO.
AND BEFORE YOU SAY IT... CHRISSY AND MATHIAS KNEW THE RISKS. I GET IT. DOESN'T MEAN I WON'T EVER SEE THOSE TWINS AS ANYTHING BUT A DIRECT TRADE FOR THE FRIENDS I LOVED.
SO, TELL ME WHY EXACTLY YOU'VE COME BACK TO SILVER BAY AND PUT THOSE ASSETS WE LIBERATED DIRECTLY IN HARM'S WAY?
THEY WERE NEVER ASSETS, CRESTON. IT WAS THE RIGHT THING TO DO. BACK THEN, IT WAS OUR CHOICE. BUT THIS TIME--
VALENCIA THREATENED TO LEAK OUR LOCATION TO MUSE UNLESS WE HELPED HER.
SHE WHAT?
YEAH. I KNOW. NOW YOU UNDERSTAND.
TO WHAT END?

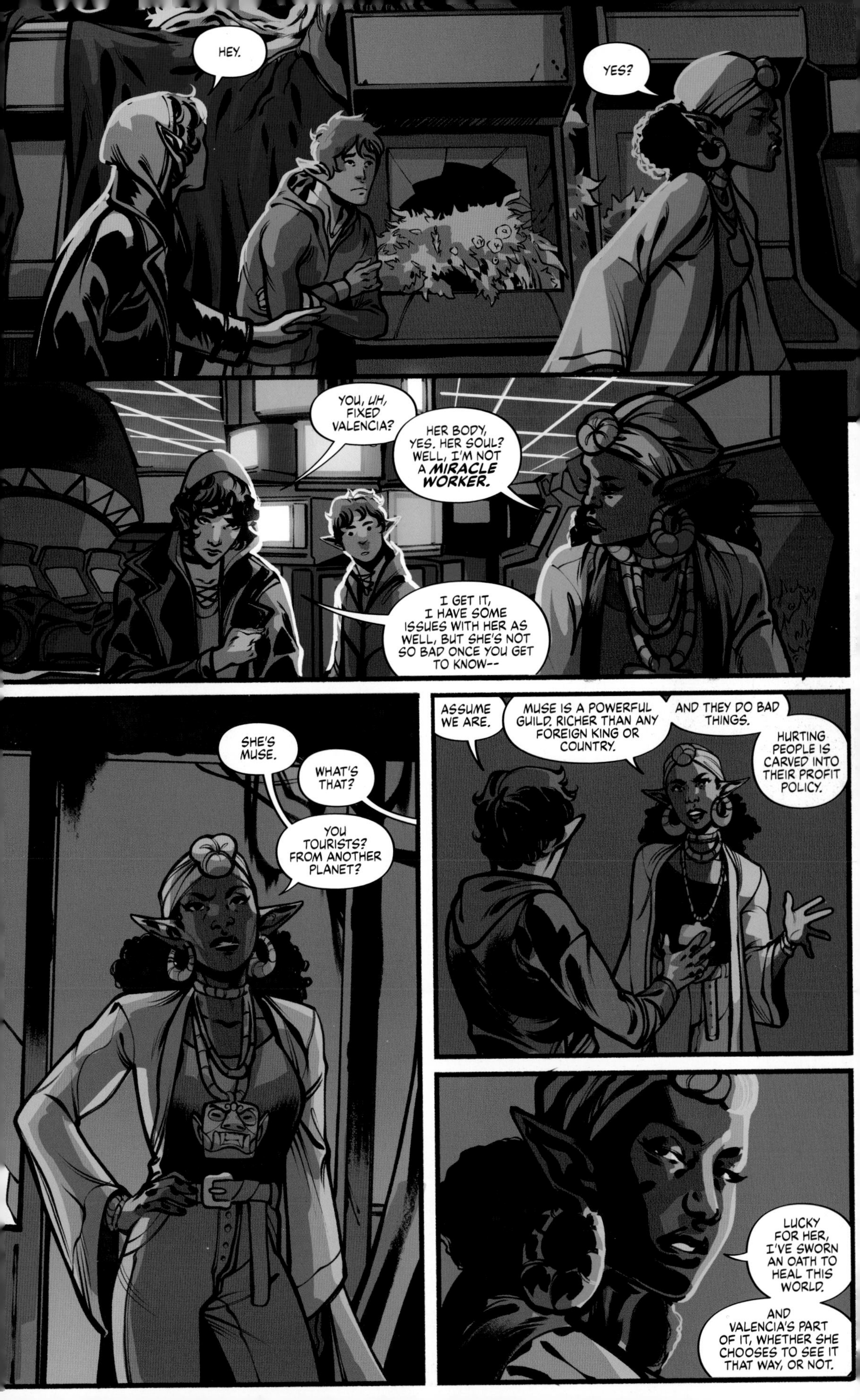
HEY.
YES?
YOU, UH, FIXED VALENCIA?
HER BODY, YES. HER SOUL? WELL, I'M NOT A MIRACLE WORKER.
I GET IT, I HAVE SOME ISSUES WITH HER AS WELL, BUT SHE'S NOT SO BAD ONCE YOU GET TO KNOW--
SHE'S MUSE.
WHAT'S THAT?
YOU TOURISTS? FROM ANOTHER PLANET?
ASSUME WE ARE.
MUSE IS A POWERFUL GUILD, RICHER THAN ANY FOREIGN KING OR COUNTRY.
AND THEY DO BAD THINGS.
HURTING PEOPLE IS CARVED INTO THEIR PROFIT POLICY.
LUCKY FOR HER, I'VE SWORN AN OATH TO HEAL THIS WORLD.
AND VALENCIA'S PART OF IT, WHETHER SHE CHOOSES TO SEE IT THAT WAY, OR NOT.

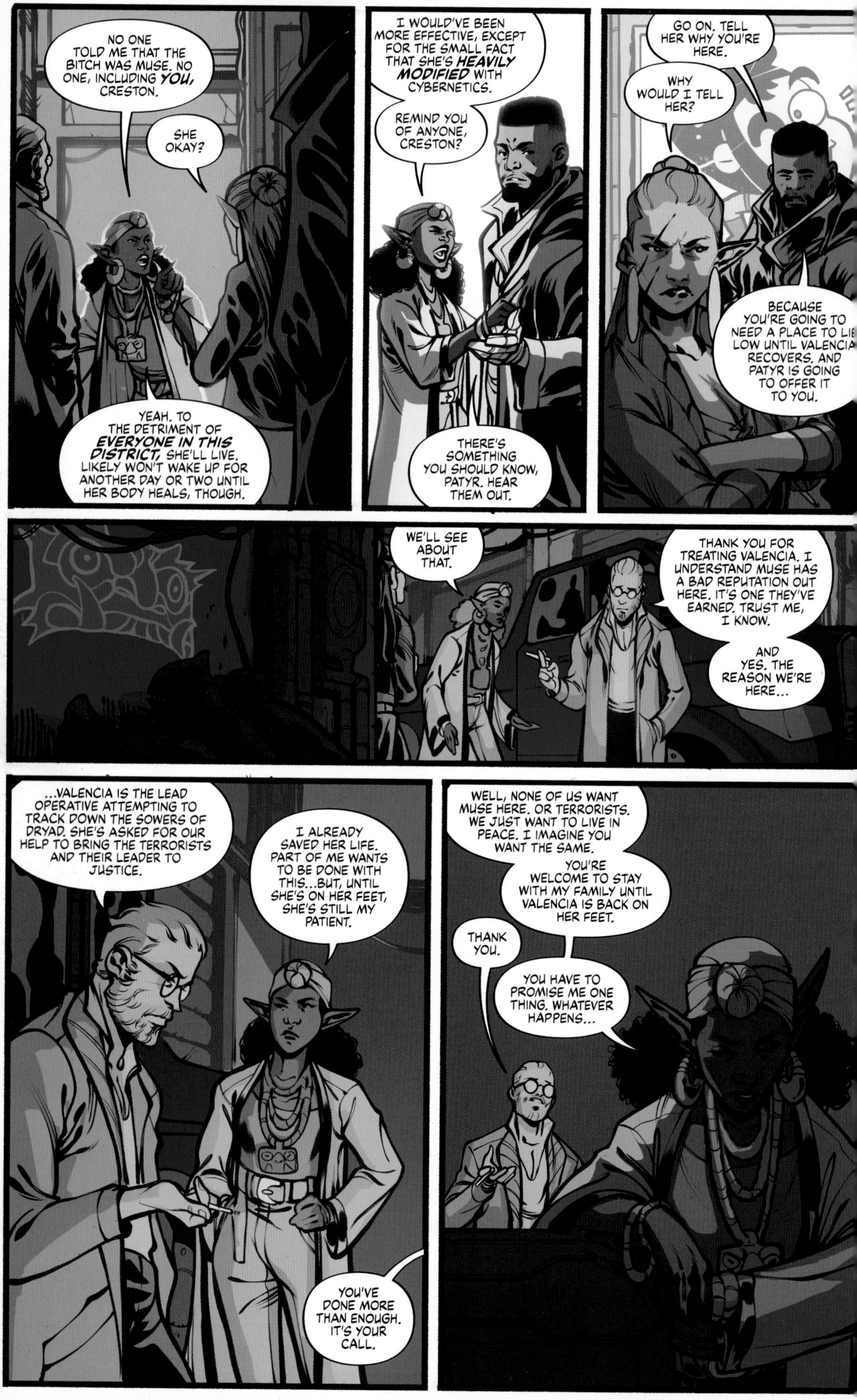
NO ONE TOLD ME THAT THE BITCH WAS MUSE. NO ONE, INCLUDING ***YOU,*** CRESTON.
SHE OKAY?
YEAH. TO THE DETRIMENT OF ***EVERYONE IN THIS DISTRICT,*** SHE'LL LIVE. LIKELY WON'T WAKE UP FOR ANOTHER DAY OR TWO UNTIL HER BODY HEALS, THOUGH.
I WOULD'VE BEEN MORE EFFECTIVE, EXCEPT FOR THE SMALL FACT THAT SHE'S ***HEAVILY MODIFIED*** WITH CYBERNETICS.
REMIND YOU OF ANYONE, CRESTON?
THERE'S SOMETHING YOU SHOULD KNOW, PATYR. HEAR THEM OUT.
GO ON. TELL HER WHY YOU'RE HERE.
WHY WOULD I TELL HER?
BECAUSE YOU'RE GOING TO NEED A PLACE TO LIE LOW UNTIL VALENCIA RECOVERS. AND PATYR IS GOING TO OFFER IT TO YOU.
WE'LL SEE ABOUT THAT.
THANK YOU FOR TREATING VALENCIA. I UNDERSTAND MUSE HAS A BAD REPUTATION OUT HERE. IT'S ONE THEY'VE EARNED. TRUST ME, I KNOW.
AND YES. THE REASON WE'RE HERE...
...VALENCIA IS THE LEAD OPERATIVE ATTEMPTING TO TRACK DOWN THE SOWERS OF DRYAD. SHE'S ASKED FOR OUR HELP TO BRING THE TERRORISTS AND THEIR LEADER TO JUSTICE.
I ALREADY SAVED HER LIFE. PART OF ME WANTS TO BE DONE WITH THIS...BUT, UNTIL SHE'S ON HER FEET, SHE'S STILL MY PATIENT.
YOU'VE DONE MORE THAN ENOUGH. IT'S YOUR CALL.
WELL, NONE OF US WANT MUSE HERE. OR TERRORISTS. WE JUST WANT TO LIVE IN PEACE. I IMAGINE YOU WANT THE SAME.
YOU'RE WELCOME TO STAY WITH MY FAMILY UNTIL VALENCIA IS BACK ON HER FEET.
THANK YOU.
YOU HAVE TO PROMISE ME ONE THING. WHATEVER HAPPENS...

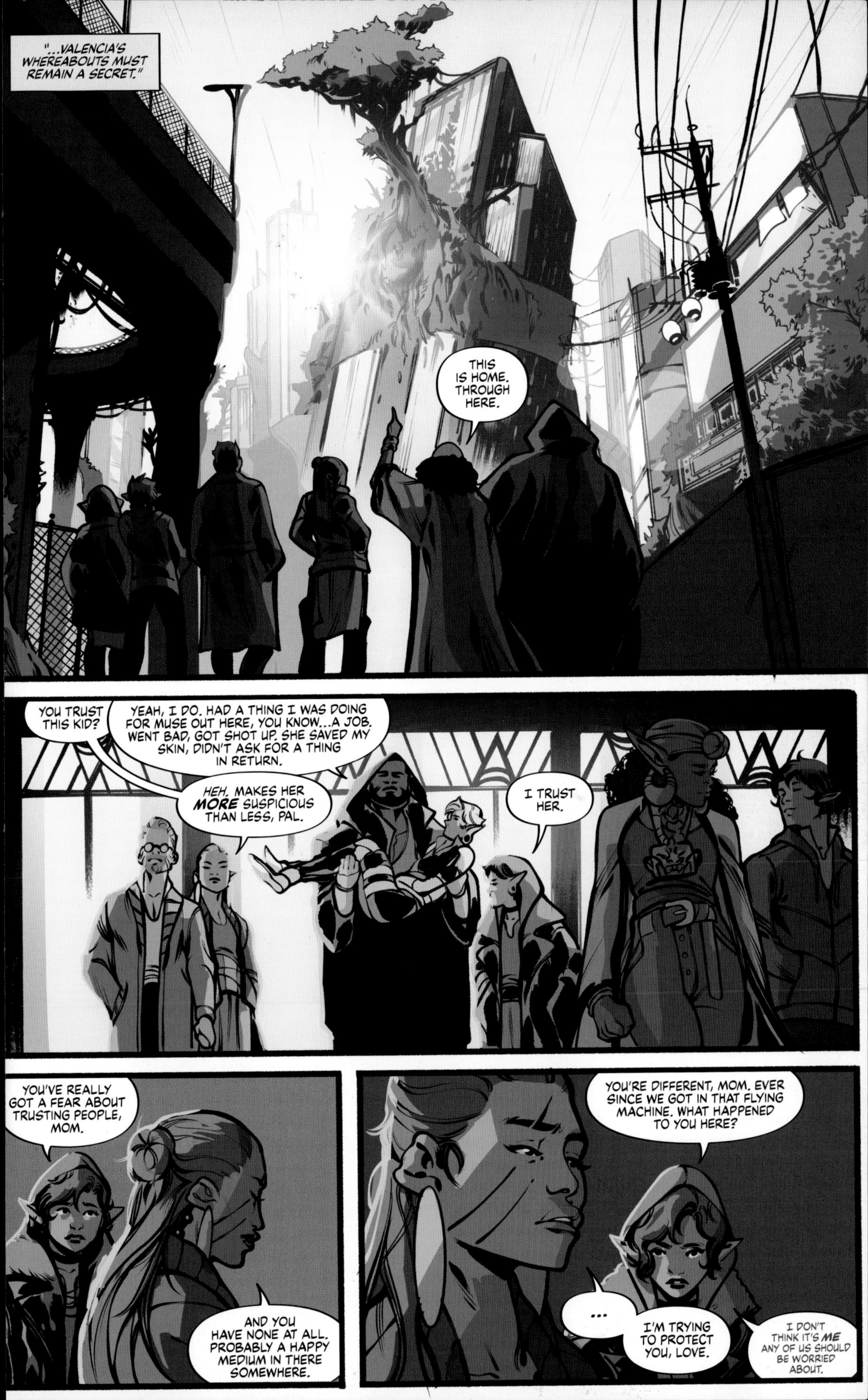

"...VALENCIA'S WHEREABOUTS MUST REMAIN A SECRET."
THIS IS HOME. THROUGH HERE.
YOU TRUST THIS KID?
YEAH, I DO. HAD A THING I WAS DOING FOR MUSE OUT HERE, YOU KNOW...A JOB. WENT BAD, GOT SHOT UP. SHE SAVED MY SKIN, DIDN'T ASK FOR A THING IN RETURN.
HEH. MAKES HER MORE SUSPICIOUS THAN LESS, PAL.
I TRUST HER.
YOU'VE REALLY GOT A FEAR ABOUT TRUSTING PEOPLE, MOM.
AND YOU HAVE NONE AT ALL. PROBABLY A HAPPY MEDIUM IN THERE SOMEWHERE.
YOU'RE DIFFERENT, MOM. EVER SINCE WE GOT IN THAT FLYING MACHINE. WHAT HAPPENED TO YOU HERE?
...
I'M TRYING TO PROTECT YOU, LOVE.
I DON'T THINK IT'S ME ANY OF US SHOULD BE WORRIED ABOUT.

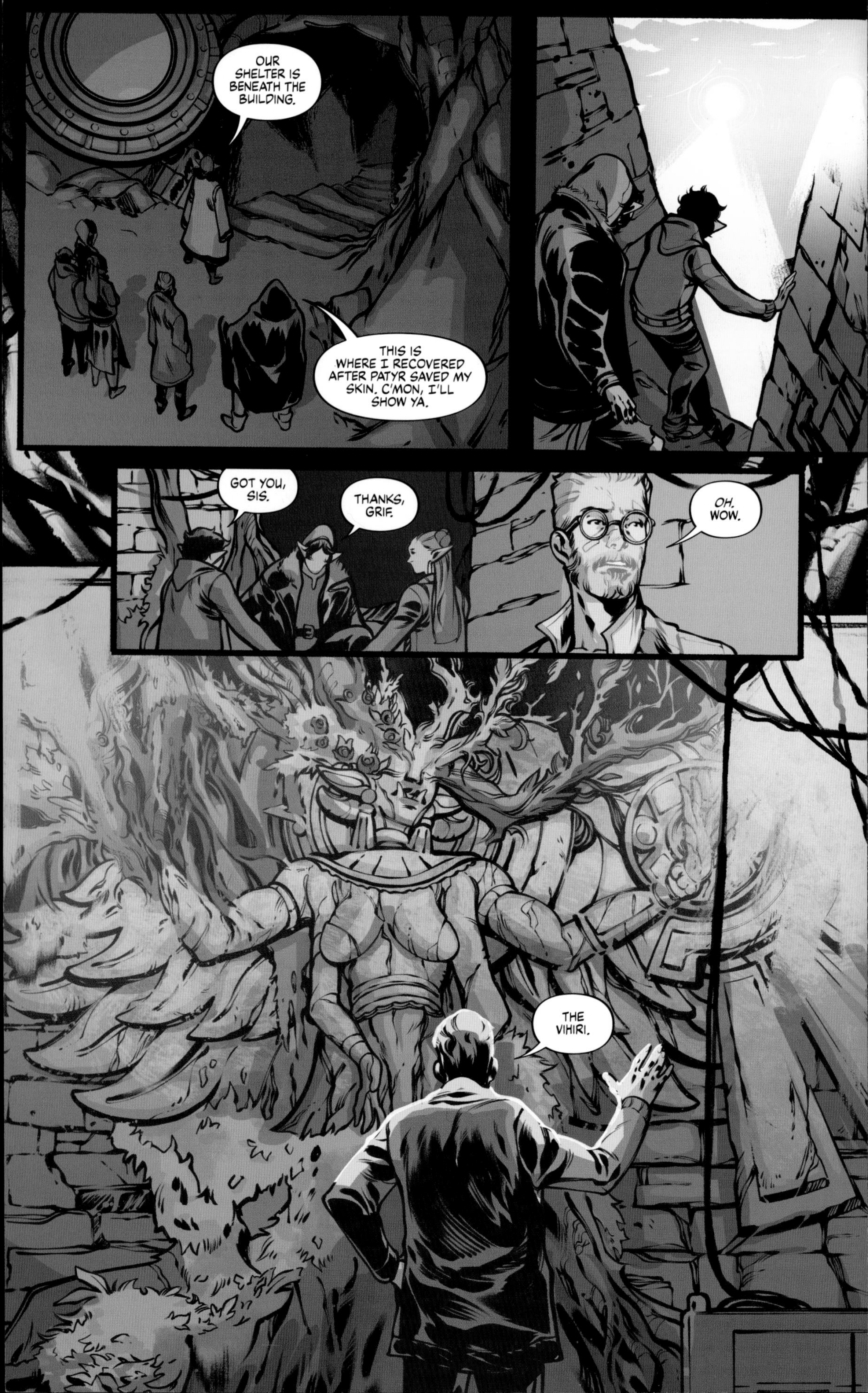
OUR SHELTER IS BENEATH THE BUILDING.
THIS IS WHERE I RECOVERED AFTER PATYR SAVED MY SKIN. C'MON, I'LL SHOW YA.
GOT YOU, SIS.
THANKS, GRIF.
OH. WOW.
THE VIHIRI.

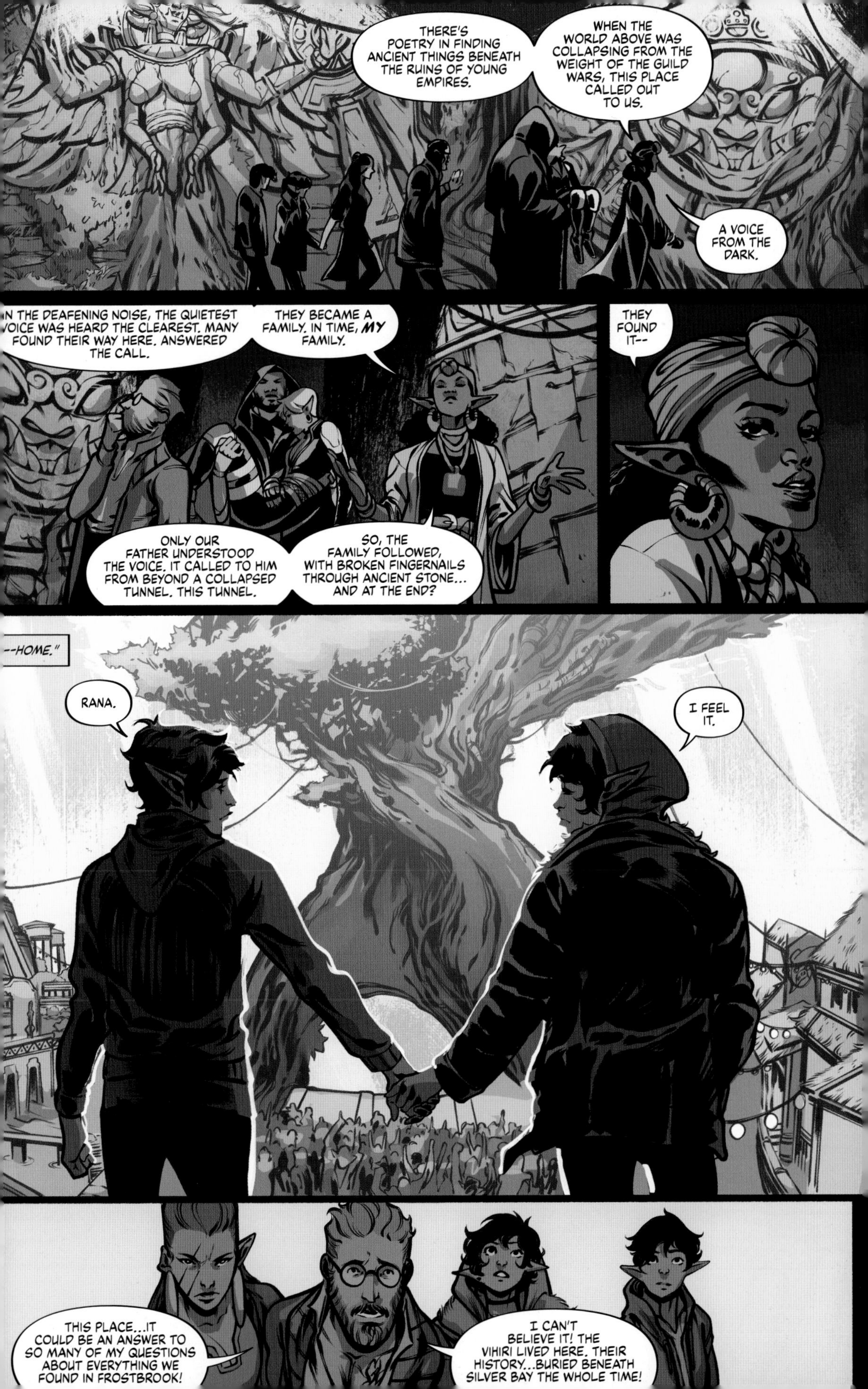
THERE'S POETRY IN FINDING ANCIENT THINGS BENEATH THE RUINS OF YOUNG EMPIRES.
WHEN THE WORLD ABOVE WAS COLLAPSING FROM THE WEIGHT OF THE GUILD WARS, THIS PLACE CALLED OUT TO US.
A VOICE FROM THE DARK.
IN THE DEAFENING NOISE, THE QUIETEST VOICE WAS HEARD THE CLEAREST. MANY FOUND THEIR WAY HERE. ANSWERED THE CALL.
THEY BECAME A FAMILY. IN TIME, MY FAMILY.
ONLY OUR FATHER UNDERSTOOD THE VOICE. IT CALLED TO HIM FROM BEYOND A COLLAPSED TUNNEL. THIS TUNNEL.
SO, THE FAMILY FOLLOWED, WITH BROKEN FINGERNAILS THROUGH ANCIENT STONE... AND AT THE END?
THEY FOUND IT--
--HOME."
RANA.
I FEEL IT.
THIS PLACE...IT COULD BE AN ANSWER TO SO MANY OF MY QUESTIONS ABOUT EVERYTHING WE FOUND IN FROSTBROOK!
I CAN'T BELIEVE IT! THE VIHIRI LIVED HERE. THEIR HISTORY...BURIED BENEATH SILVER BAY THE WHOLE TIME!

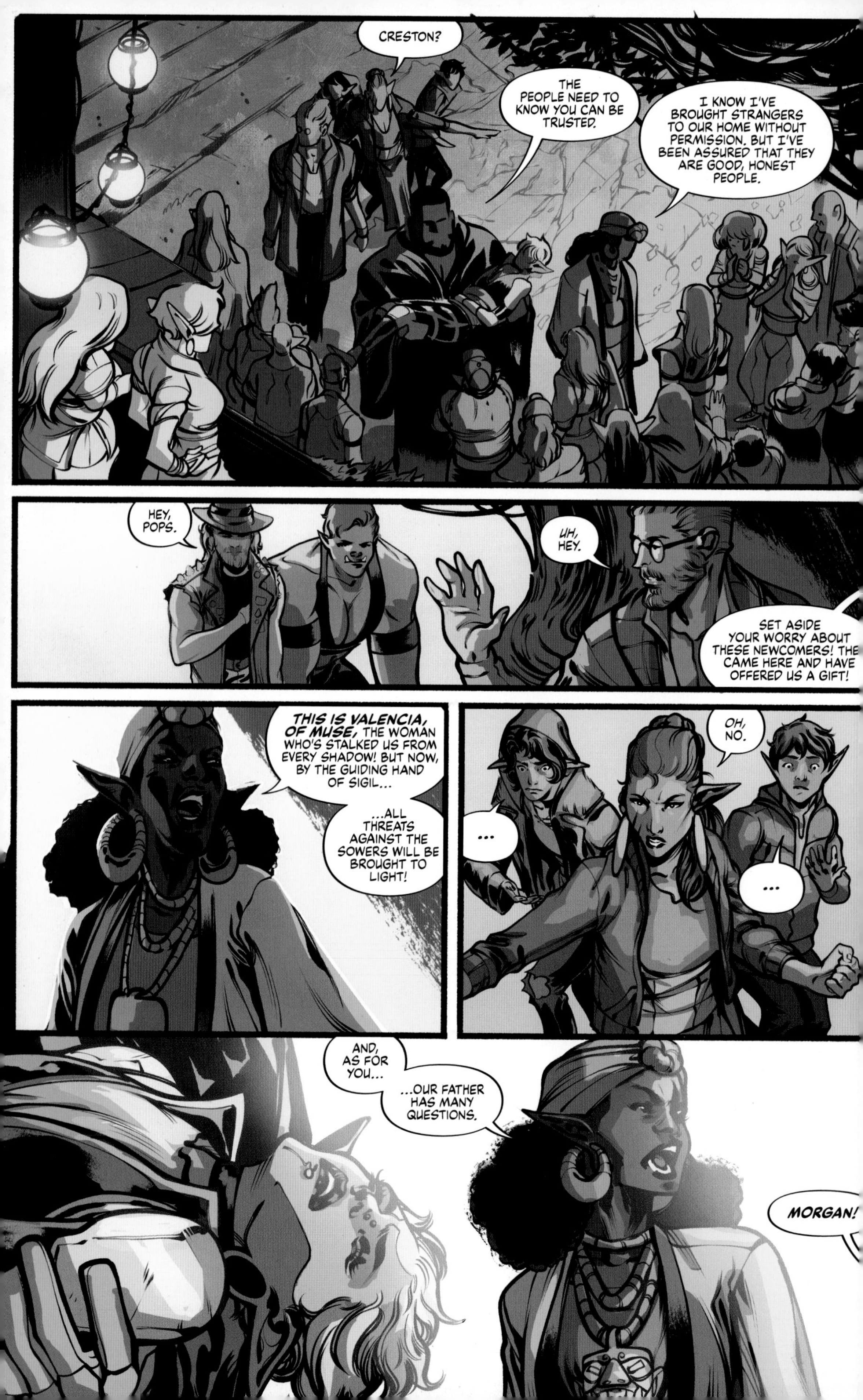
CRESTON?
THE PEOPLE NEED TO KNOW YOU CAN BE TRUSTED.
I KNOW I'VE BROUGHT STRANGERS TO OUR HOME WITHOUT PERMISSION. BUT I'VE BEEN ASSURED THAT THEY ARE GOOD, HONEST PEOPLE.
HEY, POPS.
UH, HEY.
SET ASIDE YOUR WORRY ABOUT THESE NEWCOMERS! THE CAME HERE AND HAVE OFFERED US A GIFT!
THIS IS VALENCIA, OF MUSE, THE WOMAN WHO'S STALKED US FROM EVERY SHADOW! BUT NOW, BY THE GUIDING HAND OF SIGIL...
...ALL THREATS AGAINST THE SOWERS WILL BE BROUGHT TO LIGHT!
OH, NO.
...
...
AND, AS FOR YOU...
...OUR FATHER HAS MANY QUESTIONS.
MORGAN!

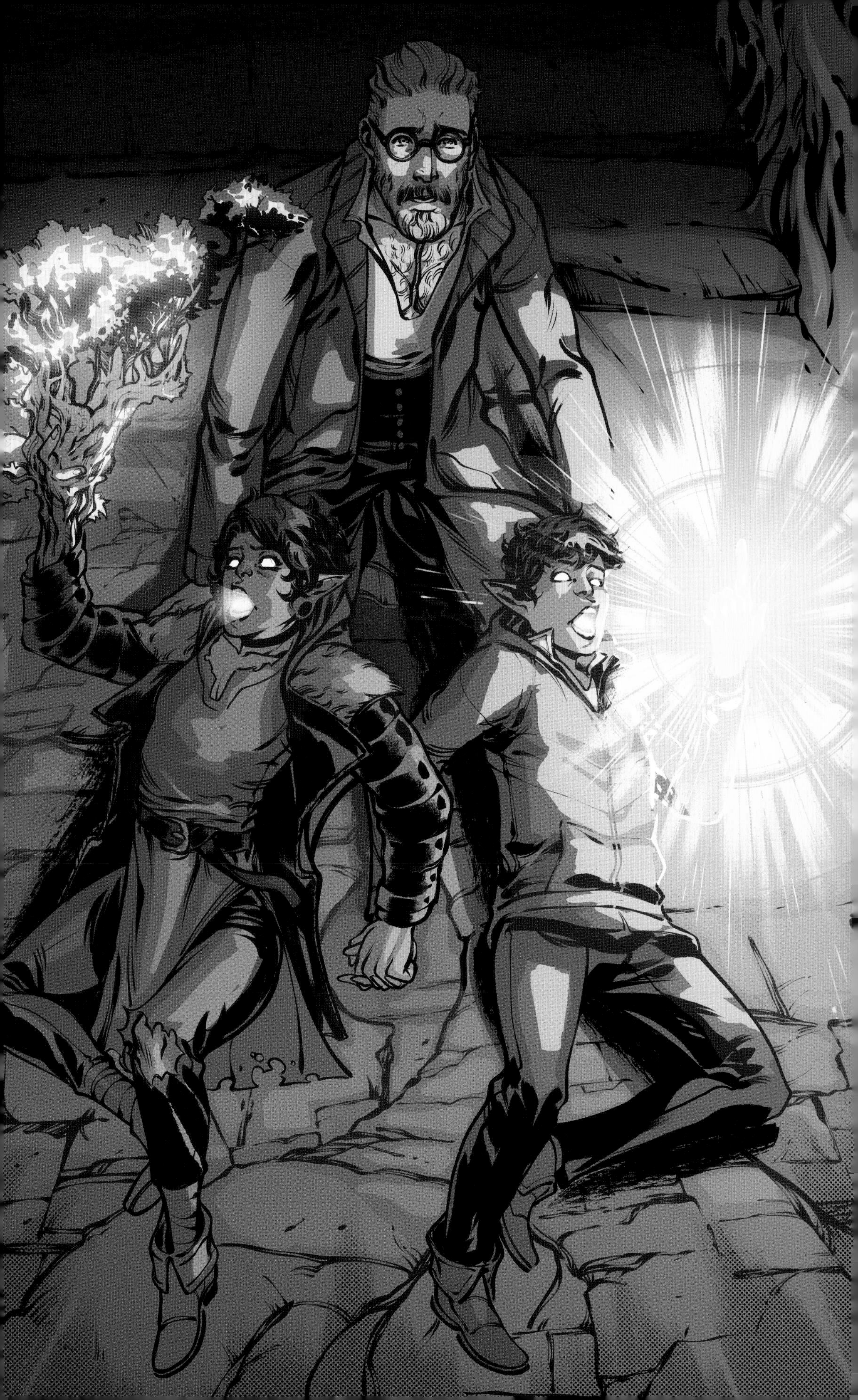

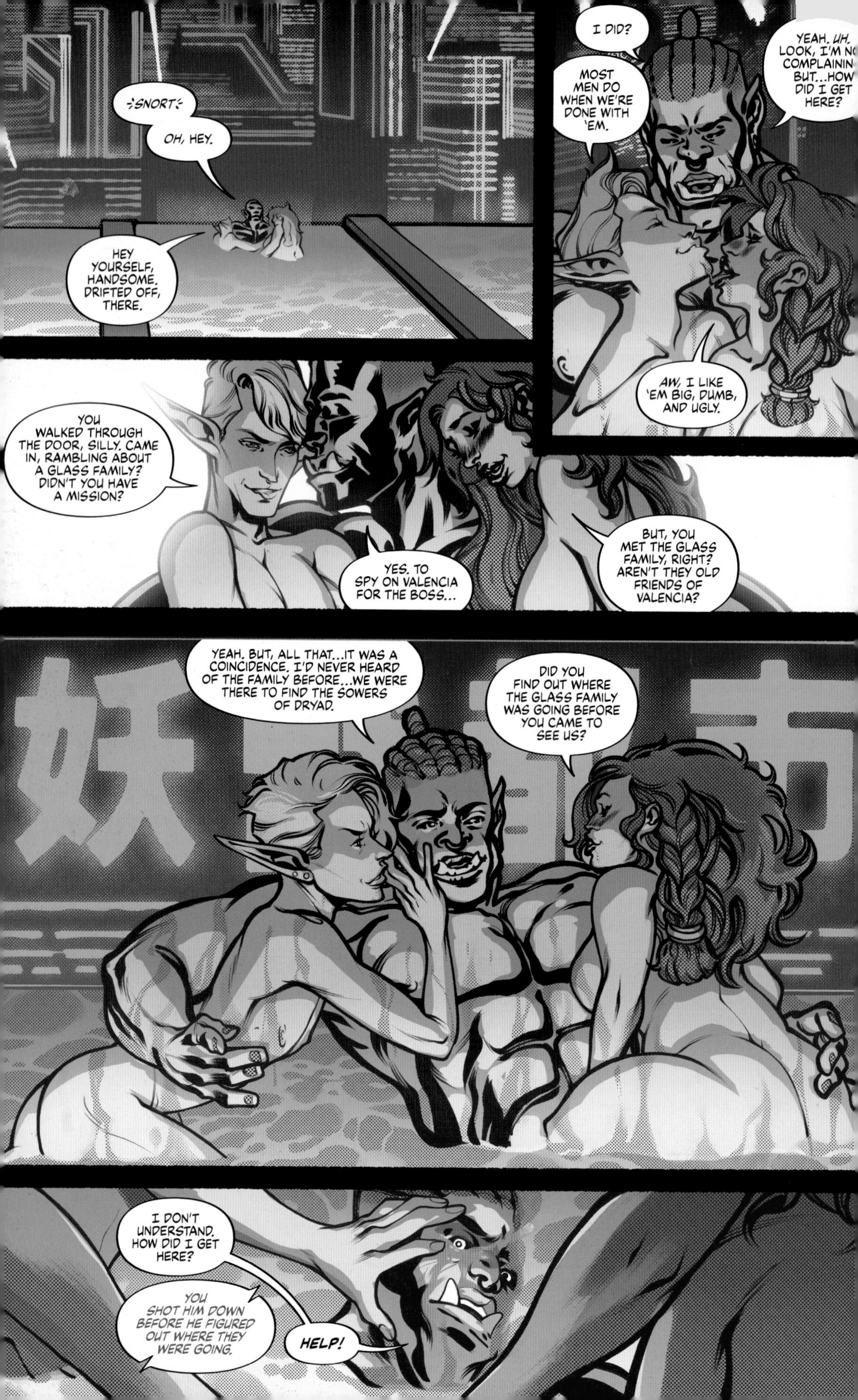
SNORT
OH, HEY.
HEY YOURSELF, HANDSOME. DRIFTED OFF, THERE.
I DID?
MOST MEN DO WHEN WE'RE DONE WITH 'EM.
YEAH. UH. LOOK, I'M N COMPLAININ BUT...HOW DID I GET HERE?
AW, I LIKE 'EM BIG, DUMB, AND UGLY.
YOU WALKED THROUGH THE DOOR, SILLY. CAME IN, RAMBLING ABOUT A GLASS FAMILY? DIDN'T YOU HAVE A MISSION?
YES. TO SPY ON VALENCIA FOR THE BOSS...
BUT, YOU MET THE GLASS FAMILY, RIGHT? AREN'T THEY OLD FRIENDS OF VALENCIA?
YEAH. BUT, ALL THAT...IT WAS A COINCIDENCE. I'D NEVER HEARD OF THE FAMILY BEFORE...WE WERE THERE TO FIND THE SOWERS OF DRYAD.
DID YOU FIND OUT WHERE THE GLASS FAMILY WAS GOING BEFORE YOU CAME TO SEE US?
I DON'T UNDERSTAND. HOW DID I GET HERE?
YOU SHOT HIM DOWN BEFORE HE FIGURED OUT WHERE THEY WERE GOING.
HELP!

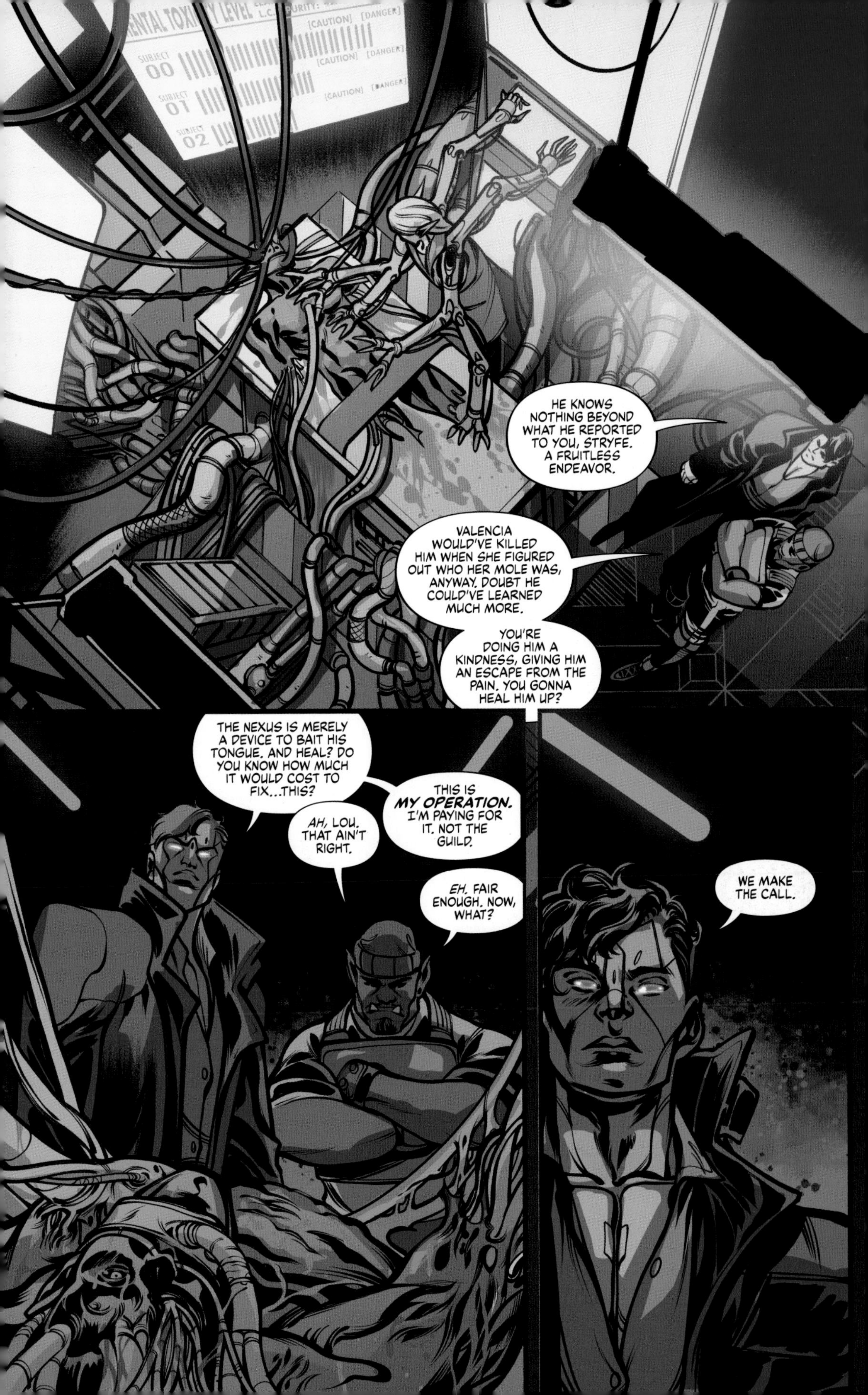
ENVIRONMENTAL TOXICITY LEVEL
[CAUTION] [DANGER]
SUBJECT 00
SUBJECT 01
SUBJECT 02
HE KNOWS NOTHING BEYOND WHAT HE REPORTED TO YOU, STRYFE. A FRUITLESS ENDEAVOR.
VALENCIA WOULD'VE KILLED HIM WHEN SHE FIGURED OUT WHO HER MOLE WAS, ANYWAY. DOUBT HE COULD'VE LEARNED MUCH MORE.
YOU'RE DOING HIM A KINDNESS, GIVING HIM AN ESCAPE FROM THE PAIN. YOU GONNA HEAL HIM UP?
THE NEXUS IS MERELY A DEVICE TO BAIT HIS TONGUE. AND HEAL? DO YOU KNOW HOW MUCH IT WOULD COST TO FIX...THIS?
AH, LOU. THAT AIN'T RIGHT.
THIS IS MY OPERATION. I'M PAYING FOR IT. NOT THE GUILD.
EH. FAIR ENOUGH. NOW, WHAT?
WE MAKE THE CALL.

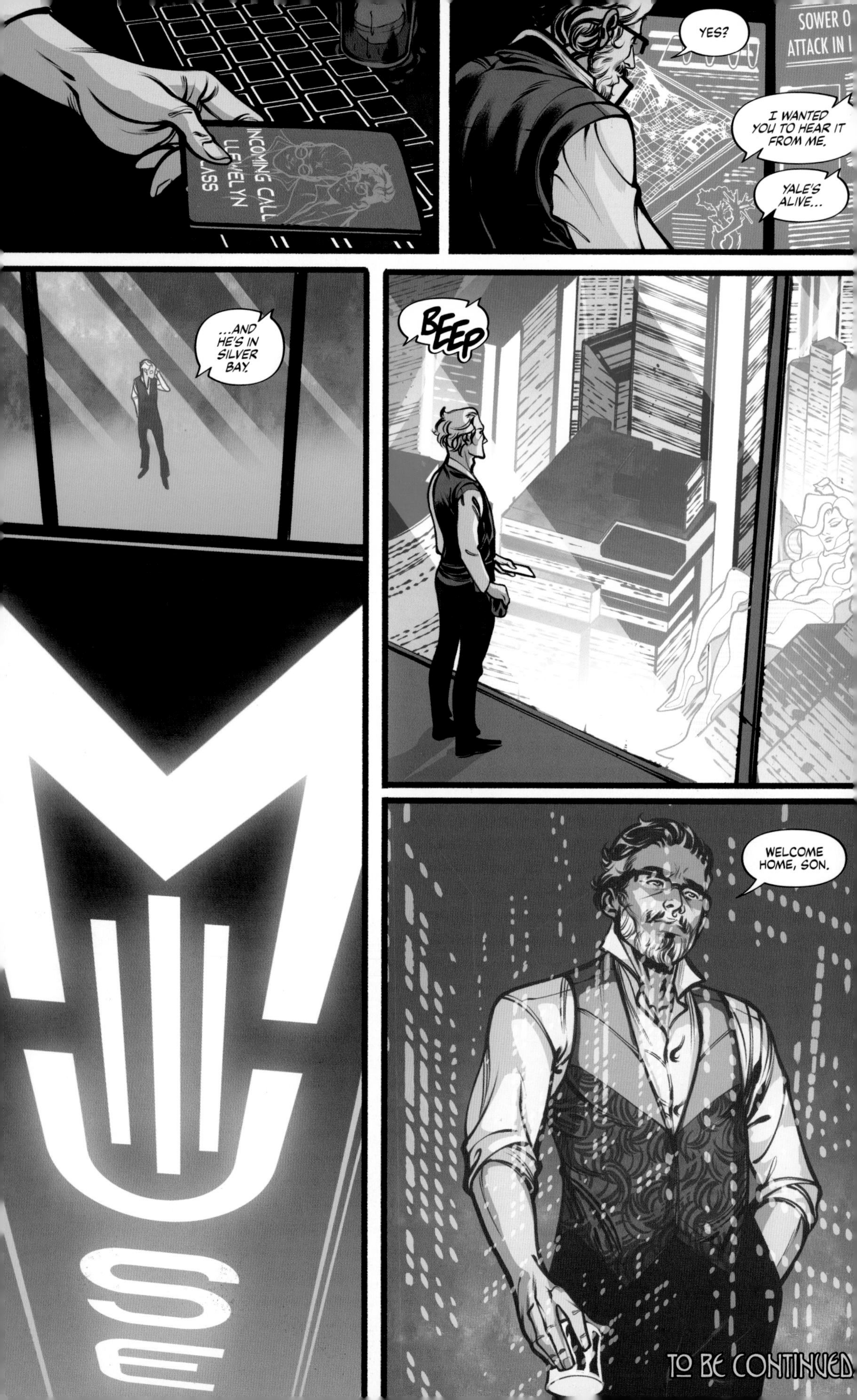
INCOMING CALL
LLEWELYN
LASS
SOWER O
ATTACK IN I
YES?
I WANTED YOU TO HEAR IT FROM ME.
YALE'S ALIVE...
...AND HE'S IN SILVER BAY.
BEEP
WELCOME HOME, SON.
TO BE CONTINUED

DRYAD

SKETCHES & COVER GALLERY

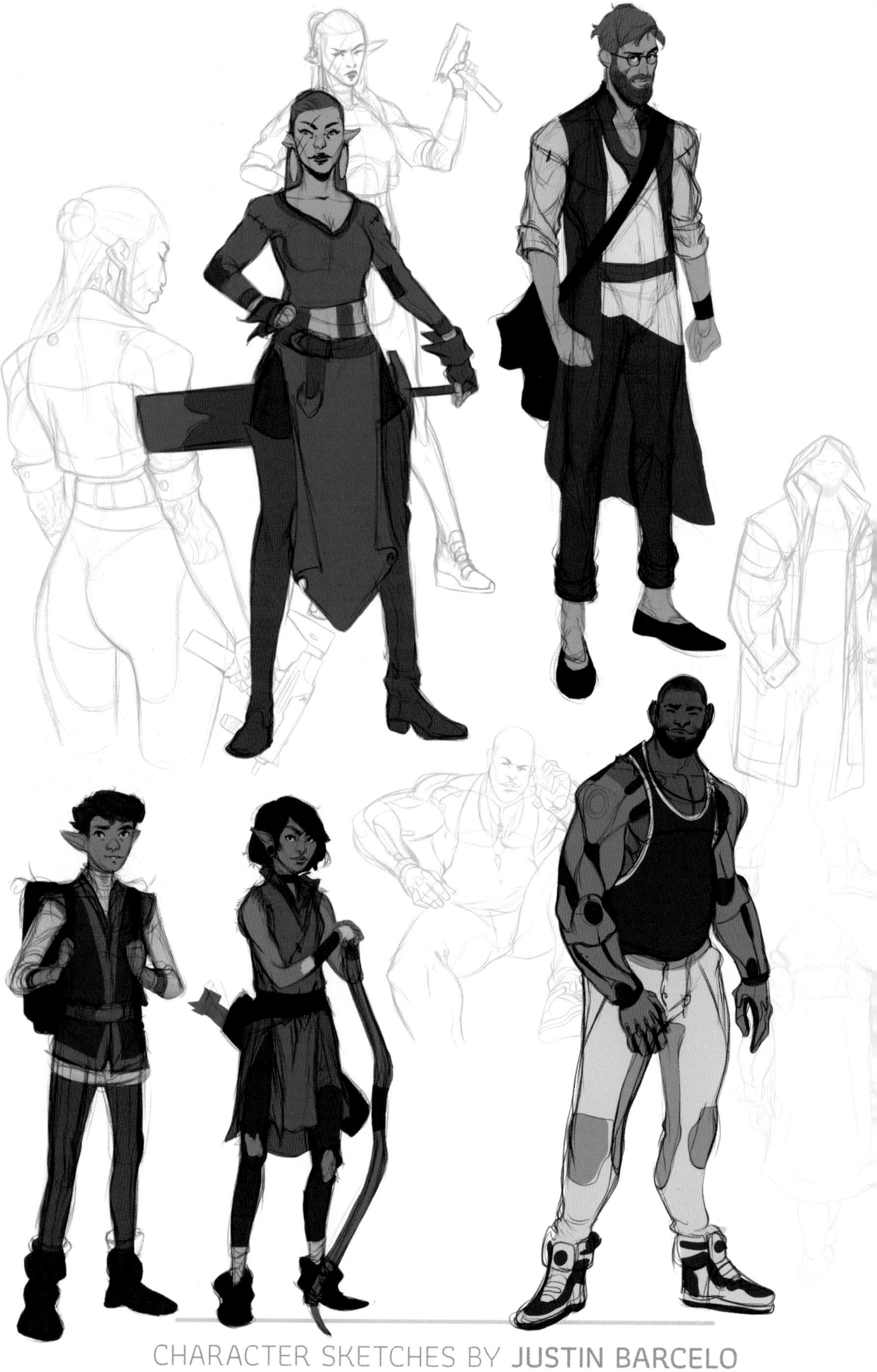

CHARACTER SKETCHES BY **JUSTIN BARCELO**

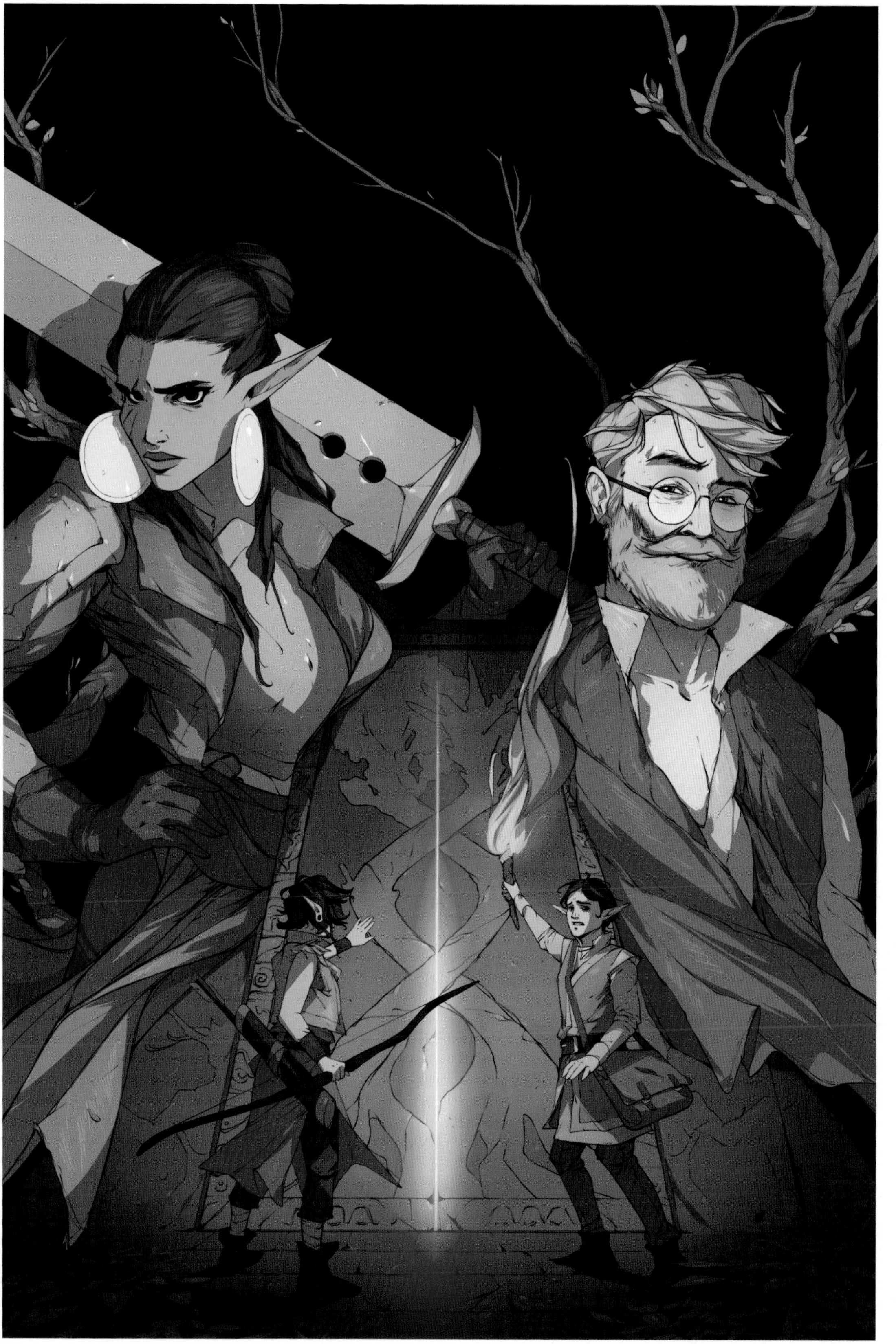

ISSUE #1 COVER • ARTWORK BY **TOMAS OLEKSAK**

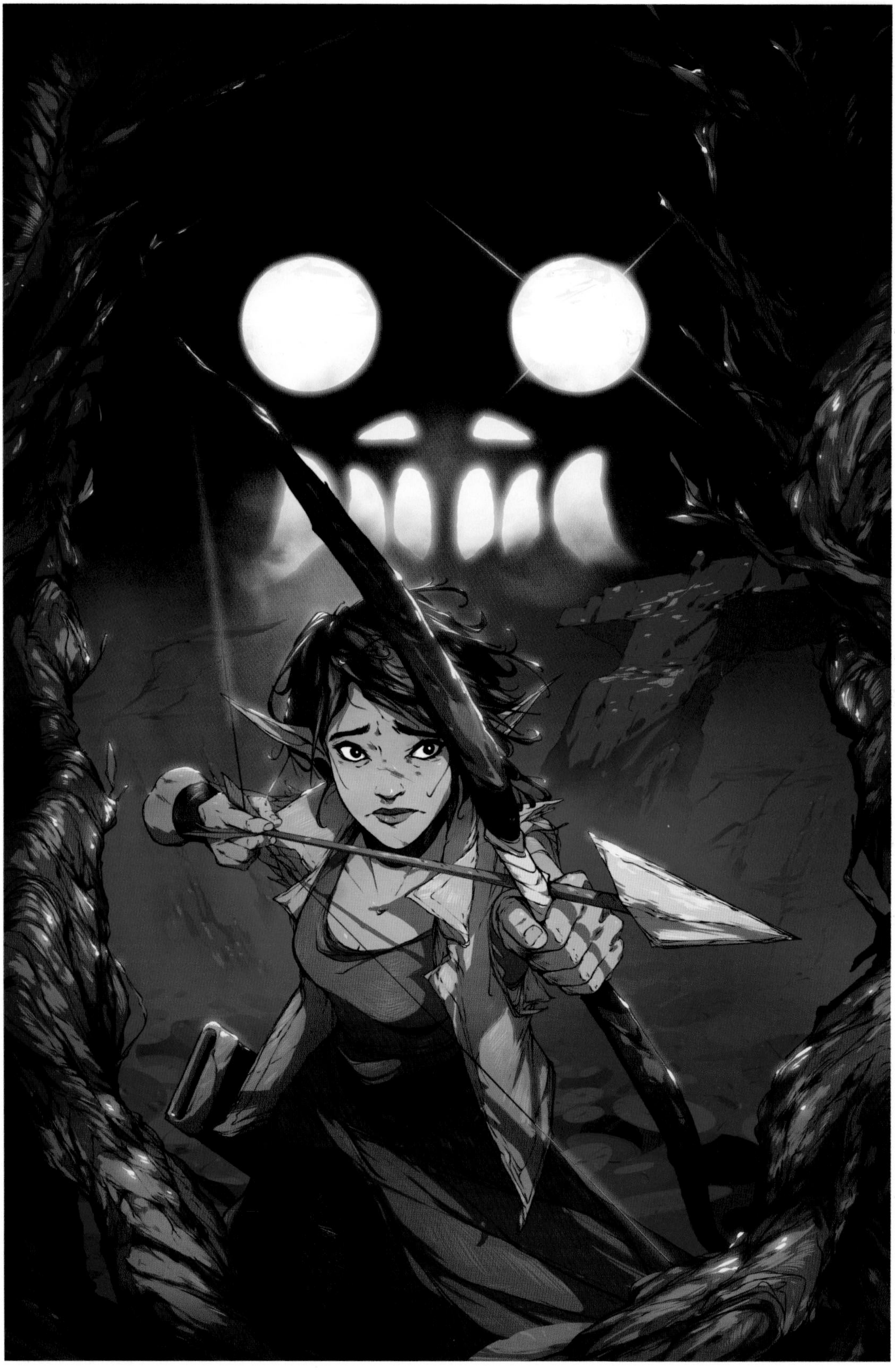

ISSUE #2 COVER • ARTWORK BY **TOMAS OLEKSAK**

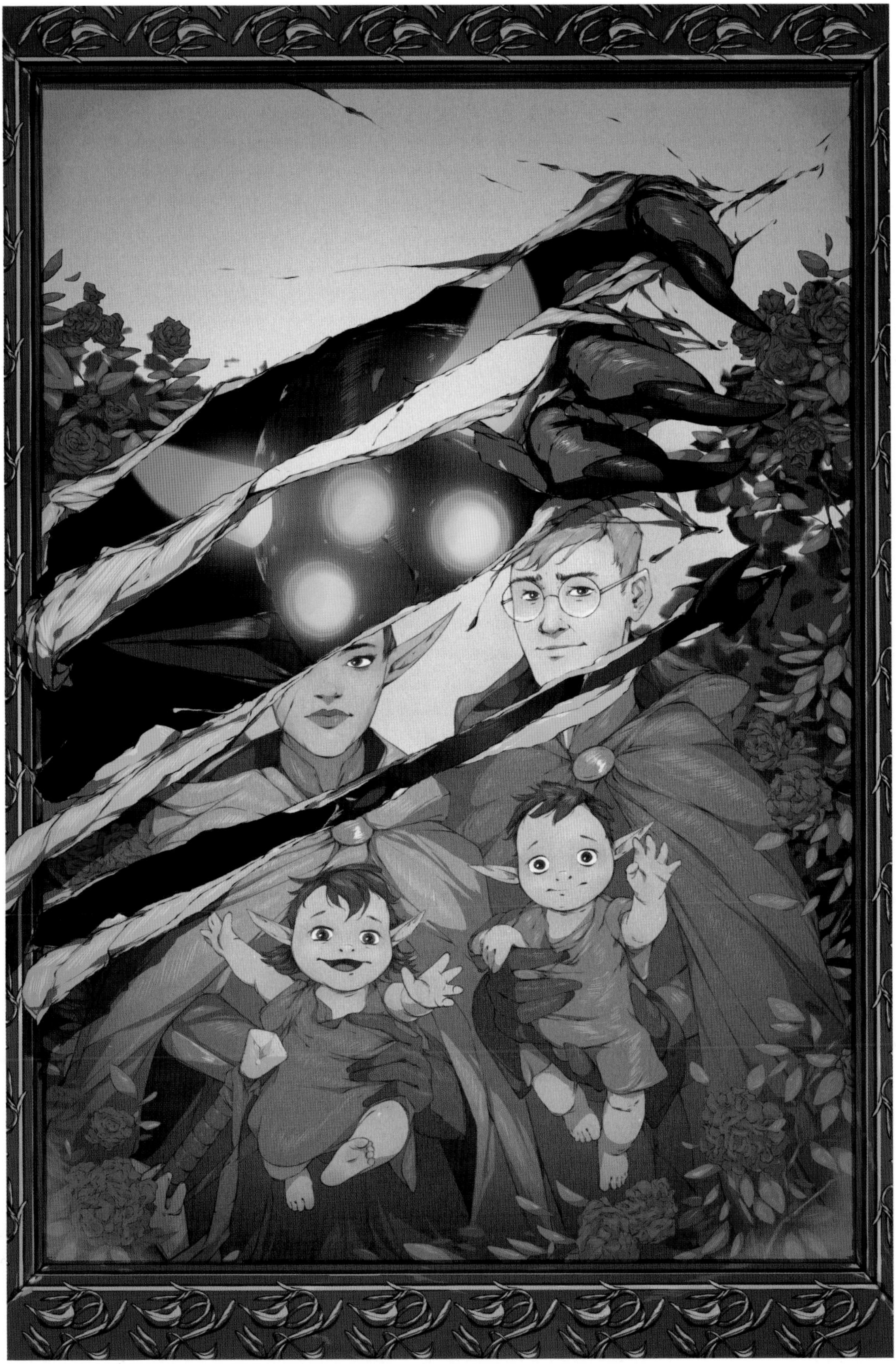

ISSUE #3 COVER • ARTWORK BY **TOMAS OLEKSAK**

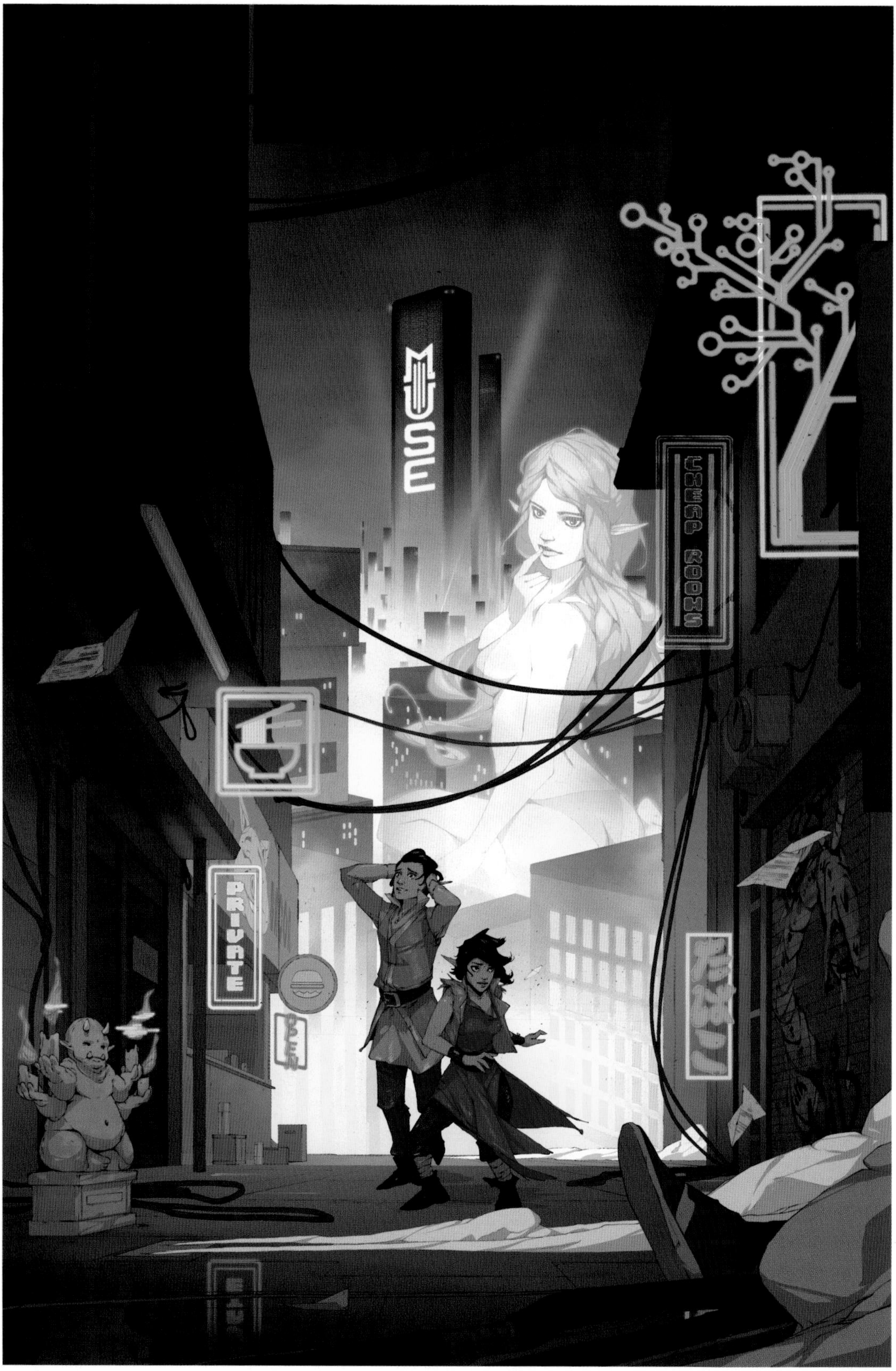
MUSE
CHEAP ROOMS
PRIVATE

ISSUE #4 COVER • ARTWORK BY **TOMAS OLEKSAK**

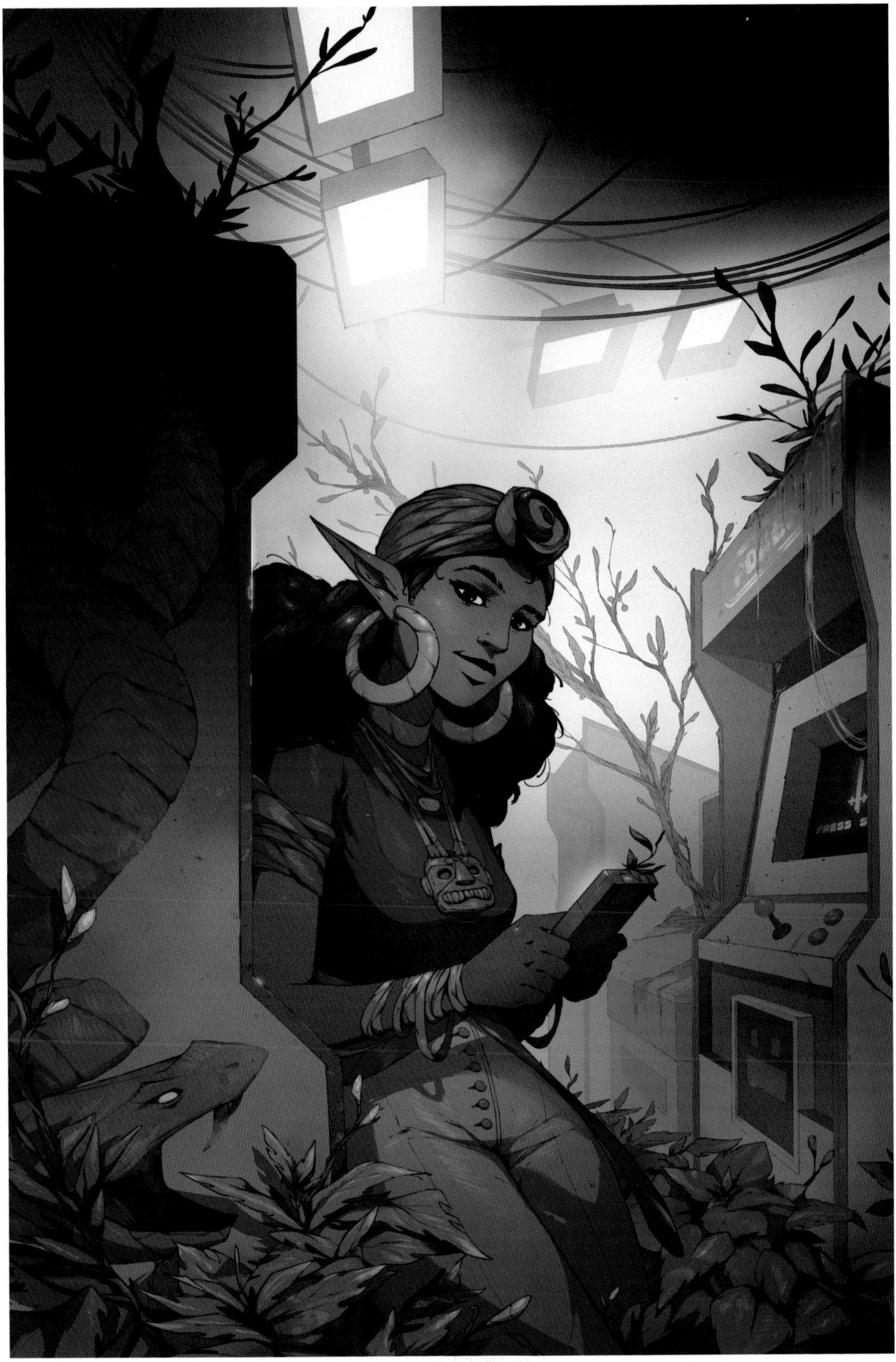

ISSUE #5 COVER • ARTWORK BY **TOMAS OLEKSAK**

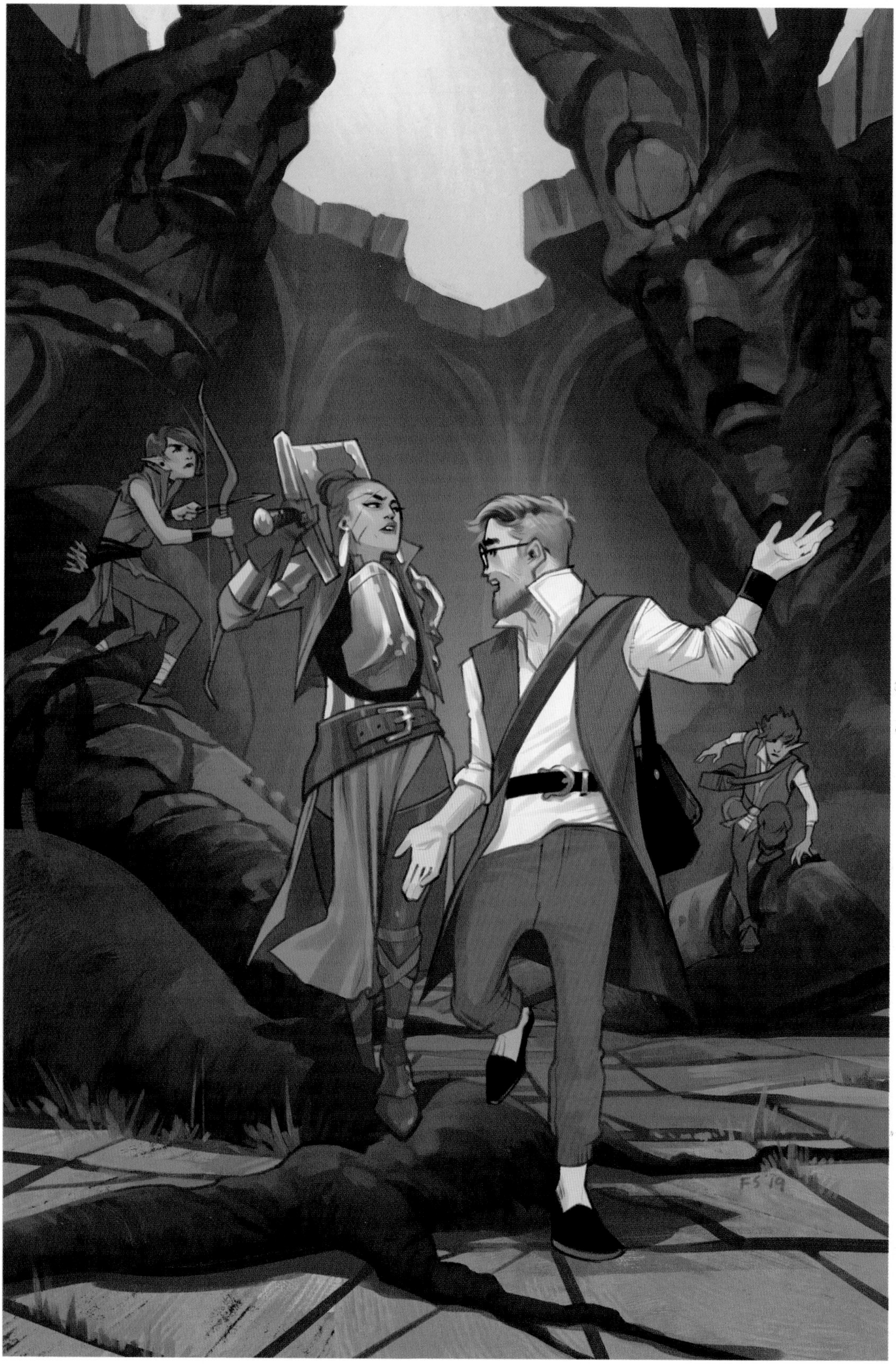
FS '19

ISSUE #1 VARIANT COVER • ARTWORK BY **FIONA STAPLES**

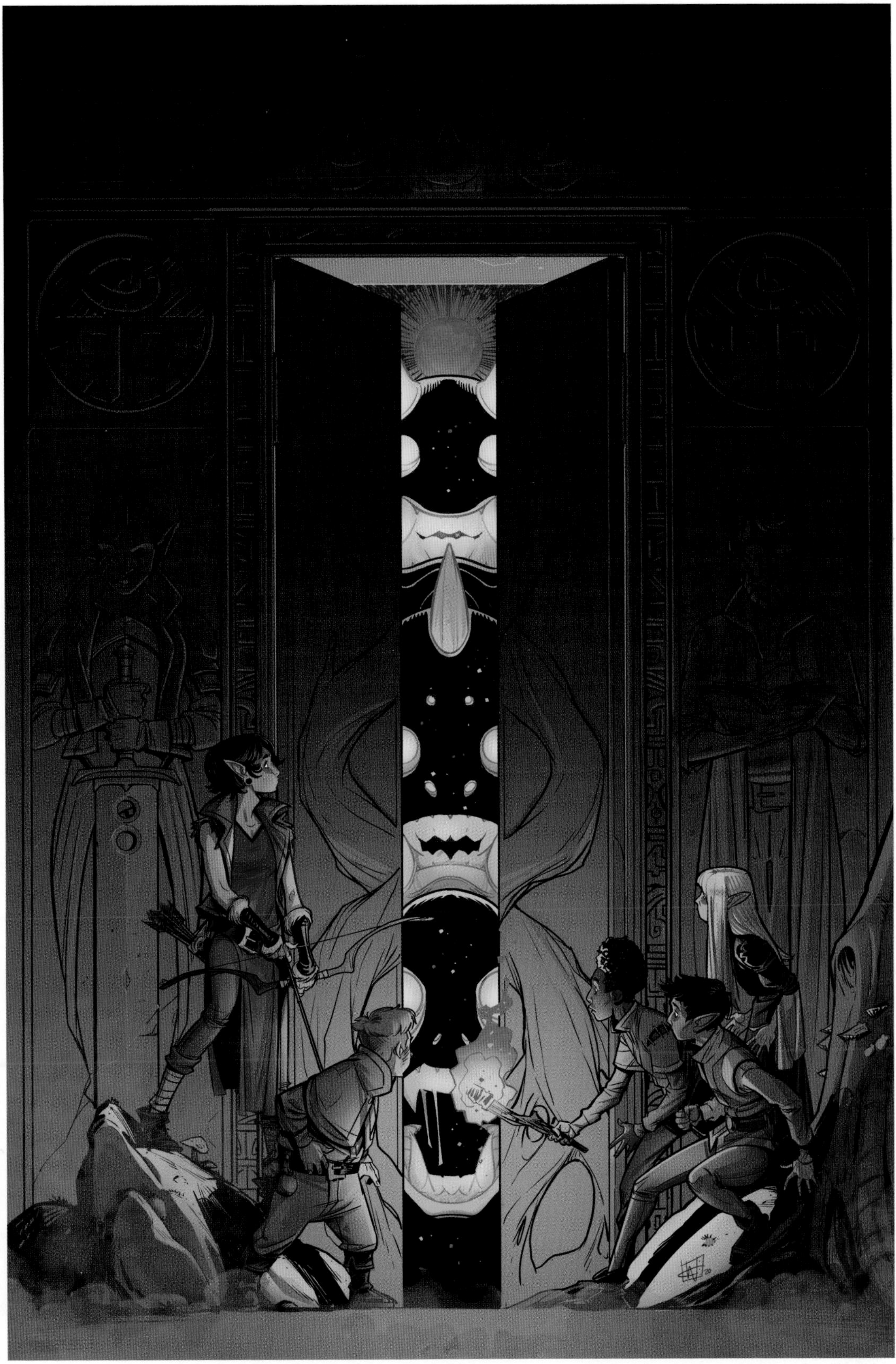

ISSUE #1 VARIANT COVER • ARTWORK BY **CHRIS WILDGOOSE**

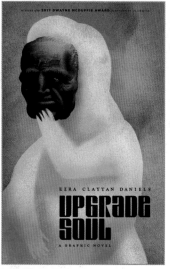